CATHER, CANON,
AND THE
POLITICS OF READING

Cather, Canon,

«««« AND THE »»»»

Politics of Reading

DEBORAH CARLIN

The University of Massachusetts Press

AMHERST

Printed in the United States of America
LC 92–12670
ISBN 0–87023–822–1
Designed by Jack Harrison
Set in Adobe Minion
Printed and bound by Thomson-Shore, Inc.

Library of Congress Cataloging-in-Publication Data

Carlin, Deborah, 1958–
Cather, canon, and the politics of reading / Deborah Carlin.
p. cm.
Revised version of the author's thesis, Harvard University.
Includes bibliographical references and index.
ISBN 0–87023–822–1 (alk. paper)
1. Cather, Willa, 1873–1947—Political and social views.
2. Feminism and literature—United States—History—20th century.
3. Reader-response criticism. 4. Sex role in literature.
5. Narration (Rhetoric) 6. Canon (Literature) I. Title.
PS3505.A87Z5916 1992
813'.52—dc20   92–12670
CIP

British Library Cataloguing in Publication data are available.

Acknowledgment is made to Alfred A. Knopf for permission to reprint short
selections from the following works by Willa Cather: *My Mortal Enemy*, copyright
1926 by Willa Cather and renewed 1954 by Edith Lewis, Executrix and the City
Farmers Bank Trust Co.; *Shadows on the Rock*, copyright 1931 by Willa Cather and
renewed 1959 by the Executors of the Estate of Willa Cather; *Obscure Destinies*,
copyright 1930, 1932 by Willa Cather and renewed 1958, 1960 by the Executors of the
Estate of Willa Cather; *Lucy Gayheart*, copyright 1935 by Willa Sibert Cather and
renewed 1963 by Edith Lewis and the City Bank Farmers Trust Co.; *Sapphira and the
Slave Girl*, copyright 1940 by Willa Cather and renewed 1968 by Edith Lewis
and the City Farmers Trust Co.

For Renée and David,
who remain,
and for Deb,
who has come to stay

Contents

Acknowledgments   ix

1
Categorical Cather: Reading the Canon(s)   3

2
Design, Duplicity, and Reading:
Narration in *My Mortal Enemy*   27

3
Tales of Telling and Fictions of History:
Casting *Shadows on the Rock*   59

4
Obscuring Destinies:
Threading the Narrative of "Old Mrs. Harris"   89

5
Lucy Gayheart:
The Bildungsroman as Grecian Urn   116

6
Enslaved by History:
The Burden of the Past and Cather's Last Novel   150

Notes   177

Index   197

Acknowledgments

As others have said before and said more eloquently, a book is always a curiously collaborative artifact, despite the single name on its title page. There are many people to whom I owe a warm thanks, but none more so than Clark Dougan, who believed in this book long before I myself did and whose enthusiasm was contagious. I would also like to thank Pam Wilkinson and Catlin Murphy of the University of Massachusetts Press for all their efforts on my behalf.

Colleagues and friends who have also shaped my writing and thinking include Emily Bartels, Deborah Browning, Chris Flug, Judith Fryer, Howard Horowitz, Paul Howe, Barbara Johnson, Chris Norris, Sharon O'Brien, Mary Rimmer, and Carolyn Stack. To one and all, many thanks.

Finally, I wish to recognize especially Eleanor Drey, whose patience and generosity supported this project in its early incarnation, and Susan Rosowski, whose wise and perceptive advice helped shape its end.

CATHER, CANON,
AND THE
POLITICS OF READING

Categorical Cather:
Reading the Canon(s)

When one starts out to write about Willa Sibert Cather, distin-
guished Nebraska novelist, he must approach his subject with simplicity and sincerity. If he does not he will sin . . . against the canons
of art.   —EVA MAHONEY, *Omaha World-Herald*, 1921

I think we should all, in our school days, be given a chance at
Shakespeare, Milton, Fielding, Jane Austen—coming down as late
as Thackeray, George Eliot, George Meredith, and Thomas Hardy. I
don't mean that *MacBeth* or *The Egoist* or *Henry Esmond* can be
"taught" at all. I mean that the students can be "exposed," so to
speak, to the classics. If the germ "takes," even in very few, it will
develop, and give them a great deal of pleasure in life. And those
who do not catch the infection will certainly not be at all harmed.
     —WILLA CATHER, 1939

When Betty Jean Steinshouer began touring her one-woman Willa
Cather performance, she tried "to duplicate Cather's evening dress. I got
a lot of brocade, shawls, and brightly colored things because I knew she
liked to dress up and wear hats and all that."[1] But her audiences, Steinshouer soon realized, were upset. They had a different vision of Cather in
their minds' eye. So she began to wear the costume made famous by a
photograph Edward Steichen took of Cather in the 1920s, in which the
author sports a sailor's middy blouse, red tie, and dark skirt. "The middy
blouse and the tie is sort of the Cather symbol," Steinshouer admitted. "I
decided, at least in that way, to give people what they wanted and what
makes them feel comfortable—that they're really seeing Willa Cather."

And according to Steinshouer, people *do* want to see and experience

Cather. "Everybody loves Willa Cather. People just come out of the woodwork. I am always astonished at the level at which she moves people, and it pretty much extends across all boundaries—economic, class, race, everything." Steinshouer does not work from a script, and each of her performances includes a period during which she takes questions from the audience in character. When asked what essential attributes of Cather she tries to re-create in her performance, Steinshouer replied, "I use a lot of her humor. She's very, very funny and people don't expect that because they think of her as having this somber tone of hardship and sternness. There's no sag in her. She's very opinionated. She loved to debate. I tried to bring out that part of her that would find the winners of the debates at the University of Nebraska and then debate them in public where she could humiliate them. She has some sharp edges."

Steinshouer believes that one reason that Cather appeals to the public at large is because "she is so fully balanced. To use Maswell's term, she's 'self-actualized.' She writes about everyday people who struggle. Only a well-adjusted person could take all of the pain and failure and problems of everyday life and exalt it to the level she does. So that a young person reading her books might think, 'Oh, this is terribly boring: there's no sex, there's no real violence' (the violence that's in there is so real it's almost unbearable). But she makes the everyday lives of Americans significant." With Cather, Steinshouer has realized over the years, "people see an inner glimpse of themselves."

While Steinshouer quite literally takes Cather to the people, the Willa Cather Pioneer Memorial Society and Education Foundation is busy preserving and promoting the life and art of Willa Cather within Nebraska and throughout the world.[2] Both academic and popular, the Willa Cather industry that operates out of Red Cloud, Nebraska, is akin to a small business run by a family utterly passionate about and deeply devoted to its product. The Cather Historical Center houses not only a significant collection of Cather's letters and papers, but also displays scenes from her novels in dioramas.[3] Officials of the Memorial have retitled the Red Cloud environs "Catherland," offering guided and self-guided tours through many of the places that appear in Cather's fiction. An advertisement of "Extraordinary Christmas Ideas" touts Cather Country Confections (six different jellies) and Willa Cather Limited Edition Brass Bookends. Girl Scout National Headquarters even created a Willa Cather Merit Badge in 1963.[4] One 1988 letter, written by Nancy

Picchi from South Orange, New Jersey, and published in the *Willa Cather Pioneer Memorial Newsletter,* typifies what constitutes Cather's popular appeal for these devotees.

It's been difficult getting back to the mundane details of work after the excitement of the Amtrak Sisters' Western Tour. Again, I would like to express my appreciation to you for your hospitality and attention. When I should be writing a grant proposal, I find myself day-dreaming about Red Cloud. I am very impressed by the work that you and your dedicated band of Catherites have accomplished in Red Cloud. The restoration of the Cather Homestead is a gift to all of us; it preserves an important place in American literature and a special time in American history. . . .

I have begun my Willa Cather Society proselytizing and have a core of believers ready to sign on the dotted line. I am always surprised by how many well-educated Americans have never read a novel by Willa Cather. I have now taken to carrying copies of *O Pioneers!* and *My Antonia* with me and distributing them to these poor souls. I feel as if I am distributing manna in the wilderness. . . .

Yesterday my husband, Bern, and I received a letter from the Statue of Liberty-Ellis Island Foundation describing the work that has been done to restore Ellis Island as a monument to the immigrants that helped to build this country. As I read this letter, I kept thinking of Red Cloud and Catherland; while Ellis Island symbolizes the beginning of the American dream for these immigrants, Red Cloud and Nebraska represent the actual realization of that dream.[5]

For Nancy Picchi, the Cather Homestead, like Ellis Island and the Statue of Liberty, is a historical monument because of its place within a particular national and even mythic grid of American history. The historical narrative within which Picchi locates and is able to read both *O Pioneers!* and *My Antonia* is one of immigration and "realization." The relevance of Cather's America is its continuation of and progression within a narrative that posits the "American experience" as one of late-nineteenth-century immigration to the United States and early twentieth-century accommodation to an expansive landscape and culture in which the self could be defined anew. The yawning Nebraska prairie then is not so far removed, at least imaginatively and ideologically, from the Lower East Side tenements, and both mark particularly "American" spaces of experience. Picchi's reading of the American dream as a drama of rebirth parallels her own conversion to Cather, and prompts her, with the conviction of the newly enlightened, to disseminate the gospel of Cather in an urban, northeastern wilderness that has not read and does not appreciate her work. Picchi, in other words, has been awakened to the historical and American significance of Willa Cather, and like all acolytes ("Catherites"), she resolves to share her newfound knowledge with an ignorant world.

Such passionate devotion constitutes simply one of the reading communities in which the person and the prose of Willa Cather are appropriated, claimed, and somehow signified.[6] Such reading communities organize themselves unconsciously around what Barbara Herrnstein Smith has termed "contingencies of value," an evaluative frame of reference in which an object, a text, or an author "is likely to perform certain particular (though taken-for-granted) functions for some particular (though only implicitly defined) set of subjects under some particular (unspecified but assumed) set or range of conditions."[7] Though such significations of value characterize virtually all critical treatments of "major" writers, Cather, because she "belongs to no school,"[8] is especially subject to the revision, reification, and renunciation of widely disparate readerly contingents. Whether viewed as an American icon, a woman writer, a lesbian, a cosmopolitan Midwesterner, a conservative Republican, a scathing journalist, an antimodernist, or an embittered elegiast, Cather remains an anomaly in American literature and her fiction is peculiarly hard to place. Despite her popular appeal, Cather lingers in the margins of the American literary canon. As Sharon O'Brien has noted, Cather's literary rank "is not a high one; she has been considered an important writer and yet somehow not a major one, somehow not an equal colleague of Hawthorne, James, or Faulkner, and perhaps not even in the same realm as Fitzgerald, Hemingway, or Dreiser."[9] The current and frequently rancorous debate about canons and the curriculum seems to bear this out. In a 1988 letter to the *New York Times Magazine*, responding to a previous piece on the controversies surrounding the literary canon, C. Webster Wheelock closed his jeremiad with the following peroration: "Any professor who lets [Charles Brockden] Brown or [Zora Neale] Hurston shoulder aside works by James, Melville, *or even Cather*, ought to be required personally to give a tuition refund to *her* students" (emphasis added).[10] Though one might wonder why Wheelock imagines the offending professor to be female, it is nonetheless interesting that removing Cather from the canon constitutes a criminal offense in his scheme, if, albeit, a lesser one.

Wheelock's qualified inclusion does suggest, however, that Cather has made it into some versions of an American literary canon. But what soon becomes apparent about canonical inclusions of Cather is that they are limited to the first half of her oeuvre, those early pioneer novels—*O Pioneers!* (1913), *The Song of the Lark* (1915), and *My Antonia* (1918)—that celebrate American manifest destiny and the settling of the West. Spanning both popular and critical assessments, Cather's canonical value resides in the heroic myth of national destiny that a vast array of readers recognize in these early novels. In the 1978 "Films for the Humanities" series, "Exploring American Literature" and "Women in American Literature," for example, "Willa Cather's America" is composed of "the wild American land and the people on it, and the heroism required to transplant the Old World culture to the harsh, vast New World." What is unique about this version of Cather's literary relevance is its staying power; nearly fifty years earlier, Alfred Kazin praised Cather's early novels for their ability to inspire "the individual discovery of power, the joy of fulfilling oneself in the satisfaction of an appointed destiny."[11] What designates these early novels as canonical then is their appeal to reading publics as stories already inscribed within the national imagination. They are recognizable versions of what Sharon O'Brien characterizes as "America's story," yet startlingly original in their evocation of the pioneer experience as, essentially, "epics of women."

> Unlike many of her female literary predecessors and contemporaries . . . Cather did not limit herself to telling a conventional female narrative. Alexandra Bergson's taming of the wild land embodies the history of her culture as Cather makes a female character representative of the American experiment without seeming to be self-conscious about doing so. Having experienced dislocation, loss, and resettlement herself, unlike her contemporaries Edith Wharton and Ellen Glasgow, Cather could claim this dominant subject in American culture and literature as her own and envision the heroic leader of the pioneer venture as female.[12]

Because of this mythic and historical resonance, Cather's early novels are the ones regularly taught in high schools and colleges. Of the seventeen Cather texts appearing on the progressive college and university syllabi collected by Paul Lauter in *Reconstructing American Literature,* only one, *Death Comes for the Archbishop* (1927), is drawn from the eight novels Cather wrote after 1925. *My Antonia,* conversely, appears six times, *O Pioneers!* four, and *A Lost Lady* (1922) and *The Song of the Lark* each turn up once. Early short stories account for the final four inclusions.[13] What is identifiably canonical within Cather's nearly fifty years of fiction writing then is, paradoxically, a small number of texts that embody the expansive West of the American imagination.

To say that Cather's fiction is noncanonical then is not entirely accurate, for obviously the early novels have attained a kind of thematic, canonical inclusion.[14] But certain, persistent questions remain about Cather and the canon generally, and this study will attempt to articulate at least some of them. Why, for instance, are the majority of Cather's late fictions rigorously unread?[15] Why are they either ignored in or excluded from canons? What is it exactly that renders them, if not absolutely noncanonical, then conventionally unclassifiable in the prevailing critical assessments of Cather's work? Why, in other words, are they difficult to read?

Such questions necessitate an examination of the way differing contingents of academic readers have addressed the late novels—those written after 1925 and until Cather's death in 1947—because public and popular acceptance of the late fiction kept Cather on best-seller lists throughout her career. These *academic* reading communities fall, broadly, into four categories: those concerned with art, style, and form in Cather's fiction; those who attempt to place Cather historically and thematically in the "main currents" of twentieth-century American literature; feminist critics; and lesbian feminist scholars. Each of these contingents have a vested interest in the politics of its own reading(s), and each represents the *idea* of Willa Cather in a radically different way.

Looking at Willa Cather as the consummate artist whose works are best understood as being fundamentally about art itself is the most prevalent approach in Cather studies, and for good reason. Begun by the pioneering work of Mildred Bennett, whose 1951 *The World of Willa Cather* introduced readers to the midwestern and biographical concerns informing Cather's fiction, this method is most closely associated with scholars at the University of Nebraska and with that university's press, which has published virtually all Cather's writing on art.[16] Composed predominantly of New Critical textual readings, investigations of Cather's artistry locate recurring biographical and thematic issues that center around what Cather firmly believed was the exceptional and necessary role of the artist in society: to preserve that which is true and good by a careful attention to human nature and a command of one's artistic medium. The Willa Cather enshrined within the Nebraska community is the embodiment of American individualism; her diligence and talent enabled her to achieve her dream of becoming the (dis)embodiment of artistic distance, intensity, and integrity. The more personal and private aspects of her life are carefully veiled and ultimately subordinated to a biographical history determined solely by artistic growth and achievement.[17] What such an approach ignores, however, are the ramifications of Cather's gender and presumed sexual preference upon her choice of subjects and strategies of representation. In this reading, art becomes the ultimate "meaning" of her considerably diverse novels.

More recently some critics have attempted to redefine Cather's work within the boundaries of canonical modernism or as arising out of and consequently affiliated, in style and technique, with a modernist impulse. Susan J. Rosowski, for instance, in her important study of Cather's novels entitled *The Voyage Perilous: Willa Cather's Romanticism* (1986), contends that "the essential characteristic of romanticism concerns a mode of perception by which the imagination is used in its synthesizing or creative powers to transform and give meaning to an alien or meaningless material world. In this sense, the Romantics inaugurated modern literature." Tracing thematic manifestations of both romanticism and gothicism throughout Cather's fiction, Rosowski charts Cather's sensitivity "to feelings we term modern: a sense of alienation and historical discontinuity."[18] What is liberating about this approach is that by arguing that experimentation with content and/or form is what characterizes both Cather's fiction and standard texts of high modernism, Rosowski's proposition allows for the incorporation of the later novels into the critical debate on canon. Phyllis Rose, who, along with Rosowski, argues pointedly for an essentially modernist interpretation of Cather's work, has suggested that impulse and design are relevant categories to examine in evaluating Cather as a canonical modernist.

> In modernist critical writings, including Cather's, certain themes recur: an urge to shake loose of clutter, a refusal to accept the mimetic function of art as previously defined, a feeling that a certain "spirit" was escaping the older forms, an urge toward anonymity. The vessel is emphasized rather than the content; art is imagined as a fragile container for the ineffable substance of life. The modernists were aware of art as a created artifact, not as a mirror reflecting reality or a camera eye absorbing and imprinting it.[19]

The critical writing to which Rose alludes is Cather's best-known essay, "The Novel Démueblé," in which she seems to move away from certain aspects of literary "realism" toward some allusive and purpose-fully indefinite articulation of her own method. Cather begins the essay by redefining what realism is *not;* it is, she suggests cryptically, "an attitude of the mind," not "the cataloguing of a great number of material objects, in explaining mechanical processes, the methods of operating manufactories and trade."[20] Though she purposefully reduces realism to an aesthetic she can then discard, what Cather does advocate in the title of her essay is a housecleaning of sorts, a stripping down of narrative to its essential minimum, unencumbered by too many "realistic" details and by authorial intervention. She praises the artistic innovation of those "younger writers [who] are trying to break away from mere verisimilitude, and, following the development of modern painting, to interpret imaginatively the material and social investiture of their char-acters; to present their scene by suggestion rather than by enumeration" (48).[21] "The higher processes of art," she concludes, "are all processes of simplification" (48–49), of "unfurnishing" the too cluttered house of fiction. What Cather arrives at finally in the essay is an aesthetic method determined by absence and allusion: "Whatever is felt upon the page without being specifically named there—that, one might say, is created. It is the inexplicable presence of the thing not named, of the overtone divined by the ear but not heard by it, the verbal mood, the emotional aura of the fact or the thing or the deed, that gives high quality to the novel or the drama, as well as to poetry itself" (50). What leads critics like Rose and others to identify this elusive definition as somehow modernist is its seeming repudiation of definite and explicable form, its emphasis on "presence," "mood," and "aura," and its implication that audience response is dictated more by divination than by apprehension.

Janis P. Stout, in her recent *Strategies of Reticence* (1990), suggests that this textual "reticence" in Cather's fictions is intimately linked to the loud silence surrounding issues of sexual preference in her life: "The aesthetic principle that Cather consciously and capably defended and that she followed in so craftly a fashion was chosen, at least in part, because it accorded so well with her need to find a strategy of avoidance and suppression. The need fueled the theoretical affiliation that gave it aesthetic respectability."[22] Hermione Lee, Cather's most recent biogra-pher, also examines Cather's life and fictional language through the lens of a modernist sensibility. Lee, in her *Willa Cather: Double Lives* (1989), suggests that Cather's conscious aesthetic of elimination and excision in language "isn't just a matter of making a sophisticated narrative read like the story-tellings of an oral culture. It is a communication (more 'modernist,' ambiguous and strange than it looks at first sight) which can find a way into the incommunicable; the silent; the obscure."[23] Avoiding the interrelation between biography and aesthetics that Stout and, to a lesser extent, Lee persuasively suggest, other critics have turned to language alone as the arena in which to locate Cather's modernism. Robert J. Nelson, for example, in his *Willa Cather and France: In Search of the Lost Language* (1988), argues that Cather's refusal to conform to knowable and signifiable language practices creates a radical modernism, resulting in "a countertext if not an antitext . . . by the author's own desire."[24] And Jo Ann Middleton, in *Willa Cather's Modernism: A Study of Style and Technique* (1990), appropriates the biological term "vacuole," using it as a way to better "understand Catherian absences." Despite such silences, gaps, and absences, Cather's novels, as Middleton points out, remain "deceptively simple to read" and, on several levels, to comprehend, which is what accounts for her particularly broad and popular appeal.[25] Wallace Stevens, one of Cather's many admirers, cautioned a friend in a letter that "she takes so much pains to conceal her sophistication that it is easy to miss her quality."[26] Indeed, I would suggest that it is the lucidity and seeming readability of Cather's concise prose that make her novels difficult to place squarely within canonical modernism as we know it, despite the efforts of critics to redefine the parameters of what "modernism" as a term signifies and, more important, to extend what is excluded a priori within that signification.[27]

Hugh Kenner's intriguing essay, for example, "The Making of the Modernist Canon" (1984), illustrates the numerous ways in which the conventional definition of modernism would necessarily not concern itself with Willa Cather.[28] In Kenner's historical narration of modernism, it is an engagement with international influences and movements that makes the modern artistic sensibility.

> As the capital [London] ingathered, the provinces stirred. Poems were mailed to *The Egoist* by William Carlos Williams from New Jersey and by Marianne Moore from New York. Williams had known Pound at college; Miss Moore revered the example of James. Though they stayed settled in America all their lives they were never tempted to make easy rhymes for the natives. Their generation, aware of emissaries in London—Pound, Eliot, H.D.—could look toward London for contact with more than mere Englishness. The next American generation, that of Hemingway, Fitzgerald and Faulkner, also drew profit from the transatlantic example. By

the time of its apprenticeship there were modern masterworks to study, notably *Ulysses* and *The Wasteland*. However rootedly local, American writing, thanks to twenty years of looking abroad, has enjoyed ever since an inwardness with the international, the technological century. (370)

Kenner's ostensible purpose in this essay is to pose the questions: "The canon of literary modernism: how did that get made? Is it made yet?" (365). But in his own history of modernism, Kenner is himself making the canon in the narration of its making. He establishes two conditions: first, that Americans who claim title to modernism transcend their own provincial literature by never making "easy rhymes for the natives." In other words, to write either for or within the literal confines of an American sensibility is to remain stuck in the mire of popular, not high (modernist) art. Kenner implicitly links Williams to Pound, Moore to James, thereby providing proof that each moved beyond his and her own national borders toward modernist pioneers who had already made the literal move to Europe. This requisite club membership in the modernist canon is especially problematic for Cather whose first novel, *Alexander's Bridge* (1912), is a "failed" imitation of James, and whose artistic mentor was the extremely marginalized and conceptually provincial regionalist Sarah Orne Jewett.[29] "Easy rhymes for the natives" also condemns economic success as a sign of the fatal popular embrace, excluding from consideration such "best-selling" authors as Cather herself.

Kenner's second condition is an artistic incorporation of continental models, what he refers to as "an inwardness with the international." The models he singles out, significantly, are *Ulysses* and *The Waste Land,* both of which originate from writers in exile from their own, limiting national conditions. The way one locates "an inwardness with the international," however, must necessarily be within a text, an *external* manifestation which then Kenner, or any critic, reads, interprets, and signifies as the product of this "inwardness with the international." In other words, the proof again lies in what any critic valorizes in a text as "modernist," which then is read as the causal effect of a writer's internalization of "modern masterworks." By this logic, *Ulysses* and *The Waste Land* become the ur-texts through which all subsequent *American* modernism is defined.

It seems also worth noting that within this passage Kenner has, in effect, created his own modernist canon, one that includes Williams, Moore, Pound, Joyce, James, Eliot, Hemingway, Faulkner, and Fitzgerald. This is less an examination of how the modernist canon was made and more a reiteration of what we already know it to be. And within the definition Kenner provides, Cather could not possibly be identified as or even remotely considered to be a modernist. Despite her own cosmopolitan travels, interests, and affinities, Cather remains somehow too American, too nationally oriented. The answer to Kenner's second question then, "Is [the canon] made yet?" is an unequivocal "yes," because the question itself, as the essay articulates, is a purely rhetorical one.

Cather, however, has not simply been ignored within critical studies of the modernist canon such as Kenner's. Rather, from the 1930s onward, she has been labeled as and harangued for being, quintessentially, an antimodernist. And certainly her own critical writing during this period did nothing to repudiate this image. On the contrary, Cather seemed to delight in fanning the flames of critical indignation, an act that had particular consequences on her literary reputation for approximately forty years.

The contemporary critical attack on Cather began in 1933 with the publication of Granville Hicks's essay, "The Case against Will Cather."[30] In it Hicks critiqued what appeared to him to be "the political conservatism" evident in all Cather's work, embodied most clearly in her nostalgic evocation "of the frontier, and . . . the heroism of earlier days" (140). Though Hicks conceded that both *O Pioneers!* and *My Antonia* "have their importance in American literature" because they contain "a basis in reality" (141), he was less charitable toward Cather's subsequent fiction. Essentially, Hicks was the first critic to align Cather's personal sensibility with the work she produced, arguing that Cather could not sustain her vision of America's heroic idealism in the midst of the modern world: "as she looked at the life about her, her despair grew" (143). Hicks's final assessment of Cather is harsh. Concluding that "her romantic dreams involve the distortion of life" (146), he dismisses Cather as a writer who has nothing relevant to say about the twentieth century: "Miss Cather has never once tried to see contemporary life as it is; she sees only that it lacks what the past, at least in her idealization of it, had. Thus she has been barred from the task that has occupied most of the world's great artists, the expression of what is central and fundamental in her own age" (144).

Cather, not surprisingly, perceived these to be fighting words. And the critical essays she wrote during the thirties respond to Hicks's attack with a rhetoric of hyperbolic posturing and defensive rationalization. The Preface to *Not Under Forty* (1936), for instance, announces dramatically that "the world broke in two in 1922 or thereabouts, and the persons and prejudices recalled in these sketches slid back into yesterday's seven thousand years." Rather than counter Hicks's characterization of her as antimodern, Cather embraced it. "It is for the backward," she declared unapologetically, "and by one of their number, that these sketches were written. . . . the book will have little interest for people under forty years of age." In that same year she published her specific response to Hicks in a letter to the *Commonweal* entitled, "Escapism." In it Cather begins with the rhetorical question, "What has art ever been but escape?" and justifies her position by arguing that art is devoted to universal, human experiences, not simply contemporary, economic ones.[31] The difference between Cather and Hicks lies in their separate notions of what, literally, escapism means. Cather adopts one sense of the word—the diversion of the mind to purely imaginative activity—to insist that "true" artists must be allowed to exist in their own separate sphere, "left out of the social and industrial routine" (21). Art, she implies, is by necessity apolitical, because only then does it transcend social propaganda and the petty details of daily life that weigh down and ultimately destroy the human and experiential "truth" to which all "great" fiction aspires. Hicks, conversely, conceives of literature as essentially and necessarily political. Escapism in his terms constitutes a betrayal of one's social and human responsibility, an evasion of unpleasant reality through what he characterizes as Cather's compensatory nostalgia. Both believe that art should aspire to "truth," but each defines it legitimately and oppositionally, within the operative meanings of the word "escapist" itself.

Confirming rather than contradicting Hicks's reading of her fiction, Cather's theoretical writing inadvertently contributed to the critical devaluation of her work throughout the thirties and forties.[32] Sharon O'Brien has commented on how certain critics during these decades— Hicks, Kazin, and Trilling especially—engaged in an ad feminam attack of Cather that was in part motivated by their desire to define themselves in opposition to the paternal power and influence of the literary critics who had immediately preceded them: "At the same time they were sons confronting a maternal presence their fathers had left as a literary legacy, a woman writer of the first rank. In attacking Willa Cather, the leftist critics who came of age in the 1930s were thus engaged in a complex oedipal drama, seeking both to replace the older generation of male critics and to repudiate a powerful maternal literary figure by defining her as limited." O'Brien accounts for the virulent antifeminism of these attacks by historicizing the role that gender played in the formation of the canon. Noting that increased professionalization of American literary studies occurred during these decades, she surmises that critics regularly delegated women writers to lesser and "minor" ranks so as to ensure that a vigorous, virile, and national American literature existed to rival that of an English tradition in which the male masters—Chaucer, Shakespeare, and Milton—had already been enshrined.[33]

O'Brien's work is important in determining why Cather was the brunt of such vicious attacks during these decades, but it does not discuss fully the canonical consequences of this critical invective, especially upon Cather's late fiction that was being both written and published at the time.[34] For what distinguishes the critical rhetoric of this decade is not only a none too subtle misogyny about what is "feminine," and therefore, nostalgic and regressive, in Cather's fiction, but also an interpretation that links explicitly Cather's personal life to her fictional texts. Alfred Kazin, for example, simply reiterates Hicks's claims that Cather's early fiction was her only important contribution to American literature, and that as her career progressed, her novels deteriorated. Kazin himself charts a teleology of personal and artistic decline that exactly parallels what he reads as the "meaning" of Cather's later fictions: "The climax in Willa Cather's career came with two short novels she published between 1923 and 1925, *A Lost Lady* and *The Professor's House*. They were parables of the decline and fall of the great tradition, her own tradition. . . . Later, as it seemed, she became merely sentimental, and her direct criticism of contemporary types and manners was often petulant and intolerant."[35] Equating Cather personally with her texts ("They were parables of the decline and fall. . . . she became merely sentimental"), Kazin identifies the "climax" of her career in the years between 1923 and 1925, when Cather was nearing fifty. What is telling in his diction, however, is his characterization of both her and her work as "petulant," "intolerant," and "sentimental," words frequently associated with the elderly, especially women.

Other attacks are more relentlessly personal. Leon Edel argues in his ironically titled "Homage to Willa Cather" that after 1922 Cather "was a creature of old and fixed habits and she could not swim with the stream. This made for deep loyalties and abiding affections. It also tended to dry up the fount of her inspiration; there was no sustenance in the present."[36]

In this extraordinary passage, Edel equates Cather's inability to produce what he deems "great" fiction with an encoded asexual signification: she is a "creature" in his diction, "old and fixed," whose "fount" has dried up, offering "no sustenance" in the present. In one sense, Edel is describing what he sees as Cather's refusal to accommodate herself to the modern American world of the twenties, thirties, and forties. Yet the associations conveyed by his imagery suggest as well that Cather had herself become an aged crone, whose withered body (fount/breasts) betrays her inability to offer "sustenance in the present" (both for herself and for the reader), during precisely that period in which she wrote her final seven major works of fiction. Edel's critique is, essentially, a postmenopausal condemnation of Cather and her late fiction as being past their prime; they are outdated, they are uninteresting, they are old-womanish.

The canonical consequence of such psychologizing has been the creation of an entire school of criticism that reads Willa Cather the author as virtually indistinguishable from her works, especially the later ones.[37] Moreover, these later assessments accept unquestioningly the early critical formula that Cather's novels climax in the twenties, then spiral downward in a trajectory of despair, decline, and artistic degeneration. Such assumptions allow both John H. Randall and David Daiches, for example, to conflate Cather with her late novels in the following critical evaluations.

> Another sign of artistic weakening makes its appearance about this time: the main characters, when the stress becomes too acute, beat a mental retreat to an earlier and less frustrating phase of their existence; in other words, they regress. . . . the actions of her later protagonists seem to be projections of some unfortunate personal traits of her own. . . . The kindest thing which can be said of the later crisis novels is that they present a world-view at once idiosyncratic and bizarre. I am inclined to make the severer judgment that they embody an outlook on life so distorted and falsified as to be practically worthless as an interpretation of human experience.[38]

> A strong inventive imagination was not one of Willa Cather's gifts. Her memory had to be stirred, her emotions involved, some autobiographical impulse had to be touched, however indirectly, before she could produce her best and strongest work. And her best work *is* strong: she possessed the kind of masculine sensibility which drew nourishment from simple, elemental situations to subtilize them and make them persuasive symbols of aspects of experience. . . . In retreating from the earthy situations of her

earlier Midwestern novels she had finally lost altogether the epic touch, and, though she had gained other qualities, none of them were so convincingly her own.[39]

The biographical basis of these readings is self-evident; Cather's art weakens as her life progresses. Yet these passages impart an interpretation about Cather and her fiction that prevails even today. This reading centers upon the idea that Willa Cather's life and art embody a traditionalism that is vigorous when it evokes the pioneer West, but rigid and genteel from the 1920s onward. Accordingly, Cather lost herself and her artistic strength within the wasteland of an urban, postwar world. She could not regain the "masculine sensibility" that invigorated her early, manifest destiny fiction. Instead, she became feminized; she weakened artistically, she retreated, she regressed, she began to see the world in "idiosyncratic and bizarre" ways. As the scope of society Cather explores in the late fiction narrows, so does her art devolve. This logic is exacerbated by the fact that most of the later novels and stories are concerned primarily with female protagonists who struggle with and even sometimes resist the social constraints imposed upon them because of gender. The late novels are devalued not specifically because they are less masculine, but because they are about telling women's stories. Thus do critical judgments reveal themselves to be a thinly disguised misogyny. Lionel Trilling's pronouncement then, that "so self-conscious and defiant a rejection of her own time must make her talent increasingly irrelevant and tangential—for any time,"[40] stands as only one of many such interpretations that have contributed to the now canonical acceptance of the "fact" that Cather's late works are artistically inept, tired failures not worth reading.[41]

One might suppose that the surge of feminist criticism in the early seventies would have addressed this devaluation of the late works, especially since they are, for the most part, stories about women. Yet in certain instances just the opposite was true. Carolyn Heilbrun, in a curiously reductive reading of the late novels, bemoans what she sees as the loss of "strong heroines" in Cather's late fictions: "Equally indicative of the female urge toward the destruction and denial of female destiny is the woman novelist who manages to achieve an autonomous woman character in perhaps one or two novels, and then relinquishes the central role to men. Willa Cather is such an author. . . . After *My Antonia*, the struggle is over, the imagination has failed in its creation of women, and has shifted to male heroes."[42] This is essentially the same attitude toward the late works as that entertained by male critics from the thirties through the sixties, only it offers an opposing explanation for failure. Heilbrun reads Cather's work as becoming more, rather than less, masculine. One wonders how she manages to ignore the female heroines in *My Mortal Enemy* (1926), *Shadows on the Rock* (1929), "Old Mrs. Harris" (1931), *Lucy Gayheart* (1936), and *Sapphira and the Slave Girl* (1940), except for the possibility that she may not find them all likable or admirable and thus refuses to designate them as "heroic." A similar, though thematically unrelated, elision of the later novels occurs in Gilbert and Gubar's analysis of Cather in *Sexchanges*, volume two of their *No Man's Land*. Though Gilbert and Gubar's premise, in keeping with the larger intent of their investigation, is that "Cather quarreled with contemporary America in general and with the 'laws' that govern heterosexual relations in particular," they spend the majority of their chapter examining the ways in which the women construct autonomy in the early novels and mention the later ones only in passing.[43] Within feminist studies on Cather, Judith Fryer's *Felicitous Space* devotes sustained analysis to two of the later novels as they represent imagined and real spaces inhabited by women characters.[44] Susan Rosowski, Janis Stout, and Hermione Lee, however, have pioneered feminist approaches to Cather's fiction which encompass issues either expressed in or related to the later novels. Rosowski (1986) and Lee (1989) address Cather's entire oeuvre (including the later novels) from a feminist perspective in their thematic and biographical studies, respectively. Stout, similarly, argues that, in general, Cather's works could be termed feminist in that they alternate between "sometimes proclaiming a feminist vision, sometimes depicting the perniciousness or merely the invalidity of the varying forces arrayed against a feminist vision, or, more simply, arrayed against women."[45] Important as these works are, they do not address what I will argue are not so much differences as readerly difficulties that arise in the later texts but are not in the earlier ones. The focus of these feminist critics is more sweeping and synthetic in approach; my methodology will tend toward the more disjunctive and particular.

Lesbian feminist criticism has not, curiously, expressed an interest in Cather's late fiction, despite the numerous critiques of heterosexuality throughout the late novels and the presence of subtle, homoerotic, and homosocial allusions within them. Though Cather was explicitly introduced as a lesbian writer by Jane Rule as early as 1975,[46] it was not until the publication of Sharon O'Brien's ground-breaking essay, " 'The Thing Not Named': Willa Cather as a Lesbian Writer" (1984), which was followed by her 1987 psychoanalytic biography charting Cather's emergence as a female-identified writer, that Cather's lesbianism became common parlance in academic conferences and critical essays. And while the term "lesbian" undoubtedly makes some readers and critics of Cather uncomfortable, and perhaps even raises the hackles of others, it also raises the political stakes of Cather criticism generally. For the impressive array of scholarship O'Brien has marshaled—especially her discovery of Cather's love letters to Louise Pound which hint at Cather's own awareness that her feelings for Pound would be viewed as "unnatural"[47]—makes it difficult, if not impossible, to ignore Cather's sexual and emotional preferences in critical works linking the life with the works that still predominate in Cather scholarship.[48] O'Brien's work, in other words, constitutes a watershed in Cather criticism and raises the following inevitable questions: What does it mean to read Cather as a lesbian writer? If, indeed, we acknowledge that Cather was a self-identified lesbian, as O'Brien claims, then does it necessarily follow that she was, because of this erotic preference, a *lesbian* writer? How can we, and do we, read lesbian traces in Cather's fiction?

In her 1984 essay, O'Brien suggests that Cather's use of the phrase "the thing not named" in "The Novel Démeublé" marks a particularly significant instance of absence in Cather's work and raises the problem of unnameability in general: "Whereas phrases like *overtone, verbal mood* and *emotional aura* suggest ineffable realms of experience and feeling— complex or barely sensed signifieds for which there is no precise verbal signifier—Cather's startling phrase *the thing not named* has another connotation: an aspect of experience possessing a name that the writer does not, or cannot, employ." O'Brien herself suggests the connection between what she calls "Cather's startling phrase" and Oscar Wilde's coining of "the Love that dared not speak its name," and concludes that though Cather appears in the passage as "the modernist writer endorsing allusive, suggestive art and inviting the reader's participation in the creation of literary meaning," she must also be read as "the lesbian writer forced to disguise or to conceal the emotional aura of her fiction, reassuring herself that the reader fills the absence in the text by intuiting the subterranean, unwritten text."[49] O'Brien's essay has been formative in the subsequent lesbian-centered criticism of Cather. By naming the unnameable thing "lesbian," O'Brien transforms a reader's interaction

with the multiple significations of Cather's texts—"presence," "overtone," "mood," and "aura"—and instead *seems* to suggest that one can
"fill the absence in the text" with the "unwritten text" that is lesbian
experience. Though O'Brien will later in her essay complicate the reading of lesbianism as the "unwritten text" of Cather's novels, most critics
who have appropriated Cather as a lesbian writer read quite literally the
existence of a "subterranean, unwritten text" that is, essentially, lesbian.[50]
In these readings, considering Cather as a lesbian writer not only illuminates unexamined or contradictory aspects of the texts, but it also
constitutes the repressed *meaning* of the texts as well.

In order to arrive at a lesbian-centered interpretation of a text that
inscribes lesbianism as an unnameable absence, critics have begun to
read the fictions as either coded or engaged in an elaborate masquerade
that displaces their lesbian nature. Early in the critical formulation of
lesbian criticism, Catherine Stimpson argued that because "the violent
yoking of homosexuality and deviancy has been so pervasive in the
modern period," the lesbian writer who "wished to name her experience
but . . . feared plain speech" would of necessity "encrypt her text in
another sense and use codes."[51] Reading Cather's fiction as sexually
coded is prevalent among current scholarship; at the 1989 Santa Fe
Conference on Willa Cather, for example, a number of papers directed
their interpretations toward the "unwritten" text. Focusing primarily on
the early fiction, the papers had titles ranging from "Unnatural Excitement and Narrative Masquerade: The Lesbian Aesthetic in *Alexander's
Bridge*," and "The Sub/Versions and Silences in Alexandra's 'White
Book': A Lesbian Feminist Reading of *O Pioneers!*" to "The Unescapable
Ground in Another Form: Lesbian Identity in Willa Cather's *O Pioneers!*" Masquerade, subversion, silence, *another* form: what distinguishes these readings is the implicit assumption that the fiction masks,
submerges, and even distorts the lesbianism that resides, albeit coded, in
the texts. The critical task then becomes one of decoding, uncovering,
and recovering what has been unwritten, unmentionable, and unnamed.
Yet it also involves a mode of interpretation that reads between and
beyond what is literally inscribed on the page, basing its interpretive
burden of proof on the life rather than the text. It is because Cather is a
lesbian that Judith Fetterley can claim, for instance, that "the central
situation in many of her novels and stories is an indirect expression of a
lesbian sensibility,"[52] *not* because that sensibility is necessarily readable in
the text.

Another method of coding to which critics point in Cather's fiction is her use of male narrators in love with, usually, women unavailable to them. Read as a persona of the author, these male narrators allow Cather, as Bonnie Zimmerman suggests, "to express safely her emotional and erotic feelings for other women."[53] Joanna Russ also reads the novels in this way: focusing primarily on *O Pioneers!* (1913) and *One of Ours* (1922), Russ contends that the sexually ambiguous heterosexual relationships in these novels (between Emil and Marie, and Claude and Enid respectively) embody masquerades of Cather's own relations with unattainable women, emphasizing "emotional deprivation" and "the impossibility and hopelessness of the situation." Like many Cather critics before her, Russ is trying to account for the markedly nonsexual nature of heterosexual relationships in Cather's fiction. Her conclusion is that "if one goes back and translates the situations in Cather's novels into lesbian situations, the fictions often make clearer sense."[54]

Yet "clearer sense" is ultimately *not* what Sharon O'Brien advocates in the essay that informs many of these readings. Though O'Brien frequently employs the terms "masquerade," "disguise," and "displacement," she cautions against what is at once a too literal and, paradoxically, nonliteral reading of the fiction, which would claim "that the overt, written text conceals a subtext that is the 'real' story Cather would have written had she been able." O'Brien instead offers a dialectic of reading, suggesting that "we need to examine . . . what is named and what is not," keeping in mind that "authorial intention and meaning may oscillate between the two and thus be indeterminate." We misread Cather's work altogether, she insists, if we assume "that what is not named is the 'real' text, the one Cather would have written in a different social environment."[55]

Despite O'Brien's well-reasoned cautions, an emphasis on the "real" lesbian text is precisely what characterizes the majority of lesbian-centered readings of Cather.[56] Even more problematic is the way such readings continue to valorize the early fiction at the expense of Cather's later work. Deborah Lambert, for example, seems to reiterate Heilbrun's argument when she asserts that "after certain early work, in which she created strong and achieving women, like herself, she abandoned her female characters to the most conventional and traditional roles; analogously, she began to deny or distort the sexuality of her principal characters."[57] Equating Cather the woman with her female characters—a move extraordinarily similar to the one made by the early male critics of the thirties—Lambert identifies a "lesbian" text as one that features "strong and achieving women" who in some way parallel the personal attributes of their author. In this reading, only those novels that conform to a standard of politically correct representation both valorized by the critic and read as part of the author's lesbian character ("strong and achieving") are themselves lesbian texts. Bonnie Zimmerman warns that "there is a danger in this attempt to establish a characteristic lesbian vision or literary value system. . . . In an attempt to say *this* is what defines lesbian literature, we are easily tempted to read selectively, omitting what is foreign to our theories."[58] Despite this caution, what is excluded from lesbian feminist explorations of Cather's novels is the way in which the later fiction examines and self-consciously addresses not only the social and gendered conventions within which women try to create space for the self, but also the kinds of narrative conventions that shape how one tells a woman's story. In viewing the novels solely as a reflection or a masquerade of Cather's life, lesbian feminist readings necessarily ignore the ways in which Cather's lesbianism might affect textual representation, complicating and even contradicting the representation of heterosexual romance that Lambert identifies as too "conventional and traditional."

It is necessary to return then to the question of why these late novels seem so difficult to place in any critical category. Part of the reason, at least, seems to be that no critical vocabulary exists with which to discuss them, other than one that affixes derogatory labels—petulant traditionalism, too conventional, a failure of the imagination—in order to dismiss them entirely from critical discourse. The later novels then, do not conform to any of the paradigms through which we have been conditioned to read Cather's fiction. Yet another reason why Cather's late fiction eludes easy classification is that she was self-consciously experimenting with both narrative structure and technique after 1922. Her "Four Letters"—"On *Death Comes for the Archbishop*," "On *Shadows on the Rock*," "Escapism," and "On *The Professor's House*"—address the new techniques she was attempting to incorporate into her novels, which she alluded to as "experiments in form." These experiments were primarily worked out through "different kinds of method" in narrative, which Cather signified as perhaps a more appropriate term than "novel" for some of her work. One of these "experiments" was "that of inserting the *Nouvelle* into the *Roman*,"[59] the self-conscious placement of separate and distinct short stories within the novel as a whole. One effect of such experimentation is the decentering of her narratives, which are marked by a shifting and mercurial focalization rather than a single determining and easily apprehensible vision. Multiple perspective and narration figure prominently in these novels and often occur in deliberate opposition to the attempt of a particular text to sustain thematic coherence. A certain textual self-reflexiveness operates in all Cather's late works consequently; her fictions recognize and frequently comment upon their own status as fiction. Art and artifice become permeable, and thus confusing categories.

In a 1933 NBC radio broadcast, Cather commented on what she saw as the limitations in form of the contemporary American novel, which she believed was confined "to two themes; how the young man got his girl, whether by matrimony or otherwise, and how he succeeded in business."[60] As a woman novelist interested in telling stories about women in American society, Cather concluded that only "when we learn to give our purpose the form that exactly clothes it and no more; when we make a form for every story instead of trying to crowd it into one of the stock moulds on the shelf, then we shall be on the right road, at least. . . . We won't face the fact that it's the formula itself which is pernicious, the frame-up" (170). In her late fiction especially, Cather experiments with these "pernicious formulas" and the ways in which women have been (re)presented within them. As Susan J. Rosowski has noted in her trenchant analysis of women in Cather's fiction, "Cather devotes works long recognized as among her most powerful to gradually narrowing the question of what it is to be a woman. She places her female characters within increasingly complex and restrictive contexts."[61] Thus the seemingly more "conventional" and "traditional" kinds of novels Cather writes late in her career—the novel of romance, the historical novel, the bildungsroman, and novels that return to her familial and midwestern origins—self-consciously address the difficulties and tensions of writing women's stories within conventional narrative frames. The late texts experiment with genres generally, exploring how written history is created from an oral tradition of tale-telling, for example, and specifically, in their self-reflexive revision of inherited notions of what exactly constitutes a woman's tale, or a tale about a woman.

One would think then that feminist critics would have immediately embraced Cather's analysis of gender and of gendered plots in the late fiction, had it not been for the problematic "heroines" whose stories she tells. The late novels offer two types of female protagonists: powerful and embittered middle-aged women whom it is difficult to like, much less sympathize with, and more conventional, young, pliable, and almost too good ingenues. Neither of these categories of characters makes possible a feminist interpretation interested in praising "strong and admirable" heroines like Antonia Shimerda, Alexandra Bergson, or Thea Kronberg. Moreover, as Gilbert and Gubar have noted, Cather's work in general and the late novels in particular "expressed skepticism not only about conventional sex roles but also about the possibility of changing them."[62] In other words, Cather's late fictions incorporate what are commonly understood as feminist issues—power, autonomy, career aspirations, financial independence—but are not necessarily feminist. Transgressive gestures of sexual expression, of power, of role reversals appear early in the novels, but are contained, managed, and sometimes even contradicted within each text by its end.[63] Thus the problems and disruptions that the stories of these female characters engender—such as the way in which "the figure of the crippled or ill matriarch represents the limitations of women's power in patriarchy"[64]—are resolutely rewritten into some kind of narrative, if not textual, containment. The feminist critic Adrienne Munich has suggested why such interior narrative contradictions inevitably arise in women's novels. Such a female-centered tale exhibits, she argues, "profound disjunctions and throws barriers around its 'feminist consciousness' that betray profound discomfort about what is being expressed. I would argue that all western literature will exhibit some defensiveness about this subject. Female authored work cannot escape varieties of sexual malaise; identification with dominance has colonized most imaginations."[65] The narrative disjunctions in Cather's texts cut two ways. It is just as impossible to read those novels unambivalently as feminist as it is to accept the frequently conventional way they will attempt to negotiate their own closure, believable only if one represses or ignores meanings that the texts have raised earlier in their narratives. One way then to reclaim the later novels as "women's texts" is to acknowledge just how frustratingly feminist and potentially antifeminist they are simultaneously. Cather, one is forced to accept, will always demand to have her texts read both ways, and at once.

Cather's late novels, in fact, all attempt to inscribe what Ross Chambers defines as "readability," a concept I will use throughout this study as the focus of my own reading. "Readerly texts," according to Chambers,

> claim the power to produce new meanings in ever new circumstances (they lay claim to status as artistic discourse), but at the same time they are

concerned, if not to claim a single univocal sense as central to their meaning, then at least to define the range of possible meanings that they can admit, to the exclusion of other possible meanings and relevances. This is what is meant as their "readability." It is as if for them the deferring of meaning from which they benefit as art requires careful control so as not to get out of hand—and it would be possible to show in many texts of the nineteenth century, for instance, that their sense of writing as a phenomenon of entropy, of slippage, or of drift is carefully balanced by a negentropic appeal to the act of reading as an ordering, fixing, or channeling phenomenon.[66]

Chambers's characterization of a nineteenth-century authorial sensibility that appears in certain texts sums up the feelings of many critics about how Cather herself escapes into art in these late novels and about how her art constitutes a reaction against the entropy, slippage, and drift of the modern world. Yet each of the late works examined in this study—*My Mortal Enemy, Shadows on the Rock,* "Old Mrs. Harris," *Lucy Gayheart,* and *Sapphira and the Slave Girl*—questions the very possibility of arriving at any ordered or fixed meaning through the process of reading and interpretation. At the same time that the texts elicit certain readings, by trying to enclose the story within a conventional ending, they inevitably confound the reader's ability to affix an order or a meaning by incorporating within the narrative a multiplicity of contradictory perspectives and interpretations. Cather's late texts then are essentially at odds with the limits of interpretability posed throughout their narratives. They desire comprehension and readability, while they simultaneously encode a sense of narrative deferral and artistic self-referentiality. They both are and are not readable, and they incorporate this difference within their own complex and complicating narratives.

My desire in this book is to challenge previous canonical assumptions about the late novels, though I do not wish to argue that they are necessarily "better" or more complex than the earlier fiction. I wish primarily to bring these texts back into the critical discourse about Cather's work in general, now reread with increasing interest and theoretical sophistication.[67] I have, consequently, tried to be rigorously honest in these readings by framing them as exactly that, readings in the plural rather than the singular sense. For I am certain that these texts have the capacity to elicit and inspire other readings, which I hope will contribute to the critical dialogue and debate about Cather, whose narratives are some of the most complex and subtle in all twentieth-century American literature. I must also acknowledge the important study on Cather's late novels that precedes mine. Merrill Maguire Skaggs's *After the World Broke in Two: The Later Novels of Willa Cather*, addresses the same texts and time frame as my own study. Skaggs, however, conceives of and interprets these late novels within the perspective of an intellectual biography, assuming "that this most autobiographical of writers leaves traces of her intellectual struggles and passions in the texts of her novels."[68] As will become apparent, my own critical approach differs dramatically from Skagg's, yet our respective analyses might best be read as complementary rather than as contradictory.

During the long process of reading and writing about these texts, I have been consistently challenged, frequently frustrated, always intrigued, but never bored. Their ability to sustain my interest and curiosity over a period of years testifies, I think, to their complexity and their readability. And though I resolutely believe that Cather's texts are not reducible to a simple moral or unified meaning, I have learned one significant lesson: reading Willa Cather is never as simple as it seems.

2

Design, Duplicity, and Reading: Narration in *My Mortal Enemy*

> In the last analysis all criticism is purely subjective, and any man's conception of the ultimate meaning of a work of art must be merely a personal impression.
>
> —WILLA CATHER 27 May 1899, *Pittsburgh Leader*

> I think mine is the part where Alice, with maidenly compassion, picked up the Duchess' poor, abused baby and, while she was carrying it off, it turned to a pig. Dear me! how many of us have taken up projects—and people, for that matter—tenderly to our hearts and seen them turn to pigs in our arms. I am not sure but most things turn to pigs with us after awhile.
>
> —WILLA CATHER on her favorite scene in *Alice in Wonderland*,
> October 1897, *Home Monthly*

In her 1983 biography of Willa Cather, familiarly entitled *Willa*, Phyllis Robinson records Cather's own response to what strikes readers as one of the more persistent ambiguities of *My Mortal Enemy*, namely, who is the signified enemy of the title:

> In a captious letter Willa's old friend George Seibel put the matter to her squarely. He had personally decided that Myra's husband was her enemy, but he found that most readers thought it was Myra. . . . He pressed Willa to tell him exactly what she had intended. " 'Of course you are quite right,' " she answered, and then went on to state with some impatience: " 'I can't see much in this particular story unless you get the point of it. There is not much to it but the point.' "[1]

Cather's declaration of how *My Mortal Enemy* ought to be read curiously reiterates a comment made early in the novel by the ingenuous fifteen-

year-old narrator, Nellie Birdseye. Disappointed that the marriage between Myra Driscoll and Oswald Henshawe has only made them "as
happy as most people," because for her "the very point of their story was
that they should be much happier than most people,"[2] Nellie's narration
of Myra's story searches for the correct "point" to it, since her relentlessly
romanticized plot expectations cannot accommodate the incidents that
compose this novel.

Part of the "point" here certainly is that Nellie must learn to become a
better reader *as* she tells her story; the novel, in fact, embodies two
versions of Nellie's narrative perspective, one at age fifteen in part one,
and the other at age twenty-five in part two. Yet each of these first-person
accounts is located in a narrative past, since the last lines of the novel, "I
have still the string of amethysts, but they are unlucky" (104), situate her
voice in an unidentified present. Nellie has *authored* this novel, telling
both Myra's story and the story of her own two narrative accounts. We
then, along with Nellie, who is a recognizably limited narrator and
character within the larger framework of the novel, follow the narrative
to learn what is the "very point" of this story. For, according to Cather,
not only is there a point to this story, but this story consists almost
entirely of its point. If the reader doesn't get it right, the story will
evaporate; we not only won't "see much" in the story, but there won't be
"much to it" if we don't see.

And what is this *it?* What is the "very point" of the story? "Very point"
suggests at once both the farthest end of the story—its destination or
ending—and its ultimate truth. Meaning and closure coincide, or at least
they seem to. This configuration inevitably returns the reader to the
frankly ambiguous sentence from which the novel takes its title: "Why
must I die like this, alone with my mortal enemy!" (105). Authorial
intention notwithstanding, the meaning of this utterance is not so
simple. It, like the rest of the novel, is bound within Nellie's own
interpretation as the novel's first-person narrator, her own attempt to
shape meaning out of the story of Myra Driscoll's life. Nellie's last line is
itself an interpretation and an ending to any "love" story, including the
one she has just related: "Sometimes, when I have watched the bright
beginning of a love story, when I have seen a common feeling exalted
into beauty by imagination, generosity, and the flaming courage of
youth, I have heard again that strange complaint breathed by a dying
woman into the stillness of the night, like a confession of the soul: 'Why
must I die like this, alone with my mortal enemy!'" (104–5). Nellie's

authorial recall creates meaning in this closing passage. To a certain kind of narrative, "the bright beginning of a love story," she will supply indefinitely the same ending, "I have heard again that strange complaint breathed by a dying woman." This "complaint" too carries meaning only through Nellie's rhetorical power; her smile shapes it into "a confession of the soul," into a final utterance with the status of truth. And perhaps most important, there is a double claim for authority in the last line of the text. "Why must I die like this, alone with my mortal enemy!" is uttered as a question by Myra Henshawe earlier in the novel (95); Nellie, as narrator and author, transforms Myra's query into an exclamation, altering it to confer meaning. The question itself becomes the answer for which it is searching.

In many ways, this creation of meaning through selective reiteration is not unlike the critical act. It is ultimately less relevant what the meaning is (who constitutes the "mortal enemy") than who (re)constructs the elaboration of meaning, be it narrator or critic or both. In *My Mortal Enemy,* Cather has, through an authorial sleight of hand, constructed an extremely clever trompe l'oeil, despite her insistence on *seeing* the point. To look at "the very point" of the novel as both destination and illumination is to witness the act of interpretation made possible by the recall and placement of certain textual utterances. Nellie, like a critic, reconstructs the text of Myra's life into a narrative in order to make some sense of it. And why does she do this? Again, we must return to initial utterances, to Nellie's early anticipation of what "the very point of their story . . . should be" (17). Nellie functions in *My Mortal Enemy* as the disappointed and disillusioned reader who stumbles upon what she thinks is a romance in medias res, only to discover that it is something quite different and quite incomprehensible.[3] Her telling of the story records the process of her dismantling all of her previous conventions and expectations about what this story is. Discovering that the "very point" of the story Nellie wants to tell will not arrive, the interest in this novel for the critical reader reading the fictionalized reader lies in seeing how she does manage to construct and to deconstruct different expectations of "meaning" as it progresses. As Susan Rosowski has perceptively noted, "In asking the same question—what is the point of the Henshawes' story?—we realize there is neither a single point nor a single story."[4] *My Mortal Enemy,* perhaps more than any other book Cather wrote, suggests through its own, deceptive metanarrative some of the difficulties her novels pose to the reader about the acts of reading and interpretation. It is a cautionary tale for critics about reading Cather's works as simple, cautionary tales. It is also a story not without meaning, but about the creation of meaning.

Before I begin, however, to read and construct my own rereading of the story, it might be useful to examine some of the ways in which the novel has been read previously, the ways in which critics have constituted the story as a story, and at what meaning(s) they arrive when they reach, conceptually and narrationally, "the very point of the story."

My Mortal Enemy is a novel that eludes easy classification with, or even among, Cather's other fiction. As Hermione Lee, Cather's most recent biographer, notes, "it has always been a hard book to 'place' in her work." The consensus is that it is a transitional, "curious little book" and the "most radically *démeublé* of Willa Cather's novels," owing to her intensified experimentation with concise, elliptic prose. Many readers also find it insufficient as a work and read it as a "kind of pendant to *The Professor's House*," or as a failed revision of *A Lost Lady*. Virtually no one likes the novel. Its heroine is "thoroughly unpleasant," "malicious— though magnetic," "a wicked, tyrannical woman," and "an aggressive woman who trampled on her husband"; such opinions lead some readers to identify Cather herself as Myra ("The strong-willed, tyrannical heroine of the novella seems to me at some points to resemble Willa Cather herself"), while others locate "little Willa Cather" in the guise of Nellie. Despite wherever Cather may or may not be within the novel, this "most bitter piece of fiction she ever wrote" is interpreted as having a cathartic rather than a deleterious effect on the rest of her work:

> Beneath the smooth, classical prose surface of this book there may lie the author's attempt to see herself honestly and to reconcile herself to her own personal situation. And perhaps the recognition that one's own worst enemy is often oneself allowed the author to return to happier, creative spirits again.
>
> It apparently drained the last bit of gall from her system and cleared the way for the serene historical novels of her next half decade.[5]

One kind of critical meaning is conferred in these passages, that of value. Despite its unlikable protagonist, and the perception of its diminished artistry after *The Professor's House* and *A Lost Lady*, the critics who comment on the novel assert that *My Mortal Enemy* retains a useful, if not important, position within Cather's canon, an accolade usually denied the later fiction. It may be a lesser novel, but psychologically it is a boon, a necessary evil, a trial by fire to move Cather's fiction to a higher and happier plateau. The skull beneath the skin, to our surprise and relief, has a smile on its face.

It should come as no surprise then that the thematic readings of this novel neatly parallel the critical and biographical urge to account for the rage and rancor expressed in this story. These thematic interpretations, though disparate, share a singleness of intent; each attempts to place the novel on a track moving toward some kind of moral lesson or epiphany. Interestingly enough, in this most economic of narratives, many readings of this novel see its moral as above all an economic one. For Philip Gerber, *My Mortal Enemy* embodies "Cather's last direct thrust at the materialism rampaging throughout contemporary society," while John Randall complains that "the values of the book seem to be entirely perverse, since they consist chiefly of the exaltation of money and brute power. Above all, the lesson driven home is that of the sanctity of success and the blasphemy of failure."[6] For each of these critics, the economic moral is tied directly to "the very point" of the story, because the novel chronicles a financial decline leading to the death of the impoverished heroine. David Stouck, however, reads a different meaning into this trajectory. For him, the novel "moves toward a final Christian reckoning. . . . that the quest for power and possessions must end in failure and that only in religion and art is there any source of permanent values."[7] Even when the thematic focus shifts to the failure of love and marriage, the oracular signification of the novel's end remains. In Susan Rosowski's feminist reading of the novel, the awakening of both Myra and Nellie "to the personal consequences of [Myra's] romantic elopement with Oswald,"[8] can only be achieved by the correct understanding of Myra's "strange complaint" (105) about her husband as a "mortal enemy" (95, 105). Again, we inevitably must arrive at meaning when we reach the novel's end. There is and must be some kind of thematic and moral value—a Christian reckoning, a lesson, an awakening—or we will leave this novel of almost oppressive despair feeling cheated and duped. Our reader's contract for attention in exchange for revelation will have been broken. We will have no way to contain and to explain the rage, discontent, and bitterness in this story.

Many readers, in fact, do have these feelings, a response that casts suspicion on the sufficiency of thematic interpretations to account for the disturbing questions this novel raises. The critic Dorothy VanGhent, for example, writing in 1964, can locate nothing in the novel that will "account for the slight feeling of puzzled dissatisfaction with which one turns from it. . . . the book leaves one with the unsatisfied sense of something unseated and unreferred . . . something whose resolution here is perhaps too facile."[9] What is unsettling is described here as "too facile." Likewise, another early Cather critic, René Rapin (1930), notes that the reader of *My Mortal Enemy* "becomes discouraged" from being told too little, and consequently "takes but a perfunctory interest in the book, leaves it unsatisfied and hastens to forget it."[10] For John Randall, however, "the novel (once read) is unforgettable. It is the most fascinating and least likeable of Willa Cather's books."[11] What, then, are we to make of these readerly contradictions? Why, in a novel in which we are told by both author and narrator that the point of the story is necessary to understanding and is, moreover, understandable, do readers feel discomfited after they reach this point? If Cather's novels shape and elicit interpretation to make a claim for readability, then what kinds of limitations does Cather throw up around the construction of reading meaning into this work? When and why does the security of meaning turn from a baby to a pig in our arms? Why, in other words, is this novel hard to read?

As many recent critics of the novel have argued, part of the frustration a reader experiences in *My Mortal Enemy* is that the desire to become engaged in *a* story is thwarted; the novel itself denies the wish by foregrounding the acts and processes of storytelling as its central "story."[12] This multiplicity of stories in the novel is complicated even further by the different ages and voices through which Nellie Birdseye narrates her perceptions of events. As Jo Ann Middleton has noted, "With Nellie, Cather creates several viewpoints within one center of consciousness, constructing a multiple viewpoint point of view in the first-person. . . . The effect is that we see Myra . . . from many angles, but here the use of first person deliberately intensifies our identification with Nellie as we see Myra through her eyes."[13] Nellie Birdseye's is the perspective through which the novel is experienced and as such will be shaped by the text's necessity and the reader's desire for some kind of thematic coherence and narrational subtlety. Yet Nellie Birdseye, the narrator, is also a fictional character whose changing perceptions about Myra Henshawe reveal a more complex "reading" of this enigmatic woman, one that Susan Rosowski argues fundamentally shapes the way we inevitably experience the "story" of this woman: "Cather has pitted Myra Driscoll Henshawe against her narrator's and her reader's expectations of a female character and, by her character's complex richness, has exposed those expectations as stagnant and self-limiting."[14] Nellie's narrative then cannot be read solely as "an indifferent or transparent medium for imparting information or thematic content," but rather must be experienced both as a narration of the text and as a representation of her character (and of her character's limitations) simultaneously.[15] To recognize such a difference in this novel not between but rather *within* thematic coherence and narration is to address how the text both creates and confounds its own ability to be read. *My Mortal Enemy* can be viewed as a test case for much of the late fiction because it takes for its focus a difference within the novel of subjects, of voices, of stories and, most important, of the ways in which these stories can be read.[16] It exemplifies in Cather's late work what Ross Chambers has identified in some novels generally as "a constant tug-of-war between conflicting strategies—between narrative self-referentiality whereby the story draws attention to its status of art and forms of narrative duplicity whereby the story pretends to be concerned only with its informational content and yet reveals in unobtrusive ways (usually by slight discrepancies) that this is not so."[17]

As I hope my reading of *My Mortal Enemy* will suggest, narrative self-referentiality and narrative duplicity merge, more often than not, into a deceptive design in the late fiction, rather than into an elucidatory difference. For every clear meaning *or* subversive inference Cather constructs, there is a qualifier not far behind. Narrative self-referentiality continually rends the illusion of the text's presentation of itself as readable, thematically cohesive, and artistically contained. And nowhere is this design so clear and, paradoxically, so obscure as in the story about a story that Nellie Birdseye learns to tell in *My Mortal Enemy*.

The story of *My Mortal Enemy* which Nellie begins in the first line of the text—"I first met Myra Henshawe when I was fifteen, but I had known about her ever since I could remember anything at all" (3)—is already a story in bas-relief, a story raised upon and arising out of another story. Myra Driscoll-the-woman appears first in this text as Myra Driscoll-the-myth, a myth whose tale is ritually recounted on special occasions: "She and her runaway marriage were the theme of the most interesting, indeed the only interesting, stories that were told in our family, on holidays or at family dinners" (3). The "interest" for Nellie lies in the romantic daring of the Henshawes, who get married by defying Myra's uncle and eloping. Indeed, it is an old story in more ways than one. This information, however, is introduced in the second chapter of the novel, so that when we encounter the sentence above at the beginning of the text, its ambiguity and duality seem deliberate. Myra's "runaway marriage" is both one effected by running away and one that is out of control. Since these two interpretations will jockey for position in the young Nellie's narrative, one suspects that the more sophisticated narrative voice which closes the novel has intentionally added another level of "interest" to the story. This halving of narrative consciousness between an ingenuous and an ironic reading of the romantic ethos in the novel is an early indication of how the text asks to be read. We may follow the fifteen-year-old narrator through the first half of the novel, but it will be at a distance.

The first narrated story Nellie relates in the novel is of her meeting with the Henshawes when they pay a stopover visit to her Aunt Lydia in Parthia, Illinois. Her own sense of fiction is at once fascinated and frustrated, for the Henshawes are not what she has imagined. Myra especially, "a short plump woman in a black velvet dress" (5) who "was beginning to have a double chin and was sensitive about it" (6), fails to conform to Nellie's romanticized expectations. Yet curiously, both the real and the fictive Myra converge with Nellie to become dual subjects in this introductory and descriptive moment. Nellie and Myra are, and are introduced to the reader as, mirror images of one another. The moment in which Nellie gazes upon the seemingly diminutive Myra, the latter glances in her direction, while the text records that "she saw my reflection in a mirror" (5). This conflation of the singular, nominative pronoun "she" with the possessive form "my" confuses the reader's syntactic expectations. Both subject and direct object merge into a mirrored reflection of one another.[18] Nellie and Myra, both in this opening chapter and throughout the novel, will vie for attention as competing subjects. We, with Nellie, will attempt to read Myra while we simultaneously read Nellie reading Myra.

This task is especially difficult at first because Nellie openly acknowledges her limitations as a reader. Most of her reactions to Myra-the-heroine-come-alive are a mixture of "bewilderment and concern" (5). Nellie is "fascinated, but very ill at ease" (7) in Myra's presence and feels "quite overpowered by her" (6). She cannot keep pace with the alternating pleasant and then caustic turnings of the older woman's conversation, and consequently she is "never sure whether she was making fun of me or of the thing we were talking about" (7). Halfway through this first chapter then, we are confronted with a narrative constructed upon

Nellie's remembrance of scattered and seemingly random details; we seem to experience them with as much confusion and abruptness as Nellie, who is continuously "some time in catching up with the situation" (8). Nellie cannot yet give up the coherence of the story she has heard for the complexity of the one she is telling.

Nowhere is this narrative incongruity more pronounced than in her recall of the Henshawes as a couple. Oswald Henshawe first seems to her "less perplexing than his wife" because his appearance more closely approximates her fantasy of a romantic hero; "he looked more as I had expected him to look" (8). What Nellie expects are typical and conventional masculine attributes, "a rather military air . . . personal bravery, magnanimity, and a fine, generous way of doing things" (8). This is her interpretation of what he is, which is colored by her interpretation of what she wants him to be; "something about him" has "suggested" these characteristics to her. Yet when Nellie describes Oswald physically, she notices a "perplexing combination of something hard and something soft" (10) in his face, owing perhaps to his soft, half-moon eyes and his "limp, drooping moustache" (8). This ambiguity seems to suggest a kind of impotence, magnified by the single scene Nellie chooses to remember from that night. Oswald and Myra quarrel briefly because she has, without consulting him, given away his six new shirts to the janitor's son. Certainly her extravagance will become a prominent theme of the novel, but in this scene she blithely informs everyone that she has disposed of the shirts because they "bulge in front" and "give [Oswald] a bosom" (9). Nellie notices only his returned look of "amusement, incredulity, and bitterness" (9), and does not seem to register the implied feminization of Oswald in the face of Myra's economic and sartorial power. It is not who wears the pants in the family, but who is allowed to wear the shirts that seems to be at issue here.[19]

Though part of Cather's technique in the "novel *démeublé*" is to record information with no authorial intervention or elaboration, Nellie does react to this scene in her narration. While the chapter seems to end with Nellie listening raptly to Myra's retelling "all the old stories and old jokes that had been asleep for twenty years" (10), what in fact happens is that Nellie herself interrupts Myra's authorial role with her own narrative overlay, and begins to recount the story that we have as yet not heard, the story of Myra's youth and subsequent elopement with Oswald. Why does she do this? Why does the old story intrude upon the present one? Before attempting an answer, it is necessary to note that within this interlude Nellie tells not one long story, but four separate ones. Each attempts to counter and repress the "real" story with which the novel begins, the story of the dramatic and disillusioning power Myra Henshawe possesses that will deny Nellie's desire to script properly the love story she wishes both to read and to tell.[20]

The first of these four stories describes Myra's origins; she was an orphan raised by her great-uncle "in the finest property in Parthia," which Nellie can remember "only as a convent" (11). The "point" of this story centers on two facts, Myra's similarity to her uncle ("she was a good deal like him; the blood tie was very strong" [13]), and the economic pressure he puts on her in order to control her desires. He threatens to "cut her off without a penny" (15); she defies him and marries the Protestant Oswald Henshawe. This first account briefly outlines the salient plot details of the story—the wealth to which Myra has become accustomed, how the conflict between uncle and niece arises out of a familial stubbornness, how Myra and Oswald carry on their romance secretly. It ends with a dry account of their elopement (15) and their departure on "the Chicago express" out of Illinois altogether.

The second version of, or addition to, this story picks up the emotional pace. It, like the first, begins with a memory of the Driscoll house as a convent, counterpointing Myra's wild romance to the nuns "pacing two and two under the apple trees" (15). Promenading around the Driscoll grounds as "a little girl" (15), Nellie remembers hearing her aunt Lydia "tell me again about that thrilling night (probably the most exciting in her life)" (15–16). Lydia's story in Nellie's memory focuses cinematically on Myra leaving the house for good—the sleigh's waiting for her in the snow, the lights in the house, Myra's bouncing step as she comes down the walk. Lydia ends her story with the consequence of this scene, Myra's being cut out of the will. It is at this point that Nellie asks for the real end of the story, if the Henshawes have been "happy," and is distressed to learn that they have only been "as happy as most people" (17). For Nellie, "that answer was disheartening; the very point of their story was that they should be much happier than other people" (17).

Failing to get the kind of ending she desires, the third story in the interlude is Nellie's own construction of a fictional framework through which to understand events. Again watching "the nuns pacing so mildly and measuredly among the blossoming trees," Nellie romanticizes the scene into a kind of religious fairy tale: "I thought of the place as being under a spell, like the Sleeping Beauty's palace; it had been in a trance, or lain in its flowers like a beautiful corpse, ever since that winter night when Love went out of the gates and gave the dare to Fate. Since then, chanting and devotions and discipline, and the tinkle of little bells that seemed forever calling the Sisters in to prayers" (17). Imaginative repression seems to be the operative force in Nellie's interpretation of this story. Myra and her uncle have ceased to be people and have instead become personifications, Love and Fate. The house has been transformed into Sleeping Beauty herself, waiting passively for the sexual catalyst, the entrance of the prince into the closed room and his reanimating kiss upon the lips of the "beautiful corpse." The chastity of the convent has now superseded the chastity of the princess. Nellie's story, even though she knows "that this was not literally true" (17), seems also to be waiting like Sleeping Beauty for the prince, harbinger of the proper ending, who will turn the tragic, virginal story into a happy, sexual one. The story she tells here, significantly, lacks an ending. The sisters live, "since then," in a continuous present of "chanting and devotions and discipline" and bells that are "forever calling" them to prayers. Since Nellie cannot have the ending she desires, it seems that she will have no ending at all.

In the last story she narrates, her vivid remembrance of John Driscoll's funeral, Nellie returns to the problem of ending the story to her satisfaction. Again the scene centers upon a religious edifice, this time the church to which Driscoll has left all his money. Like the Sleeping Beauty story, the account of John Driscoll's funeral carries sexual overtones. His dying suggests both his mortal and his sexual incorporation into the church: "They surrounded, they received, they seemed to assimilate into the body of the church, the body of John Driscoll. They bore it up to the high altar on a river of colour and incense and organ-tone; they claimed and enclosed it" (18). The sexual passivity of Driscoll's corpse here—surrounded, received, and assimilated into the body of the church—links him to Sleeping Beauty, at the same time that his dying is certainly phallic, in that *his* body is "claimed" and "enclosed" within the church. Though this sexual climax *is* the expected ending to the Sleeping Beauty story, Nellie interprets it as Driscoll's escaping and transcending a conclusion: "I thought of John Driscoll as having escaped the end of all flesh; it was as if he had been translated, with no dark conclusion to the pageant, no 'night of the grave' . . . from the glory of the high altar, he had gone straight to the greater glory, through smoking censers and candles and stars" (18–19). Troubled by her confrontation with mortality—the inevitability of Myra's aging from youth to a double-chinned middle-age—Nellie's smoke screen obscures death itself, which not only constitutes a kind of ending to this series of stories, but will also provide an ending to the novel itself. The story of the uncle usurps that of the niece; Nellie here is author of an ending and constructs an interpretation that fits a narrative design with which she is familiar. She has already written the end of the story at the beginning of the novel, since death, religion, and familial inheritance of character traits will reappear as aspects in Nellie's interpretation of Myra's ending.

What these four stories demonstrate is a pattern of repression and re-creation that characterizes Nellie's reading in the early part of the novel. In the first two stories the subject is Myra's elopement, and Nellie takes the role of the passive reader. These are stories that have been *told to* her. Only when the ending does not fit her expectations does she meta-morphose it into a fairy tale and then into a religious and sexual apotheosis. She does not wish to read the story as she has discovered it in chapter one, so her remembrance of the old stories intrudes and re-shapes the narration into one she can understand and tolerate: "After I went home from that first glimpse of the real Myra Henshawe, twenty-five years older than I had always imagined her, I could not help feeling a little disappointed. John Driscoll and his niece had suddenly changed places in my mind, and he had got, after all, the more romantic part" (19). The placement of Myra's uncle into "the more romantic part" of the story seems to be Nellie's attempt to reconstruct and transfer the power struggle she witnesses briefly between the Henshawes into some kind of acceptable interpretation. For the Sleeping Beauty in this story is not Myra; *she* is no passive maiden waiting to be awakened. On the contrary, she is more the moving force in the romance and in the novel. She defies her uncle to his face and marches out of the house to her husband. The passivity that exists is more properly located in Nellie's early rendering of the male characters; she registers Oswald as "something hard and some-thing soft," not unlike the way John Driscoll's entrance into the church is presented as simultaneously passive and phallic. What is noteworthy in Nellie's story of the funeral is that Driscoll not only escapes human mortality, but that the authority of the church and his easy assimilation into it—his "masculine" privilege—take precedence over the logic of narration. Nellie explicitly tells us that he has escaped his ending; he goes express, "straight to the greater glory." Fiction seems to offer an escape from reality. The nastier, move compelling facts of life can be ignored in certain kinds of stories, specifically the kinds Nellie tells in this interlude. What she cannot so easily explain away, however, is "the real Myra Henshawe"—and her "feminine" liabilities—who absolutely cannot be incorporated into any story in Nellie's repertoire. This is why the story that begins in chapter three of the novel is the story Nellie *learns* to tell *as* she tells it. It is the story of "the real Myra Henshawe" told by a narrator who not only resists this reality, but who only vaguely comprehends it by the end of her own narration. Nellie must somehow find a way to tell a variation of the love story with an unconventional and uncooperative subject.

With chapter three begins Nellie's continuous narration of what will constitute the basic plot and themes of *My Mortal Enemy*. Arriving with her aunt Lydia on Christmas Eve in New York, Nellie clearly has no intention of relinquishing her romantic fantasies. Everything for her is new, impressive, wealthy, and magical. Nellie is especially moved by a higher standard of living than she has hitherto experienced, and she revels in material pleasure: "Everything in their little apartment *seemed to me* absolutely individual and unique, even the dinner service; the thick grey plates and the soup tureen painted with birds and big, bright flowers—*I was sure there were no others like them in the world*" (27, emphasis added). Nellie behaves, as Myra notices, "fair moon struck" (26), and we are meant to regard with some skepticism the veracity of her early narration. This passage, for example, indicates twice an implicit acknowledgment of its own ironic distance. The text's coupling of the qualifier "seemed to me" with the unhesitating opinion that "I was sure there were no others like them in the whole world" directs us to see Nellie as a naïf swept up in a whirlwind of new sensations. The older narrative voice here comments upon the limitations of her younger persona. This same ironic distancing of the narrative from itself occurs in Nellie's extravagant use of hyperbolic similes. The reader is given signal after signal to recognize Nellie's telling of the story early on as another version of the fairy tale she has just recounted. Some of the more glaring similes suggest this fairy-tale quality explicitly: "like the pages' caps in old story books" (20); "like an enormous fortress with a thousand windows" (23); "like a ruddy autumn moon at twilight" (23). All of these suggest a reading still immersed in a fantasy, one that will interpret according to its own imaginative needs. And this is partly true. Nellie does wish to read this way. The story she ends up telling, however, significantly differs from the one she desires to tell. For the pattern that emerges in the first part of the novel is one that begins to dismantle Nellie's romantic expectations while she is engaged in the process of narrative, in the act of telling the story. We encounter, then, a difference within the narrative itself, and such a difference inevitably raises some questions. Why are there so many instances where Nellie fixes our gaze on the fissures in her wish for an idealized story? Why do we so often view Myra's unhappiness and bitterness? Why do aspects of Myra's considerable power continually make their way into the narrative?

The beginnings of an answer that could account for this difference within the narrative lie in what I have previously termed Cather's subversive feminism, those elements of female power that function as red herrings within the text, making more complex and confusing the search for meaning. In *My Mortal Enemy,* the power of women, and of Myra in particular, becomes the competing and antagonistic subject of Nellie's desire for a Sleeping Beauty heroine, the type of woman who properly belongs in a romantic story about women for whom love is everything and who give up everything for love. Myra Henshawe's presence in the novel, however, forces Nellie to tell a different story. Her power is the disruptive element that makes impossible Nellie's own romantic narrative ideas in the first half of the novel. Indeed, as Susan Rosowski has persuasively argued, "Nellie Birdseye tells Myra's story not as Lydia or Oswald would have it, but as Myra Henshawe taught her. In doing so Nellie completes her own awakening to a sentimentality that insists people fit themselves into simplistic roles."[21] At odds with itself, the narrative unravels in the shaky hands of its narrator.

The first fissure that slowly spreads through Nellie's idealized picture is similar to the one she encounters in her initial meeting with the Henshawes, the one that she immediately tries to repress by recalling the story of their elopement. What Nellie again witnesses is a kind of gender blurring, similar to the way the "snow blurred everything a little" (22) when she arrives in New York. Such a sexual dynamic appears especially in her vision of Ewan Grey, a young Scotsman whom Myra is encouraging in a romance: "His clean, fair skin and melancholy eyes, his very correct clothes, and something about the shape of his hands, made one conscious of a cool, deliberate fastidiousness in him. In spite of his spotty past he looked, that night, as fresh and undamaged as the flowers he wore" (28). What is interesting about this passage is the way in which Nellie's authorial gaze is turned on the young man as an object. The diction of her description, his "deliberate fastidiousness" and looks "as fresh and undamaged as the flowers he wore" are phrases, especially the lack of defloration, that would usually be reserved for women. The implied feminization of this man is augmented by Myra's comment on his role in the romance. She confounds Nellie's more conventional ideas about masculine behavior by insisting that "he's just the sort of boy that women pick up and run off into the jungle with" (23). Man, not woman, is the object of desire, just as he is the object of Nellie's gaze. Since this comment precedes Nellie's description of Grey, it seems likely that Myra's disregard for conventional gender roles has begun to influence Nellie's perceptions in subtle ways. This sexual inversion also resonates in Nellie's interpretation of winter two pages later, which she envisions as something "tamed, like a polar bear led on a leash by a beautiful lady" (25). Nor is she disturbed by the obvious androgyny of the actors she meets in Myra's apartment, such as the old man, Jefferson de Angelais, whose "painted eye-brows spread and came down over his eyes like a veil" (45), or Helena Modjeska, whose hands Nellie sees as deserving to hold both male and female objects, "a sceptre, or a chalice—or, by courtesy, a sword" (46). Passivity and powerlessness, her newfound knowledge suggests, are not only the province of women, nor is power the exclusive domain of men.

Nellie also learns through Myra a new and disturbing story about marriage and the pairing off of men and women. Myra's maxim about love, in fact, "Love itself draws on a woman nearly all the bad luck in the world" (28), absolutely refutes the Sleeping Beauty tale's conventional wisdom that happiness begins after marriage. Myra interprets the story a different way: "You send a handsome fellow like Ewan Grey to a fine girl like Esther, and it's Christmas eve, and they rise above us and the whole world around us, and there isn't anybody, not a tramp on the park benches, that wouldn't wish them well—and very likely hell will come of it!" (31). In Myra's reconstructed teleology, marriage is not the beginning of happiness, but is instead the beginning of the end. And though this passage predicts what will happen to Ewan and Esther as a couple, it is worth noting that earlier Myra voices her concern more on the young woman's behalf. Though Grey, in Myra's judgment, is "distractedly in love" (23), her overriding feeling seems to be that she "couldn't bear it if anything cruel happened to Esther" (24). "Anything" is deliberately vague, but in context it seems as if marriage is what Myra has in mind. The passage also stands out because it reiterates subtly Nellie's evocation of the end of John Driscoll's story. Myra sees no happy transmutation of a mortal state for a heavenly one. The end, as she sees it, is hell. Her refutation of the "happy ending" carries additional weight because it closes off both chapter three and the end of Nellie's first day in New York. The narrative offers no debate of this interpretation; Myra has, so to speak, the last word. However, though Nellie's narrative placement of Myra's ending seems to indicate that it possesses a kind of irrefutable logic, it remains merely another version of how romance stories end.

As the novel progresses, Nellie comes into contact not only with different endings of romance, but with different configurations of romantic pairings as well. Balancing and commenting upon the conflict of heterosexual couples in this first part are a series of female same-sex pairings, most noticeably beginning with Nellie's insistent memory of the nuns walking "two by two" (15) early in the novel. Among Myra's New York circle she witnesses this same gender division, a society "in which the women sat two-and-two, while the men stood about the refreshment tables, drinking champagne and coffee and smoking fat black cigars" (39). She notices too that Myra's relationships with women, particularly Helena Modjeska, evince a kind of romantic devotion and a profound lack of conflict directly in contrast to her marriage. In one of the longer scenes in this brief book, Nellie recounts Myra's special relationship with "a dear friend of hers, Anne Aylward, the poet" (41). What impresses Nellie about this relationship is the transformative power of Myra's intimacy with the dying young woman: "Never had I seen her so brilliant and strangely charming as she was in that sunlit study up under the roofs. Their talk quite took my breath away; they said such exciting, such fantastic things about people, books, music—anything; they seemed to speak together a kind of highly flavoured special language" (42). Though not overtly lesbian, these pairings present an implicit alternative to heterosexuality, especially in the easy equality and mutual admiration they engender. The power of animation, the "special language" the two women "speak together," and Myra's increased brilliance and charm arise from a reciprocal romantic friendship, not from the stilted heterosexuality of the fairy tale Nellie first envisions. The effect of this relationship on Myra is also telling. For Nellie notices that "Myra's look and vocative" (43) take on a particular kind of power when she "but mentioned the name of someone she admired" (43), and in this novel this circumstance only occurs when the subject is a woman. Myra, in fact, demonstrates her own authorial power over Nellie when she discusses her friends: "one got an instant impression that the person must be wonderful, her voice invested the name with a sort of grace . . . and this, accompanied by her singularly direct glance, had a curious effect. When she addressed Aunt Lydia, for instance, she seemed to be speaking to a person deeper down than the blurred, taken-for-granted image of my aunt that I saw every day, and for a moment my aunt became more individual, less matter-of-fact to me" (43). Who *is* the author here? Nellie, by responding to Myra's authorial voice, slowly learns a different way to see beyond the "taken-for-granted image" with which she initially confronts the world. Myra as subject and the power of her "look and vocative" become a competing and even vaguely antagonistic force in Nellie's narration as it progresses. For at this point, all the "taken-for-granted" ways in which Nellie has been able to read the story have been subtly undermined; marriage is at best a disagreeable and at worst a disastrous choice for women and men, and romance is more easily located in female friendship than in heterosexual bonding.[22] Myra's power in this first half of the novel is located precisely in her ability to dismantle the romance Nellie initially wishes to tell.[23] She creates both a sexual and a textual ambiguity. It is not so much the difference between, but the difference within gender that has the power to disrupt and radically detour the narrative.

Though there is something fine and purely evoked in Nellie's description of Myra and Anne, the glimpse we get of Myra's power cannot be and is not rendered unambivalently in the novel. For Cather, power invites abuses more often than not, for both men and women. In previous novels, for instance, as in this one, the power men most frequently command is tied directly to money. And this combination corrupts. Ivy Peters, in *A Lost Lady,* is viewed ungenerously in the novel as a newly monied force whose contact with society coarsens its more refined elements, specifically his sexual access to the "lost lady," Marian Forrester. In *My Antonia* as well, the unprincipled money lender Wick Cutter is also an attempted rapist, as Jim Burden discovers to his horror one night when Cutter mistakes him for Antonia in the darkness. At every juncture in Cather's works, including *My Mortal Enemy,* the attainment of power through money resides in self-made, and therefore less genteel, men such as John Driscoll, who often wield their power indiscriminately or capriciously, frequently controlling female desire or engineering a sexual relation.

Female power is treated no less critically in Cather's oeuvre, especially in the late novels. Often frustrated, women's power is usually confined to a limited sphere and appears as a kind of domestic autocracy.[24] Nevertheless, female power always carries with it a cost; someone inevitably pays a price. Literally, in *My Mortal Enemy*, it is Oswald Henshawe. For Myra conceives of power chiefly in terms of money, and her economic dependence on her husband is the root of much of their marital conflict. What money does for Myra, as the diction of her economic interactions emphasizes, is to elevate her above what she regards as the democratic mass of common people and to place her squarely within the realm of artists. In an early scene, Myra chooses a holly tree for Modjeska which Nellie describes as "easily the queen of its companions" (30). Myra sees it as "naturally hers" while Oswald counters that it is "naturally the most extravagant" (30). Her retort concerning his pettiness allows her to have her own way at the same time that it betrays his controlling the proverbial purse strings. Myra strains continually against these economic fetters. Her effort to express a capacious and generous nature within circumscribed means causes her to become a perpetual malcontent and to fall prey to what Nellie reads as "insane ambition" (41), insane chiefly because she does not possess enough power to be self-satisfied. Yet Myra refuses to relinquish her desires for money, power, and extravagance throughout the novel, and Nellie's narration of Myra's actions thus becomes increasingly ambivalent. Though Nellie would like to see only Myra's charm, generosity, and wit, she instead is forced to recognize the bitterness and despair that underlie the older woman's more attractive qualities. As the first half of Nellie's adolescent narration draws to an end, her ability to interpret becomes more and more strained. Nellie's subject has not only presented her with realities she would rather not have faced, but Myra has become almost too complex to be interpreted at all by a fifteen-year-old girl.

For Nellie to be able to tell the story, Myra's power will have to be contained in some way. Nellie must reassert her own narrative authority over her charismatic but confusing subject. A small step toward this is the incursion of specific literary allusions into the novel. When the narrator encounters her own difficulty in reading, other texts are recalled to offer and encourage interpretation. Bellini's *Norma* is the most important text that modifies and aids the reading of *My Mortal Enemy*.[25] Nellie recalls a party the Henshawes give on New Year's Eve, during which "a young Polish women who was singing at the Opera that winter" (46) is requested by Modjeska to sing the *Casta diva* aria from *Norma*. Any number of possible correlations between the two texts suggest themselves. The opera invites a comparison between Norma as a Druid high priestess who has taken a vow of chastity and Myra, whose most attractive and compelling qualities come to light in the company of women. Suggestive parallels of plot also appear. The specific moment in the opera when Norma sings the aria occurs after her discovery of her lover's, Pollione's, affair with a young woman. In the novel, Nellie has just witnessed a scene in which she suspects Oswald of fabricating a story about a gift of topaz cuff links he has received from a young lady who, he claims, "doesn't know the ways of the world very well" (33). Both lovers are seen by the women as antagonists; Pollione is Norma's "*sacrilego nemico,*" Oswald, Myra's "mortal enemy." In addition to the implication of adultery, there is the betrayal of religion; Norma breaks her vow of chastity for Pollione much the same way Myra will later believe she has broken with her faith in Catholicism in order to marry Oswald. The aria also, in both opera and novel, is a prayer for and a brief moment of peace before an acrimonious and bitter scene between the lovers.[26]

Despite many parallels, these associations expand the mystery of the moment rather than clarify specific meanings in the text. Though *Norma* provides a framework in which certain shared themes can be pinpointed, the scene affects Nellie, in her roles of *both* reader and author, as an epiphany that defies not only interpretation, but language altogether.

> For many years I associated Mrs. Henshawe with that music, thought of that aria as being mysteriously related to something in her nature that one rarely saw, but nearly always felt; a compelling, passionate, overmastering something for which I had no name, but which was audible, visible in the air that night as she sat crouching in the shadow. When I wanted to recall powerfully that hidden richness in her, I had only to close my eyes and sing to myself: "*Casta diva, casta diva!*" (48)

This passage, perhaps more than any other in all her work, typifies Cather's narrative poetics with its absence of signified meaning and its insistence on being read with something close to what Keats defined as negative capability, "of being in uncertainties, Mysteries, doubts, without any irritable reaching after fact & reason."[27] In the attempt to explain the essence of Myra's character, Nellie's narration reiterates Cather's chief principle of composition, a narrative conveyed through "the inexplicable presence of the thing not named, of the overtone divined by the ear but not heard by it, the verbal mood, the emotional aura of the fact or the thing or the deed, that gives high quality to the novel or the drama, as well as to poetry itself."[28] Such a technique paradoxically claims meaning at the same time that it asserts the inability of a text to formulate that meaning through language. Trying to grasp Myra's "meaning" in the text, Nellie can only arrive at a series of hyperbolic adjectives of power— "compelling, passionate, overmastering"—which ultimately prove inadequate to express that "something for which I had no name." Just as Myra crouches in the shadow of the singer, so too does this scene place itself behind the veil of another text. The way *Norma*, to employ Ross Chambers's paradigm of intertextuality, "determines the selective process of reading" is by dramatizing the opacity of language.[29] Though meaning is "audible" and "visible," it remains unspeakable and therefore uninterpretable. The insertion of the opera into the narrative does, chronologically, give Nellie a brief stay against confusion and against her increasing difficulty in making sense of the story. It also contains the clearest expression of how this text asks to be read.

For, curiously, this passage adopts the same narrative stance as the very last paragraph of the novel. Here, an older Nellie, conscious of having created the narrative, again attempts to explicate the "hidden richness" of her text through the recall of a specific phrase. What should not be surprising is that "*Casta diva*" is at once as evocative and as inexplicable as "my mortal enemy." Meaning is felt rather than known. In this climactic moment of *My Mortal Enemy*, the text recognizes and, in a way, avows its own fictiveness. Though we are encouraged to read interpretatively, the text refuses to assign a meaning to itself. For Nellie, who again takes up her fifteen-year-old perspective in the last two episodes of part one, the *Casta diva* scene encapsulates the problems of interpretation and understanding, which frequently overwhelm her narration in the first half of the novel and which instigate the deconstruction of meaning with which her narration ends.

It is almost as if the appearance of the authorial Nellie who can conjure Myra's "hidden richness" at this climactic point in the novel signals a move toward maturity in her younger self. This suggests itself as a possibility because of the explicitly sexual nature of the next scene and its effect upon Nellie's increasing awareness of the secrets and the secret conflicts of power relations in marriage and sexuality. Nellie arrives at the Henshawes' apartment expecting lunch and finds instead that she has stumbled upon what Freud termed the primal scene.

The third of the typical sexual theories appears in children when through some unforseen domestic occurrence they witness parental sexual intercourse, concerning which they are then able to obtain only a very incomplete idea. Whatever detail it may be that comes under their observation; whether it is the position of the two people, or the sounds, or certain accessory circumstances, in all cases they arrive at the same conclusion, that is, at what we may call the *sadistic conception of coitus,* seeing in it something that the stronger person inflicts on the weaker by force.[30]

She overhears a vicious power struggle between husband and wife, which is perhaps the most equal exchange they have in the novel. Myra's "angry laugh" (49) is met by Oswald's "distinctly malicious chuckle" (50). Nellie's rendering of the scene moves by snatches of accusation and symbolic inference. The Henshawes argue about a key belonging to Oswald that Myra has stolen from his pocket. She demands to know the "meaning" of the key, challenging Oswald for the power, suggestively phallic, that it accords him: "I tell you, I will know the truth about this key, and I will go through any door that your keys open" (49). Myra's focus here is on desire (I tell you . . . I will know . . . I will go) and on access, to be able to "go through any door" that Oswald can. The reference to keys opening locked spaces is also striking because the only other time it appears in the novel, Myra bemoans the nastiness of being poor "as she fitted her latchkey" to their apartment (41). Keys seem to signify a kind of power Myra cannot possess, the power to alter their finances or the power to know Oswald's secrets, to open doors he has the power to keep locked. The scene grows increasingly more complex and sexually confusing when Oswald insists that the key opens not a door, but a secret box, or a box of secrets, in his possession, "a safety deposit box" (50).[31] Though Myra accuses him of lying, what dominates this scene is Oswald's power of withholding, a peculiarly passive stance that frustrates both his wife and the reader. By refusing to tell the secret of the key, Oswald, in effect, denies access to interpretation, denies the power to read and to make sense of this interchange.

Nellie simply registers the fury of this struggle, especially its sexual implications, and its effect on her is one of Oedipal confusion and horror: "What I felt was fear; I was afraid to look or speak or move. Everything about me seemed evil" (51). From ignorant happiness she feels herself to have fallen "from security into something malevolent and bottomless" (51). Oswald and Myra are positioned behind closed doors, and what Nellie hears are the sounds of psychological grappling presented as a nasty verbal battle. The key, secret box, and closed doors all function as what Freud calls "accessory circumstances" and enable her to arrive at what she discovers is the Henshawes' sadistic marriage. What remains ambiguous, however, is who occupies the stronger and weaker roles. Nellie, who is taken to lunch by Oswald, feels only Myra's aggression and entertains "a conviction that I should never like Mrs. Myra so well again" (52). We must suspect such an easy judgment though, not only because Cather inverts the expected power scheme by placing power in passivity (Oswald) and weakness in aggression (Myra), but because Nellie's interpretations of, rather than reactions to, this new story begin to dominate the text.

At lunch with Oswald, Nellie's narration takes on a newly acquired subjective intensity, located in the repetitive first-person subject/verb construction of her description: "I wondered . . . at the contradiction in his face. . . . I felt that his life had not suited him. . . . I thought he ought to have been a soldier or an explorer. I have since seen those half-moon eyes in other people, and they were always inscrutable, like his; fronted the world with courtesy and kindness, but one never got behind them" (52). Interpretation becomes necessary here, because of Oswald's inscrutability and because they are sitting silently (there is nothing for her to record but her impressions). As a reader, Nellie still seems caught in the throes of her romantic fantasies. Her description of Oswald stresses the chivalry she reads in his behavior to her after the fight, and she admits a desire for rewriting his story—"he ought to have been" something more daring than she has discovered him to be. This passage also contains an early indication of the ways in which Nellie's narration will make a bid for truth and meaning. The last sentence, which again locates this reflection in a narrative present, subtly evokes a stronger sense of authority than we might first suspect. It implies the accumulation of years and experience; she has "since seen those half-moon eyes in other people," and she finds them "always inscrutable." Such a reading encompasses a sophistication beyond that possible in her previous comments, yet it is still linked to them in the text. It attempts to persuade through a rhetoric of aphoristic wisdom. This technique will occur with noticeable frequency in the second half of the novel as Nellie becomes more proficient in seeming to create a coherent reading. Here, however, it remains an anomaly in the more persistent pattern of ingenuous readings.

We see, in fact, just how limited a narrator the young Nellie is (or how limited the older narrative voice shows her to be) in the last scene of part one when Lydia and Nellie, departing New York, encounter Myra on the train. Particularly significant in this final episode is its function as neither an end nor a resolution to the first half of the novel. There is a kind of wry humor in the fact that though Myra insists she "didn't plot anything so neat as this" (53), she does engineer an ending not by running away with her husband, but by running away from him. She has ruptured irrevocably the possibility for romance with which Nellie began the story. The three women, Nellie, her aunt Lydia, and Myra are in transit; the quarrel has had no ending, either reconciliatory or tragic, which creates a lack of closure and leaves matters obscurely open-ended. The evocation of this scene too, tends toward the obscure and indecipherable, as with Nellie's reading of Myra's mouth. "It seemed to curl and twist about like a little snake. Letting herself think harm of anyone she loved seemed to change her nature, even her features" (54). Here, it is her own reflection Nellie sees, not the image of Myra. Nellie's sexual knowledge suggests the mouth as a snake, and it is *her* thinking harm of Myra that has altered the older woman's nature and features.

The scene also contains two related comments, by Myra and Lydia respectively, which are meant to be deliberately and disturbingly enigmatic to Nellie and to the reader. Myra's comment involves her discovery of the "plot" between Oswald and Lydia to invent a story about the topaz cuff links (33–34). Though she claims not to hold the lie against Lydia, to her, "it's disgusting in a man to lie for personal decorations. A woman might do it, now . . . for pearls!" (54). It is unclear what Myra intends with this final declaration. Is it merely a cynical retort suggesting that women can betray as well as, or better, than men?[32] Or does the "now" function as a catalyst of time: I can *now* conceive of betrayal and mendacity because I can see that it has been done to me? Lydia's rejoinder, that "a man never *is* justified, but if ever a man was . . ." (54) is equally confusing. On one level, it appears easy to read: A man never is justified in deception, but because Myra is so overbearing and impossible, if ever a man was . . . it is Oswald. Lydia *seems* to damn Myra, but significantly, her judgment is conveyed through ellipsis, through something that cannot be said. The ellipsis also indicates a syntactic interruption in the middle of a sentence, much the same way that Myra's flight from Oswald on the train is evidence of a rupture in her marriage and makes impossible any resolution to this part of the story. Nellie, curiously, has no dialogue throughout this entire episode, recording but not commenting upon, even in interior monologue, the scene as it unfolds.

It is as if the narrative has finally slipped out of her hands. Left midsentence, in confusion, this part of the narrative demonstrates Nellie's inability to make sense of language itself. We are left only with the fragments of a sentence, which we are unable to interpret. Language falls off and apart into the ellipsis; the narrative affirms its own uninterpretability. The only certainty remaining in these ruins of Nellie's narration is what *must* be left unsaid, what, ultimately, language is unable to say.

When part two of the novel begins, it is clear that Nellie may have become a better reader, as the shift from romance to realism indicates: "Ten years after that visit to New York I happened to be in a sprawling overgrown West-coast city which was in the throes of rapid development—it ran about the shore, stumbling all over itself and finally tumbled untidily into the sea. Every hotel and boarding-house was overcrowded and I was very poor. Things had gone badly with my family and me" (56). Gone is the "blurred" and fantastic landscape of a snow-covered New York City. In its place is what appears to be a resigned acceptance of what will be the landscape of her life. Like Myra, Nellie too has become estranged from her family, though the text provides no explanation for this occurrence. Nellie has aged ten years, plans to begin teaching English at what she calls an "experimental and unsubstantial" college, and has unexpectedly run into Oswald Henshawe on her hotel staircase. The "facts" which she claims to soon discover "about the Henshawes' present existence" (69) testify to their diminished finances, loss of hope, and Myra's illness, which turns out to be cancer. Nellie delights in seeing Myra again though, and for a moment she seems still caught in her early tongue-tied narration: "She was . . . she was herself, Myra Henshawe!" (62). Later, however, she sums up Myra's contradictions in a passage that exposes not only her increased facility with language, but also her authority to write and to read her subject:

> She sat crippled but powerful in her brilliant wrappings. She looked strong and broken, generous and tyrannical, a witty and rather wicked old woman, who hated life for its defeats and loved it for its absurdities. I recalled her angry laugh, and how she always greeted shock or sorrow with that dry, exultant chuckle which seemed to say: "Ah-ha, I have one more piece of evidence, one more, against the hideous injustice God permits in the world." (65)

This passage marks the first time that Nellie, in her narration, has ventured to speak *for* Myra, rather than simply record what she has said.

No longer a girl disillusioned and baffled by the story unfolding around her, Nellie seems to be in command of her subject and of her story. She betrays, in interjected interpretations like the one above, a consciousness of authoring her text. And it is likely that as first-time readers of the novel, we would feel ourselves to be, at last, in capable narrative hands.

But are we? A comparison between Nellie's respective narrative stance in parts one and two of the novel presents some problems with regard to continuity and focus between these two differing and differently told versions of Myra's story. Nellie is used with some dramatic distance and irony as a narrator in part one to register the undercurrents of conflict and the ambiguity of gender she witnesses as her "romance" narrative falls apart. We are, I believe, meant to read this first half as the deliberate unmaking of one kind of story. We record, consciously or not, the multiplicity of meanings with which the text confronts us, as Nellie's desires to tell one kind of story become modified by new realities in the world she rather ambivalently encounters. In this second part, however, Cather uses Nellie's narrative voice to confirm certain kinds of meaning, to remake Myra's "runaway" story into a contained, or fictionally bound, tale.[33] This kind of foregrounding of an acceptable and, in fact, rather conventional thematics at the end of the novel is characteristic of Cather's female-centered late fiction. In *My Mortal Enemy*, Myra, who has engineered the breakdown of the romance novel in part one and who, in the *Casta diva* scene, defies definition and meaning in language, must die in the second half of the novel because she cannot be contained or explained any other way.[34] It is she whose departure from her husband at the end of part one signals the rancorous and aborted ending to Nellie's story, and the resulting failure of the narrative to represent Myra in any kind of conventional marriage plot results in her increasing marginalization. Residing in an obscure and shabby hotel, impoverished and, like the imperious Sapphira Dodderidge of Cather's last novel, immobile, Myra has been completely divested of her formidable power. While only tangentially touching upon the effect that the loss of this power has had upon her character, the narrative instead seems to turn the trajectory of her story line into one concerned primarily with mortality.

Such a shift of perspective resides largely in Nellie's increased authority as *the* interpretant of events. Subtly, but insistently, what appears to be a series of unconnected comments begins to be shaped into a dual pattern of oppositions between youth and age and between free will and religion. When Nellie first moves into the hotel, for example, she notices an elderly man whose solitude and imagined deprivation make her "melancholy" and depress her "unreasonably" (58–59). She concludes that "for youth there is always the hope, the certainty, of better things" (58). Though this comment seems to be Nellie's immediate and personal reaction to an incident, after she meets up with the Henshawes, the juxtaposition of embittered aging with fondly remembered youth becomes a central theme. More often than not, Myra's ruminations on aging are filtered through the lens of loss, particularly lost chances which she believes might have changed her fate. "Oh, if youth but knew!" (75) she exclaims to Nellie about the power of love to destroy, while in another scene she recounts a dream in which "I was young, and the sorrows of youth had set me crying!" (79). For Myra, age brings with it the loss of everything: dignity, privacy, "even the power to love" (89). While this kind of embittered resignation is consistent with Myra's character as we know it, its centrality as subject within this last half of the text, along with the repeated allusions to suicide (72, 76, 80, 86), establish a reading more grounded in the human condition of mortality, than in the female condition of ambivalent empowerment which accounted for so much of the focus of part one. Again the novel returns to the unanswered question raised at the beginning of its narrative in chapter two with Nellie's four versions of Myra's past: What is the proper way to end a story in which the female subject does not fit into the expected or traditional pattern?

Myra herself offers two ways of reading and interpreting her own ending. Both return to personal and textual origins, linking the novel thematically at beginning and end. The first reading argues for a genetic predetermination of personality. Myra's reminiscence about her uncle stresses the same oxymoronic quality that Nellie notes earlier in her: "He would help a friend, no matter what it cost him, and over and over again he risked ruining himself to crush an enemy" (81). John Driscoll's recklessness succeeds where Myra's fails, primarily because "men who hate like that usually have the fist-power to back it up" (81), while women, it is implied, do not. Despite such a gendered difference in power, Myra's longings at the end of the novel are for reconciliation. Blood, it seems, is thicker than desire.

> We were very proud of each other, and if he'd lived till now, I'd go back to him and ask his pardon; because I know what it is to be old and lonely and disappointed, yes, and because as we grow old we become more and more

the stuff our forebears put into us. I can feel his savagery strengthen in me. We think we are so individual and misunderstood when we are young; but the nature our strain of blood carries is inside there, waiting, like our skeleton. (82)

The teleology here is inevitable and predetermines whatever story is to be told. Such an interpretation submerges the individual within the grander, and more depressing, scheme of human mortality. Physically we will age and become "lonely and disappointed"; psychologically we will be transformed into a replica of our genetic origins. This *is* the only end one can expect. The trajectory of life stretches unimpeded toward an ending that is already known. The simultaneity of the death of the subject with the end of the text confirms our sense of a plot bound forever by time. Its logic is not to be refuted.

Myra's second reading of her story attempts to confer meaning within this strict teleology, to hang an interpretation upon the inevitability of her end. Returning to the Catholicism of her youth, Myra is increasingly preoccupied with "holy words and rites" (85), which leads her to a reductive reading that denies the contradictions of love and hate that have characterized her life and marriage. Though she admits to Nellie that "people can be lovers and enemies at the same time" (88), she begins to see her husband as entirely responsible for the rift in her religious beliefs, and Nellie records that "toward Oswald her manner became strange and dark" (92). Such a rift has characterized Myra's religious nonchalance throughout most of the novel, from Nellie's first meeting with the Henshawes in chapter one throughout the entire first half. Myra's present "religious" interpretation, which casts Oswald as "the enemy" responsible for her unhappy life, misreads her own story as being radically more simple than it actually is. Given also Nellie's detached sympathy for *both* Oswald and Myra in this part of the novel, the text acknowledges the inadequacy of this interpretation. Myra creates a coherent reading—she links her beginning and end—only by repressing the story as we have encountered it. She appears not to be the best reader of her own text.

Nor, for that matter, does Oswald. The text also disavows his reading of events, which, like Myra's, returns to a perceived unity and coherence that the novel does not substantiate. Enjoining Nellie not to remember his wife as she exists in the second half of the text, Oswald asks that Nellie "remember her as she was when you were with us on Madison Square, when she was herself, and we were happy. Yes, happier than it falls to the lot of most mortals to be. . . . These last years it's seemed to me that I was nursing the mother of the girl who ran away with me. Nothing can ever take that girl from me" (103–4). Since we know absolutely that Myra was far from "happy" during Nellie's sojourn when they lived on Madison Square, this version of events invites disbelief. Oswald's interpretation relies upon repressing Myra as a woman; it is "the girl" who eloped with him that he fixes imaginatively in his memory. Impossible to ignore as well is the resonance of his pronouncement that they were "happier than it falls to the lot of most mortals to be," since it is a thinly disguised reiteration of Nellie's desire that "the very point of their story was that they should be much happier than other people" (17). This has already been exposed as a fiction, so the response to Oswald's interpretation must be necessarily skeptical.

The text does, however, valorize Nellie's reading in the second half, especially as it concerns her interpretation of Myra's religious and enigmatic utterances. Some are left unglossed and subsequently carry a kind of aphoristic intensity: "Light and silence: they heal all one's wounds—all but one, and that is healed by dark and silence" (73). That one wound remains deliberately unsignified; the text leaves it for the reader to approximate meaning. In other important instances though, Nellie intervenes with absolute authority to give a partial, directed explanation of Myra's words. During Myra's deathbed scene, "when she had been lying like a marble figure for a long while" (94), not unlike a Sleeping Beauty, she makes two remarks which the text signals as being central to an understanding of the novel, and both of which Nellie interprets. The first Myra speaks "in a gentle, reasonable voice" to her priest: " 'Ah, Father Fay, that isn't the reason! Religion is different from everything else; *because in religion seeking is finding*' " (94). Nellie responds to this almost as if she is an apostle being asked to interpret one of the parables of Christ: "She seemed to say that in other searchings it might be the subject of the quest that brought satisfaction, or it might be something incidental that one got on the way; but in religion, desire was fulfillment, it was the seeking itself that was rewarded" (94). Nellie comments that Myra "accented the word 'seeking' very strongly, very deeply" (94), and the text itself accents the entire last clause in italics, the only time such emphasis occurs in the novel other than in lines quoted from outside texts (*Norma*, Shakespeare). We are, clearly, meant to pay attention to this maxim, and to Nellie's reading of it. She offers an interpretation that counters Myra's desire for secular achievement, "success and a place in the world" (75), by altering the equation. Only in religion is desire fulfillment; within this system alone can Myra expect to be satisfied. Such a belief invalidates the material deprivation Myra believes herself to have suffered throughout the novel. Not only has Myra (re)converted to a different way of reading her story, but the text has converted us right along with her. Her deathbed philosophy takes on the mantle of truth; the phrase "in religion seeking is finding" makes a claim for unrevealed meaning. The "desire" for explanation is "fulfillment" enough, or if it isn't, it has to be. Meaning resides in a mystery embraced, if not understood, by human faith. It is not much different from the experience of reading this novel. While the mystery obscured within language remains, Cather's veiling of this phrase in religious terms takes a partial step toward defining "the thing not named." We at least know where to locate the answer even if we don't quite grasp what that answer is. Religion then, functions as an explanation of and a reparation for human suffering. In this context, Myra's life has "meaning."

A religious context is stressed again when Nellie relates one night that "stands out in my memory as embracing them all, as being the burden and telling the tale of them all" (94). On this evening she hears the question that will both frame the novel and be its title, the moment when she "seemed to hear a soul talking" and Myra asks: "Why must I die alone like this, alone with my mortal enemy?" (95). Nellie's physical reaction reinforces the power and authority of Myra's query: "I felt my hands grow cold and my forehead grow moist with dread. I had never heard a human voice utter such a terrible judgment upon all one hopes for. As I sat on through the night . . . I grew calmer; I began to understand a little what she meant, to sense how it was with her. Violent natures like hers sometimes turn against themselves . . . against themselves and all their idolatries" (95–96). What Nellie understands and senses is, not surprisingly, conveyed in yet another cryptogram. The violent nature Nellie ascribes to Myra confirms her blood inheritance from John Driscoll; she is her uncle's daughter. That Nellie implies Myra turns against herself in the end has given rise to the duality critics have read into the "mortal enemy" of the title. But "idolatries" remains at best vague and allusive. Myra is not given to worshipping graven images in the novel, so one wonders what immoderate attachments to or venerations of things are being suggested—Oswald, female friends, money, power? Whatever this word signifies, its effect is the same. The Myra we meet in part one has been renounced both by the Myra of part two and by the text. She is to blame for her unhappiness, and she must *be* blamed if the text is to achieve symmetry or balance as it has been constructed. The effect of turning inward against a former self applies both to this novel and to its subject. Not only Myra, but the deconstruction of meaning that the first half of the text embodies must be countered and contained by Nellie's narration in the second half. The text engages in self-contradiction in the effort to assign meaning.

What then of the reader's desire for coherence or meaning? One choice might be to approach the novel solely as dramatizing the subjectivity of reading within its many interpretations of what kind of a story this is.[35] We would see in it the failure of any reading to arrive at "ultimate meaning," which would lead us absolutely to discount whatever authority the text accords Nellie's interpretation at the end. We would conclude either that Cather is entirely conscious of undermining her narrator's authority throughout the novel or that the second half falters in its purpose and hence fails to sustain the textual self-consciousness which the first half treats so convincingly.

Another way we might read this text is to embrace unhesitatingly Nellie's interpretation at the conclusion. In it we would identify a textual unity and read Myra's end as the logical outcome of her religious training and of her familial link to her uncle's character, which the novel sets up and prepares us for at the beginning. We would, in fact, be able to point to Cather herself as proof that the novel contains a meaning since she summarily dismisses readers who can't "get the point of it." This reading would interpret Nellie's final judgments about love stories as a bleak vision of human relations generally, while simultaneously recognizing that the only hope the text offers is in religion.

My own reading of the novel encompasses parts of both these interpretations. It seems to me that the latter half of the text unqualifyingly supports Nellie's narration both of Myra's religious awakening as the proper ending, *and* of the impossibility of telling happy love stories within human relations as we know them in this novel. The text elicits a reading in which Nellie's perspective has the power to identify and to dictate meaning. Yet at the same time, the multiplicity of misreadings— Myra's and Oswald's in this second half and, especially, Nellie's in part one of the novel—suggests that reading and textual self-referentiality are also of primary interest as questions which the text poses of, and, perhaps, to itself. A partial resolution of this dichotomy might be instead a return to Nellie's four versions of Myra's family story in chapter two. For the end of *My Mortal Enemy* does indeed logically follow and relate to its beginning, but within its narration rather than within itself as a text.[36] For the story that Nellie tells about Myra in part one of the novel ends with a pronounced lack of closure, just as do the stories of the Sleeping Beauty and the nuns. Her narration in part two, on the other hand, embodies a very strong sense of closure; in fact, it ends with the same religious framework that constitutes the story of John Driscoll. There is a unity here. The female story line of part one has been overturned and corrected by the story line of part two, which has both religious authority and closure, and which has been introduced to us as a gender-signified, male story appositional to the female stories that precede it. These two halves of the novel cannot, finally, be reconciled textually as I have read them here. One has to repress either the first half of the text (Myra's subversive power within, and alternative readings of, heterosexual relations) in the interest of unity and coherence, or the second (Nellie's authority which locates meaning in religion and mortality) in order to stress the refutation of a single, correct interpretation within a multiplicity of readings. Dorothy Tuck McFarland seems also to have arrived at a similar point of interpretative paradox when she argues:

> The novel thus seems to be an experiment in the depiction of conflict in an almost pure form, and the problems of understanding its meaning have stemmed from focusing too much on, and trying to make satisfactory sense out of, the particulars in which the conflict is expressed. The whole refractoriness of the novel, its resistance to resolution, seems to be Willa Cather's attempt to forestall the natural tendency to thrust past conflict toward resolution. Instead she would have us remain, almost against our will, in the conflict situation itself.[37]

I am not so sure that Cather was as conscious of creating this effect as McFarland claims. But a curious moment in the text suggests that perhaps she might have been. When Nellie first visits the ill Myra Henshawe in part two of the novel, she provides as much "amusing gossip" as she can recall. One of these stories provokes the following unexplained response from Myra: "Go on; you say that Lydia and your mother are at present in disputation about the possession of your late grandfather's portrait. Why don't you cut it in two for them, Nellie? I remember it perfectly, and half of it would be enough for anybody!" (65). So too this novel, in which the act of remembering certain elements of the narration elicits and composes an interpretation that cannot accommodate both halves of Myra Henshawe's portrait. Nellie's second narrative recollection represses and revises her first and demands, subtly, that we as readers do the same. This textual disjunction, felt rather than analyzed by most Cather critics, seems to be why the experience of reading this novel remains so disturbing and unsatisfactory. We are directed to read the text against itself.

ꜤꜤꜤꜤ **3** ꭉꭉꭉꭉ

Tales of Telling
and Fictions of History:
Casting *Shadows on the Rock*

The earliest symptom of a process whose end is the decline of
storytelling is the rise of the novel at the beginning of modern
times.   —WALTER BENJAMIN, "The Storyteller"

And really, a new society begins with the salad dressing more than
with the destruction of Indian villages.

—WILLA CATHER, "On *Shadows on the Rock*"

Shadows on the Rock (1931) is a historical fiction.[1] It recounts the seasonal
year of 1697–98 in the lives of the early settlers of French Quebec, "the
rock" of the title. Though centered around the fictional characters of
the "philosopher apothecary,"[2] Euclide Auclair, and his twelve-year-old
daughter, Cécile, the text revivifies a number of historical personages
from seventeenth-century French Canada, and, by all accounts, Cather
read widely to achieve some kind of accuracy and authenticity in her
portraits.[3]

I wish, however, to shift the attention from history in order to offer
another kind of reading, a reading focused solely on the narrative
structure of the text. Such a reading poses and presupposes the question:
What if the novel, or narrative, or collection of sketches dramatizes self-
consciously not so much a history, or a particular kind of history, but *the
process of constructing history,* the ways in which fictions, legends, miracles, and tale-telling compose and interpret history? What if the text
embeds an acknowledgment of its own distorting power as narrative, a
recognition of tale-telling itself as an agent of history? In this reading, the

text would not only represent French Canadian and female tradition in material goods and in ways of keeping house, but would also transcribe the tradition of, and in its own telling would demonstrate, "historiography as a form of fiction making."[4] What if *Shadows on the Rock* is not really about history at all, but rather about fiction within, fiction against, and fiction *as* history?

I wish to begin with a letter Cather wrote in 1931 to Wilbur Cross, then governor of Connecticut, expressing appreciation "for the most understanding review I have seen of my book."[5] The letter remains one of Cather's rare attempts to explain her fiction, though, as usual, it obscures more than it illuminates. Praising Cross for recognizing "what a different kind of method I tried to use from that which I used in the *Archbishop*," Cather attempts to define this methodology in the letter. One passage in particular stands out as supremely paradoxical and puzzling.

> To me the rock of Quebec is not only a stronghold on which many strange figures have for a little time cast a shadow in the sun; it is the curious endurance of a kind of culture, narrow but definite. There another age persists. There, among the country people and the nuns, I caught something new to me; a kind of feeling about life and human fate that I could not accept, wholly, but which I could not but admire. It is hard to state that feeling in language; it was more like an old song, incomplete but uncorrupted, than like a legend. The text was mainly anacoluthon, so to speak, but the meaning was clear. I took the incomplete air and tried to give it what would correspond to a sympathetic musical setting; tried to develop it into a prose composition not too conclusive, not too definite: a series of pictures remembered rather than experienced; a kind of thinking, a mental complexion inherited, left over from the past, lacking in robustness and full of pious resignation. (15)

Cather's introduction of the rhetorical term "anacoluthon"—"Syntactical inconsistency or incoherence within a sentence, especially the shift from one construction, left incomplete, to another" (*Webster's Third New International Dictionary of the English Language Unabridged,* 1961)— is telling about the act of translation she simultaneously describes and performs in this passage. A "feeling" that is "hard to state . . . in language" acquires a metaphorical referent ("more like an old song") and is signified into something. The French language system of her sources is turned into English; historical figures and situations are (re)presented as fiction. More important, so too the translation of "an old song, incomplete" into "a prose composition, not too conclusive" requires what the syntax of the passage itself provides—the shift from one construction (in this case, metaphoric), left incomplete, to another; the very definition of anacoluthon.

What Cather finally arrives at is an approximate definition of the form of her text, a definition purposefully indefinite: "a prose composition, not too conclusive, not too definite: a series of pictures remembered rather than experienced." The seeming function of the colon in this compound sentence is to balance the clauses, to signify that the second clause represents a restatement or a definition of the first. It marks the contiguity between creation and memory, between the fictional present of "composition" and the historical past of "pictures remembered." Part of the tenuous balance Cather strikes here is of parallel static representation, "a series of pictures" composed by and composing "a prose composition," the lack of conclusion and definitiveness in a "remembered rather than experienced" narrative frame. What Cather describes is what Ross Chambers calls the "anti-model of plot,"[6] a narrative text marked by the absence of causality and conclusion. In this regard, its narrative is neither historical nor particularly novelistic,[7] in the conventional sense of the formal structure of a fiction (distinct from the fiction itself) determined by historical time. But if we can at least be "clear" about what the "meaning" is not, to rephrase Cather, then the burden is to show that the text means more than nothing. In one last anacoluthic turn, let us return to anacoluthon.

If we cannot immediately locate the text's meaning, we must at least be able to determine generally what the text is about. But what makes Cather's explanation so complex and slippery is that its embedded anacoluthic logic leaves incomplete all the categories through which we might define the text. One could, with some degree of confidence, say that if Cather's text is *about* anything, on the most accessible thematic level, it is about the translation of French sensibility into Canadian character, about creating another culture by transplanting received traditions into new territory. I want to suggest that where the alleged "meaning" of this text resides is within the rupture of anacoluthon, in the gap between the contiguity of "historical" and "novel." It is not merely about the translation of history into fiction, but rather, about what can be created from the slippage of the link between these two invented narratives, between these two kinds of verbal fictions.[8] It is this difference *within* narrative structures that I wish to explore as the new territory of this text.

Shadows on the Rock is composed of relatively disconnected narrative tellings and narrated re-creations of events in the past.[9] Rather than read the text as being about narrative itself though, critics have tended to look instead at the content of the narrative. In it they discover similar and/or repeated themes which they then read as the "meaning" of the text. These readings demonstrate that though the form of the text may be anacoluthon, its content is not.[10] But such an assertion is partly true and partly not true. The consistency that thematic readings depend upon *is* provided within *Shadows on the Rock,* and it comes from the narrator itself. The external focalizer of this text—what Mieke Bal calls the "anonymous agent, situated outside the fabula"[11]—seems to be primarily responsible for the thematic consistency that allows a reader to read for meaning. In its moral pronouncements about characters and actions, in its didactic interpretation of certain stories, the external focalizer suggests Cather's characterization of "a kind of thinking, a mental complexion inherited, left over from the past" (On *Shadows,*" 15). Such a "mental complexion" represents shared cultural values, and it should not be surprising, or even incorrect, that a reader could locate one kind of meaning within the novel through a voice that revivifies and makes vivid a seventeenth-century sensibility.

Yet the external focalizer also functions in *Shadows on the Rock* as a prism through which different levels of memory are refracted into told narratives. I stress the tale-telling quality of narrative here because if the external focalizer focalizes shared cultural assumptions, the "*on disait*" (it was said that) quality of its comments also suggests its role as a repository for the stories, bits of gossip, prejudice, and tales that have gone into the creation of a culture. Its role is at once teller and interpreter, though as the latter it lapses into periods of significant, and indeed, telling silence.

There are four basic constructions of remembered stories in *Shadows on the Rock.* They appear in no particular sequence or order and they tend to slip into and out of one another regularly. Such shifts, I would argue, are part of what Cather suggested was the text's anacoluthon structure. The first such construction appears in the opening line of the text: "One afternoon late in October of the year 1697, Euclide Auclair, the philosopher apothecary of Quebec, stood on the top of Cap Diamant gazing down the broad, empty river far beneath him" (3). This is an example of the external focalizer in all its omniscient authority. Drawing our eye back through time and down to this particularized starting point (both a geographical location and an individual consciousness situated above "the rock"), the external focalizer orients us within the generalized historical situation of this fiction and within the fictive treatment of this historical situation. The external focalizer tells us a historical story ("It was indeed a rude beginning of a 'new France'" [6]) through the perspective of fiction as a tale told ("Divest your mind of Oriental colour, and you saw here very much such a mountain rock . . ." [5]). This synthesis of history and fiction is *the* structure of *Shadows on the Rock* as a narrative text, with the external focalizer functioning as the agent who relates the narrative.

The second narrative construction in, rather than of, the text, amplifies the contextualizing of storytelling and stories told as both subject and form of the text itself: "Since this happened every night, Cécile thought nothing of it. Her mother had begun to look out for Blinker a little before she became so ill, and he was one of the cares the daughter had inherited. He had come out to the colony four years ago" (15). In this passage we receive the history of Blinker as a story already formed and one that, like "the cares" of the young girl, has been "inherited." The external focalizer, in this instance, relates the story through the memory of Cécile; it is already a part of her internalized sense of history. What is focalized is not so much the re-creation of a particular consciousness, as it is the retelling of what has contributed to the making of that consciousness, the way in which stories inform human history.

The third type of focalized narration appears when the story of a particular character is related through the language of an external focalizer, as in: "When he was a little boy, he used to tell Cécile, nothing ever changed next door, except that after a rain the cobbles in the yard were whiter, and the ivy on the walls was greener. Every morning he looked out from his window on the same stillness" (17–18). This construction has two effects. It is used throughout the text to articulate the stories of less than articulate characters such as the six-year-old Jacques Gaux (70–74), Blinker (160–62), and, frequently, Cécile herself (40–42, 130–36). But in this case, when the character focalized, Auclair, is more than capable of telling his own story, and which he does when the focalization shifts into character focalization in the succeeding paragraph ("Naturally," Auclair would tell his daughter, "having seen the establishment next door always the same . . ." [18]), it has another function. It represents and transforms Auclair's history into *his story*, and it collapses the difference between historical narrative and fictional narrative. This is not unlike the way in which the external focalizer works in Blinker's story, though there is one telling difference. The story of Blinker, as it is given voice through Cécile's internalized remembrance, already has been woven into the fabric of the colony's history. Cécile's recall of it through the external focalizer unveils one of these histories within the text. Auclair's story of his first meeting with Count Frontenac, however, appears in the text in the process of being passed down, in the process of becoming a story which Cécile will be able to recall at a later date. In this regard, the external focalizer not only focalizes the narrative, but also erects a superstructure of narratability within the text by retelling tales that have *been* told, and by telling tales as they are *being* told.

The fourth and final construction of narrated tales in *Shadows on the Rock* occurs when a story is focalized through a character and is *told as a story*, as in the following example.

> While her hands flew among the scraps of colour, Mother Juschereau began somewhat formally:
> "Before she had left her fair Normandy (*avant qu'elle ait quitté sa belle Normandie*), while Sister Catherine was a novice at Bayeux, there lived in the neighborhood a *pécheresse* named Marie." (37)

The text signals its acknowledgment that this is an externally narrated tale within its narrative both by describing the way it is told ("Mother Juschereau began somewhat formally") and by nodding parenthetically to the original language from which it has been translated. It is at once a part of (transcribed within) and apart from (character focalized) the externally focalized narrative text.

Such multiple layers of storytelling construct the skeleton of the narrative and are marked by subtle differences within their synthesis of history and fiction. Yet *Shadows on the Rock* is not only narrated as a series of stories, it is also composed of different story genres: legends, hagiography, personal histories, miracles, adventure stories, dreams, visions, and historical vignettes. In the story of Sister Catherine and Marie *la pécheresse*, for instance, both legend (the story of a life, as of a saint) and miracle (the dead Marie's return from purgatory to chastise Sister Catherine's lack of prayers for her soul) figure as elements within

the tale. Anacoluthic shifts in the text result not only from the difference
in the way stories are narrated, but also from the different kinds of stories
themselves that are foregrounded from one moment to the next. Rather
than tie the stories together on the basis of similarities within their
content, I would emphasize abruptness, the sudden appearance and
subsequent displacement of different stories, as the single most important subject of this text. Thus the sketchiness and brevity of the novel's
characters and scenes, which critics have complained of as imaginative
anemia and thin writing,[12] might instead be read as part of the tradition
of storytelling Cather records in, and as, the text. As Walter Benjamin
argues in "The Storyteller":

> There is nothing that commends a story to memory more effectively
> than that chaste compactness which precludes psychological analysis. And
> the more neutral the process by which the storyteller forgoes psychologi-
> cal shading, the greater becomes the story's claim to a place in the memory
> of the listener, the more completely it is integrated into his own experi-
> ence, the greater will be his inclination to repeat it to someone else
> someday, sooner or later.[13]

Benjamin's quote underscores the link between personal memory and
the "inclination" to repeat stories so that they become part of a collective,
cultural tradition. The act of repetition becomes the practice of retelling,
which in turn lends, and perhaps even grants, a certain kind of authority
to these stories. They become part of the history of a given community.
Shadows on the Rock, narrated as and composed of such stories, records
this subtle, anacoluthic shift from the fictive to the historical. Thus the
text becomes, to some extent, a historical fiction in its re-creation of how
history is recorded.

The shift from fiction to history is not the only thing that is anacoluthic in this text however. For as Freud noticed in trying to account
for the fictive history of Moses, an even greater rupture may occur in the
translation from an oral into a written tradition.

> What has been deleted or altered in the written version might quite well
> have been preserved uninjured in the tradition. Tradition was the comple-
> ment and at the same time the contradiction of written history. It was less
> subject to distorting influences—perhaps in part entirely free from them—
> and therefore might be more truthful than the account set down in
> writing. Its trustworthiness, however, was impaired by being vaguer and

more fluid than the written text, being exposed to many changes and distortions as it was passed on from one generation to the next by word of mouth. Such a tradition may have different outcomes. The most likely event would be for it to be vanquished by the written version, ousted by it, until it grows more and more shadowy and at last is forgotten. Another fate might be that the tradition itself ends up by becoming a written version.[14]

Freud begins this passage by assuming the existence of an inevitable distortion ("deleted," "altered") in the written version of history. Yet oral traditions too are susceptible to distortions in Freud's scheme, especially when they are "passed on from one generation to the next by word of mouth," when they are repeated and re-created by the individual storyteller, when the tradition is retold as a story. We confront anacoluthon not only in the translations of fiction into history (the oral giving way to the written tradition), but also in the transfiguration(s) of traditions as they are retold through generations, in the way history becomes fictionalized through its telling. What Cather attempts in *Shadows on the Rock* is to preserve the "shadowy" tale-telling tradition by inscribing that tradition *within* and by translating it *into* a written account. In *writing history* she has necessarily distorted the oral tradition and has relied upon anacoluthon to effect the shift from one construction to another. The text embodies the process by which fictions narrated in a society compose its history, while it simultaneously and self-consciously acknowledges the way in which "the tradition itself ends by becoming a written version," the way history is itself a kind of fiction. If the narrative of *Shadows on the Rock* translates fiction into history, then the text as metanarrative reinscribes history as fiction. In this respect, the novel stands as perhaps Cather's most radical experiment with the boundaries of narrative form, representing itself as a new and self-conscious version of the "historical novel."

This delicate suspension of tale-telling as the agent of shared traditions in a culture, and of the way in which it is preserved within this fictional re-creation is no better demonstrated than in the one "intertextual reference" of the novel.[15] Though stories abound in this novel, only one written text is inscribed within it. Early in the narrative on All Saint's Day, Cécile discovers "the picture of a little boy" (84) in *Lives of the Saints* who resembles Jacques Gaux, and she sits her friend down to read him the story of his look-alike, "little Saint Edmond" (84). I include the

French text as it appears in the novel, followed by a translation of it into English.[16]

> "*Edmond était tout enfant un modèle de vertu, grâce aux tendres soins de sa pieuse mère. On ne le voyait qu'à l'école et à l'église, partageant ses journées entre la prière et l'étude, et se privant des plaisirs les plus innocents pour s'entretenir avec Jésus et sa divine Mère à laquelle il voua un culte tout spécial. Un jour qu'il fuyait ses compagnons de jeu, pour se recueillir intimement, l'Enfant Jésus lui apparaît, rayonnant de beauté et le regarde avec amour en lui disant: 'Je te salue, mon bien-aimé.' Edmond tout ébloui n'ose répondre et le divin Sauveur reprend: 'Vous ne me connaissez donc pas?— Non, avoue l'enfant, je n'ai pas cet honneur et je crois que vous ne devez pas me connaître non plus, mais me prenez pour un autre.—Comment, continue le petit Jésus, vous ne me reconnaissez pas, moi qui suis toujours à vos côtés et vous accompagne partout. Regardez-moi; je suis Jésus, gravez toujours ce nom en votre coeur et imprimez-le sur votre front et je vous préserverai de mort subite ainsi que tous ceux qui feront de même.'*" (85)

["As a child Edmond was a model of virtue, thanks to his pious mother's tender care. He was never seen anywhere but at school or in church, dividing his days between prayer and study, and depriving himself of the most innocent pleasures to commune with Jesus and his holy Mother to whom he devoted a special kind of worship. One day when he was fleeing his playmates in order to meditate, the baby Jesus appears to him, radiant with beauty and looks at him with love saying: 'Greetings, my beloved.' Edmond, dazzled, does not dare to answer and the divine Savior continues: 'You don't know me then?—No, admits the child, I do not have the honor and I think you must not know me either, but take me for someone else.—What, little Jesus continues—you don't recognize me, I who am always at your side and accompany you everywhere. Look at me, I am Jesus, engrave this name in your heart forever and imprint it on your forehead and I will preserve you from sudden death along with everyone who will do the same thing.'"]

Two telling constructions of revision shape a reading of this passage: resemblance and recognition. Cécile shows the picture and its accompanying text to Jacques because it *resembles* him, signaling both the similarities between this intertextual text and the narrative text, as well as the (a)likeness (*ressemblance*) of one text to, and within, another. Even more suggestive is the "little Jesus'" insistence that the "little Saint Edmond" recognize (*reconnaissez*) him, that he perceive him as something previously known. Presumably, Cécile reads this story to Jacques so that he, having been apprised of his physical similarity, will recognize himself as "like" Saint Edmond, and so that he will also recognize Jesus as someone whom he does, and, of course, ought to know. If, then, we are asked to recognize the correlation between this text and the narrative text, since it is presented to *us* on the page to be read, what is it exactly we are supposed to see, and how will this recognition direct us to understand the text as a whole?

Cécile *reads* rather than *tells* a story to Jacques in this instance; her action is analogous to the way in which the novel is presented to a reader. Yet the text of "little Saint Edmond" nonetheless inscribes the continuous present of inscription; it holds in suspension the fictional present of stories and the historical past of this story as the "life," lived, told, and finally, textualized, of Saint Edmond. For the verb tense of the continuous present in "*gravez toujours ce nom en votre coeur*" ("engrave this name in your heart forever"), *is* the act of storytelling made textual. The continuous present of engraving (*gravez*) and imprinting (*imprimez*) signals at once the repetition of tale-telling in an oral tradition (the retelling of Jesus' visitation to Edmond) and the inscription of this tale into a text. Moreover, the apotropaic moral of this story is presented and represented as a shared understanding within the culture of seventeenth-century French Catholicism ("*tous ceux qui feront de même*"). What we are being asked to recognize then, is the continuous present of inscription in the process of becoming the text, the synthesis of *a* historical representation of a tradition in *the* fictional presentation of it.

Such a tension between the oral and the written, the narrated and the inscribed, is itself self-reflexively inscribed in the text through what Ross Chambers has defined as "figural" embedding, the "incorporation into the narrative of a 'figure' . . . that is representative in some sense of 'art,' or of the production and reception of narrative, that is, of narrative 'code' or 'enunciation.'"[17] *Shadows on the Rock,* as a text, acknowledges both synthesis and stasis as part of its own narrative code, as in the epigraph of the novel.

> *Vous me demandez des graines de fleurs de ce pays. Nous en faisons venir de France pour notre jardin, n'y en ayant pas ici de fort rare ni de fort belles. Tout y est sauvage, les fleurs aussi bien que les hommes.* (2)

> [You ask me for seeds from the flowers of this country. We are having some come from France for our garden, since there are neither very rare

nor very beautiful ones here. Everything here is wild, the flowers as well as the people.]

Before the narrative even begins, we are directed to see the transplanting of French culture (in this case, seeds) into Canadian soil as *the* central meaning of the text. But the introduction of flowers being imported in order to create a garden could also be read as a figure for the way tales are contained within the formal structure of this novel. I single out the figure of flowers because it reappears when specific productions of art are examined within the text. Right before Mother Juschereau narrates the first told tale in the novel, for example, Cécile encounters her as she busily constructs "artificial flowers": "Cécile fell to admiring the work Mother Juschereau had in hand. Her lap and the table beside her were full of scraps of bright silk and velvet and sheets of colored paper. While she overlooked the young Sisters at their tasks, her fingers were moving rapidly and cleverly, making artificial flowers" (35). This is, significantly, a work that she has "in hand," and one that represents something else. "These are the wild roses," Mother Juschereau says of her artificial flowers, "such as I used to gather when I was a child at Beauport" (35). This combination of real French flowers and artificial Canadian ones recalls the epigraph of the novel. Even more allusive however, is the figure of a work being "in hand," and the way in which an epigraph is one glimpse of a self-consciously authorial signature. In Mother Juschereau's declaration that the artificial flowers which she has "in hand . . . are the wild roses" of her childhood, the text embeds figurally its own mode of artistic reproduction. It acknowledges itself to be a re-creation of a living form in the past (the tradition of tale-telling); it recognizes itself through the figure of artifice as artificial in nature.

Another play between the living and the artistically reproduced oc-curs when Cécile visits Count Frontenac's apartment and requests to see once more something she considers to be "much lovelier than real fruit" (60): "Between the tall silver candlesticks stood a crystal bowl full of glowing fruits of coloured glass: purple figs, yellow-green grapes with gold vine-leaves, apricots, nectarines, and a dark citron stuck up endwise among the grapes. The fruits were hollow, and the light played in them, throwing coloured reflections into the mirror and upon the wall above" (59). Implicit in this description is the way light animates what would otherwise be a still life. The inverse of Mother Juschereau's re-creation of living flowers into art, the glass fruit comes alive when light is cast upon it, which in turn casts reflections within "the mirror and upon the wall above," a doubled artificiality. The narrative pictures simultaneously art and the image of art, redoubling its self-reflexive play when in the same scene Cécile gazes at the count's tapestries and notes that they "represented garden scenes" (60).[18] Again the narrative directs attention to the inscription of art within the text and demands a recognition of the text's self-consciousness of itself as representation.

Perhaps nowhere is this more pointed than the scene in which the title of the novel becomes a figure for the novel itself. While Cécile and Jacques take refuge in a church during a rainstorm, the text spends a full five pages describing the interior of the church (63–68), especially the paintings which "stood high up among the shadows," inscribed on "three tall stone towers" (65). The children decide to light a candle in order to see the paintings better, and for their religious offering they receive aesthetic satisfaction: "Sure enough, when the fresh tapers were burning well, the gold flowers on Saint Anne's cloak began to show; not entire, but wherever there was a fold in the mantle, the gold seemed to glow like a glistening liquid. Her figure emerged from the dusk in a rich, oily, yellow light" (67). Again flowers become the central motif for artistic reproduction, this time illuminated from the shadows by light. The text not only sums up and integrates its figures—flowers, shadows, light—it also embeds them pointedly within painting, within its own sense of fictive representation. Paintings, glass fruit, and artificial flowers are all representations of a static rather than a fluid disposition. Though *Shadows on the Rock* is, like the flowers on the saint's cloak, an anacoluthic series of tales told "not entire," the text necessarily sees itself as a text, as a representation of an ever-changing oral tradition in an artistically contained, and thus permanently changed, frame. This tension appears in and emerges from the figure of Saint Anne, when "the gold" flowers of her cloak, painted and fixed, begin "to glow like a glistening liquid," animated by a "rich, oily, yellow light." To cast light, in this text, is at once to illuminate flickering and partial shadows from the historical past and to give particular artistic shape to those shadows by enclosing them within the continuous present of art.

The anacoluthic shift implicitly present in the paradoxical duality of casting as both an ephemeral projection and a hardened mold of something,[19] is made explicit in the text at two significant, and similar, points. If *Shadows on the Rock* is concerned with its own distorting power as a narrative that reshapes an oral tradition of historical composition into a fictional composition of this oral tradition, then it is likely that the text would acknowledge the slippage within the shift between these two narrative modes. For, as Freud deduced in his investigation of textuality and history: "The distortion of a text is not unlike a murder. The difficulty lies not in the execution of the deed but in doing away with the traces. One could wish to give the word 'distortion' the double meaning to which it has a right, although it is no longer used in this sense. It should mean not only 'to change the appearance of,' but also 'to wrench apart,' 'to put in another place.' "[20] The salient difference between *Shadows on the Rock* and Freud's comment, is that rather than doing away with the traces of distortion, this text inscribes them as, literally, the subtext of this novel. The two footnotes that appear in the text illustrate this tendency toward self-conscious distortion in the novel.

It chanced that this one church* in the Lower Town near Jacques's little world, where he and Cécile had so often made rendezvous, was peculiarly the church of childhood.
*[The charm of this old church was greatly spoiled by unfortunate alterations in the lighting, made in the autumn of 1929.] (63)

"I suppose you do not know anyone who would care to rent the Palace? The rental would be very helpful to me in my present undertakings. No, I shall reside at the Hôpital General*"
*[Some years before he sailed for France in 1700, Bishop de Saint-Vallier had founded the Hôpital General, for the aged and incurable. The hospital still stands today, much enlarged; the wards which Saint-Vallier built and the two small rooms in which he lived until his death are unchanged.] (274)

Both of these footnotes take as their subject architectural structures that have been altered with the passing of time. In signaling this, the text alters its own architecture, in both the diminished and the expanded versions of the footnotes. In one sense, the loss of charm about which the first footnote complains *is* what it accomplishes; it spoils the "charming" description of the church by insisting extratextually that its charm, its organic unity, has been somehow spoiled. In another sense though, the text reinscribes the architectural transformation that has occurred in history by transforming itself, through a historical allusion, and rupturing the illusion of the text as fiction. These footnotes direct the reader to be conscious of the ways in which the text is subject to, and the subject

of, history, just as the buildings—the church and the Hôpital General—
are subjected to alterations by the passing of historical time. Cather
creates a structure here that is both parallel and perpendicular, juxtaposing the contiguous claims of fiction and history while simultaneously
drawing them together into an anacoluthic convergence, or parabasis,
what Paul de Man identifies as "a sudden revelation of the discontinuity
between two rhetorical codes."[21] De Man's tiered construction of anacoluthic syntax and parabastic rhetoric applies to these footnotes in two
respects. The disruption of representation engendered by the footnotes
is located in the breaking apart of the text's architecture. For the text, as
the examples of its figural embedding would imply, recognizes itself to be
a production of art that has, in a sense, captured history and preserved it
through fictional representation. Within the frame of the text, this
particularized history of seventeenth-century French Quebec can remain unchanged and, in Cather's words, "uncorrupted." Such a claim,
however, is undercut visually by the "fact" of change and alteration
documented (and historicized by dates) in the footnotes. The fiction and
the page itself are, to recall Freud, distorted. The asterisk literally changes
the appearance of the text; fiction shifts to history and back again.
Similarly, the parabastic discontinuity to which De Man refers appears in
the difference *within* the narrative text read both horizontally and vertically. Parabasis itself denotes a speech within a Greek comedy, "in
which the chorus, moving towards and facing the audience, addressed it
in the name of the poet, often abandoning all reference to the action of
the play."[22] Such a rupture within the text is what occurs in these two
footnotes, which themselves step forward to address the reader. Another
focalizer surfaces, abandons the action of the narrative, and revises the
fictional presentation of history. The narrative is wrenched apart into
two different narratives, which we are directed to read together. If we
return to the figure of Saint Anne's cloak, we notice that its gold flowers
are illuminated only "wherever there was a fold in the mantle" (67),
whenever the material is doubled up on itself. Such doubling, at once
complementary and contradictory, always paradoxical, lies at the heart
of *Shadows on the Rock.*

Doubling is similarly relevant to the tradition in the telling of this text,
the way tale-telling both creates and re-creates history. In "The Long
Winter" (117–66), Book Three of *Shadows on the Rock,* narratives become the narrative. Book Three is the culmination of the episodic
structure and anacoluthic narrative that dominates the first half of the

novel. It is also a lucid example of the textual ambivalence that is crucial for understanding the way Cather's texts elicit and undermine their own readability, in part because the entire book is what Ross Chambers terms one long "narrational" embedding.

> "Narrational" embedding is not "l'histoire dans l'histoire" . . . but narrative act within narrative act, narrative situation within narrative situation: it implies the representation, internally to the fictional framework, of a situation involving the major components of a communicational net (emitter-discourse-recipient)—and very frequently the mirroring within a story of the storytelling relationship itself: narrator-narration-narratee.[23]

Storytelling in *Shadows on the Rock* is what sustains both the text and its society. Recounted for amusement and instruction, the tale-telling of Book Three passes the bleak and frozen season within the text and gives texture to the historical sensibility that informs this culture. Though "The Long Winter" is anacoluthic in structure, composed entirely of a series of stories narrated by various characters, we again witness the contrary pull of the external focalizer which directs our reading by interpreting the tales into comprehensible moral parables. Thus while the text itself displaces meaning within the shift from one story to another, the narrative attempts to construct a coherent reading between these stories. The text asks us to read these stories *as* the history of French Quebec, collapsing the difference between fictive and historical narratives. The narrative, on the other hand, elicits a reading that acknowledges these tales to be fictional re-creations of history, which is then interpreted by the external focalizer and assigned a meaning that "says" something about the historical past. The narrative reads history through re-creating it, while the text recreates history as narrative. In the first construction the meaning is clear; in the second it is clearly anacoluthic.

There are, essentially, nine stories that compose "The Long Winter," the first (a brief history of Saint-Vallier's life and the machinations of court politics) and the last (the return of the swallow and the rebirth of spring) externally focalized. Of the other seven stories, two are reported miracles, two are saints' lives interpreted as *exempla,* two are personal histories that end in redemption, and one is a narrative with no ending or moral, the only story with this absence. This story is the character-focalized narrative of the woodsman, Antoine Frichette. Frichette arrives at Auclair's shop seeking a cure for a hernia ("A rupture, Auclair saw at once" [138]), and is persuaded by the apothecary to relate his "long story" about a perilous journey through a raging storm in order to bring back a priest for his dying brother. Like other tales in this book, Frichette's tale broadly centers on individual will and human courage in the face of a cruel and hostile environment or society. But unlike the other stories, Frichette's narrative is not affixed with a religious interpretation that reshapes it into a morality tale. What the narrative depends upon instead (and self-reflexively stresses) is Frichette's ability to read signs in the forest so that he can find his way back to his cabin during the snowstorm, *the* central and crucial action of this story.

> "Next morning when I left that place, I noticed a few trees as I went, so I could find it when I brought the priest back with me. Ordinarily I don't notch trees to find my way back. When there is no sun, I can tell directions like the Indians."
> Here Auclair interrupts him. "And how is that, Antoine?"
> Frichette smiled and shrugged. "It is hard to explain—by many things. The limbs of the trees are generally bigger on the south side, for example. The moss on the trunks is clean and dry on the north side,—on the south side it is softer and maybe a little rotten. *There are many little signs; put them together and they point you right.*" (141, emphasis added)

Though Frichette and the priest finally do arrive in time to give the brother a Christian burial, Frichette's own fate is left bleakly undecided.

> Frichette shook his head and spread his thick fingers apart on his knees. "There is no future for me if I cannot paddle a canoe up the big rivers any more."
> "Perhaps you can paddle, Antoine, but not carry."
> Antoine rose. "In this world, who paddles must carry, monsieur."
> (145–46)

Left without an externally focalized interpretation that explains human suffering as part of and triumphant within a divine plan, just what exactly does this story point toward, and moreover, how is one to tell if it is right? Though this tale is pointedly without a moral, it does, nonetheless, have a point, if only in the sense that it ends; it reaches its point. This point, curiously enough, is the acceptance of an incurable rupture, what is at once a figural *and* a narrational embedding of the text within the narrative.

Rupture frames Frichette's story. He arrives anticipating a cure; he leaves accepting the impossibility of being cured. There is, significantly, no procedure that can heal his wound, no divine agent that can permanently alleviate his trouble (unlike the way in which the spiritual wounds of Father Hector Saint-Cyr, Noël Chabanel, and Blinker are healed in their tales.) One must, according to this tale, accept an internalized rupture. The only one of its kind among all the stories in Book Three, Frichette's tale self-reflexively acknowledges the frustration of reading a text with an anacoluthic structure. In positing a tale with no closure against a series of tales which, for the most part, are either narrated (Father Hector and the story of Noël Chabanel) or interpreted (Auclair on Blinker) as comprehensible and moral, the text signals its own divisiveness, its own split between what Cather called an anacoluthic structure and clear meaning. Much of the narrative encourages, often quite obviously, the apprehension of meaning by reading correctly, as when Auclair interprets Blinker's deformity ("When God sent you that affliction in your face, he showed his mercy to you" [162]) by recalling a passage from book four of the *Aeneid:* "Having known misery, I have learned to pity the miserable" (163). Yet there are also moments, tellingly silent, when stories can only be told and not read, when the text, through such internal ruptures as the story of Antoine Frichette, eludes and even defies interpretation. At such moments we are left, perhaps as uncomfortably as Frichette himself, within an anacoluthic rupture and a textual split, neither of which will be alleviated to our satisfaction.

There is one other tale with a difference in Book Three, that of the Montreal recluse, Jeanne Le Ber. It is, in fact, two tales really: one, the miracle of the angelic repair of her spinning wheel and two, her life story or history spun out of Cécile's memory. The history of Jeanne le Ber not only stands at the center of *Shadows on the Rock,*[24] but also is the only story with two entirely different versions, one focalized through Cécile's memory, the other revised and focalized by Pierre Charron.[25] The difference between these two narrations, and their difference within the text, questions the entire process of making meaning. For one is asked, since their respective narrations are at once parallel and contradictory, to decide which is the fiction and which the history. This decision is complicated and made more difficult by the claims each narrative establishes as to its authenticity, its proper version, and its right reading of history.

The first version of Jeanne Le Ber's life appears in "The Long Winter" and is represented as a received history, focalized through Cécile's remembrance: "In her mind she went over the whole story of the recluse of

Montreal" (130). The story, which has been passed down to Cécile as history, recounts the making of a saint. It is at once a story of religious ecstasy and female desire, and its plot charts a journey from the house of the father to a room of one's own. Significantly, the story of Jeanne Le Ber repeats many of the same elements that have figured previously in the histories of female characters, especially Mother de Saint-Augustin, whose story Cécile recalls early in the text, also after hearing about a miracle (40–42). Both are stories of religious devotion conceived as the flowering of desire and carried out through the indomitable will of each young girl. Both are also stories of female rebellion against a patriarchal authority which are then converted, during the course of their telling, to tales of complete submission to a heavenly authority.

What most characterizes the story of Jeanne Le Ber is self-possession. In opposition to a doting father and a disapproving society, Jeanne Le Ber erects a series of severe and religious boundaries between herself and the world of wealth in which she has been raised. Details of obsessive self-punishment demarcate her calling: she wears "a little haircloth shirt next to her tender skin" (131); "at seventeen [she] took the vow of chastity for five years and immured herself within her own chamber in her father's house" (132); and she finally has a tiny cell constructed for herself behind the altar of a chapel in which she vows to live a reclusive life of poverty. Jeanne's all-consuming "desire was for the absolute solitariness of the hermit's life" (132), and her devotion to "so harsh a rule" (132) forbids even her presence at her mother's deathbed. It is finally with her inheritance, "that *dot*, which no mortal man would ever claim," that she "was able to accomplish a cherished hope" (134), the construction both of her chapel "for the Sisters of the Congregation of the Blessed Virgin" (134) and of her cell which, ending Cécile's remembrance of the story, Jeanne says she prefers to the rest of the entire world (136).

Though this version of the story stresses an almost selfish desire to have her own way at any cost, Jeanne Le Ber's rebellion against her father's wishes and society's dictates is valorized by her choice of a religious calling. Such mysterious and perverse behavior is tolerated because God has an authority superseding all others. The moral of this story then might be that personal desire and fulfillment for women is possible if voiced through religious devotion. Jeanne Le Ber gets to have her cell and to live in it too. Her life history as it is rendered in this story is one of private passion, obsessive self-denial, and a religious ecstasy unequaled by anything else in the novel.

To this history of Jeanne Le Ber the external focalizer affixes a pan-egyric on the social importance and benefit of the miracle story "told and retold with loving exaggeration during that severe winter" (136). Such stories, according to the focalizer, sustain the spirit of the commu-nity "because they are the actual flowering of desire. In them the vague worship and devotion of the simple-hearted assumes a form. From being a shapeless longing, it becomes a beautiful image; a dumb rapture becomes a melody that can be remembered and repeated; and the experience of a moment, which might have been a lost ecstasy, is made an actual possession and can be bequeathed to another" (137). A notice-able repetition and transformation occurs in the passage regarding some of the central images of Jeanne Le Ber's story: desire, worship, devotion, ecstasy, and possession. It is as if the story has been so intricately woven into the fabric of history that the external focalizer can describe its value only by transcribing its language. Tradition and the telling become one. The passage also echoes Cather's own description of method in her letter to Wilbur Cross, especially in its transformation from formlessness into form. In describing the legacy of art ("image," "melody") and of tradi-tion ("an actual possession . . . bequeathed to another") which such stories bestow upon a culture, this passage parallels and praises what would seem to be the larger work of the text itself. The history of Jeanne Le Ber is both what *Shadows on the Rock* retells in its re-creation of an oral tradition, and, mirroring this passage, what it textualizes and trans-forms into a shaped artifact, into the text itself as a "historical novel."

The reader is not left to be lulled by this legend, however. For what soon follows in the narrative is a second version of Jeanne Le Ber's story, this time focalized by her childhood playmate and rejected suitor, Pierre Charron. Charron's narrative claims authority as an eye-witness ac-count. Because he has transgressed twice upon Jeanne Le Ber's vow of solitude, Charron claims *to have seen* the recluse, and therefore *to know* her history more reliably than the legend told about her. Whereas the first version of Jeanne Le Ber's history records the making of a saint, Charron's revision tells the story of the unmaking of a woman.

Despite Charron's claim of authenticity, his narrative commences only after the text has acknowledged the profound bias of it. Charron begins his story of Jeanne Le Ber with an ungenerous reference to the dowry he has lost. Reproved by Auclair, Pierre rephrases his discontent by defining it as a struggle between "the venerable Bourgeoys" and himself, which he has lost: "I care about defeat" (177). Had he triumphed, in his reading, Jeanne "would be a happy mother today . . . but now she is no better than dead. Worse" (177–78). Philosophizing that "ugly, poor, stupid, awkward" (178) girls are better suited to the life of a recluse, the prejudice in his rancor raises questions about the reliability of his revision of Jeanne even before it begins.

Charron plots his story within the teleology of a rejected lover; in his tale, Jeanne begins as a beautiful girl and ends a barren, sterile hag. When he first transgresses on her solitude he hides, not insignificantly, "under an apple-tree" in her garden (179). Her response to him is firm, but kind; she advises him to separate from her father and to marry. In this retelling, Charron spends most of the narrative extolling Jeanne's femininity, her "gracious and gentle" nature, "her face . . . fresh and soft, like the apple blossoms on that tree" (179). Juxtaposed to this initial conference twenty years past is a second one which takes place in the same year as Charron's narration. Having "heard" and "seen" the recluse, Charron possesses a story no one else can tell, a story of frightening transformation. To his eyes and ears, Jeanne Le Ber has not just aged. Her face "was like a stone face; it had been through every sorrow" (182), while "her voice was so changed,—hoarse, hollow, with the sound of despair in it" (183). Interpreting the alteration in her face and the change of her voice as evidence of profound unhappiness, the implicit moral of Charron's story is that the religious intensity of Jeanne's life has exacted an enormous toll from her as a woman. The happiness achieved by the saint at the end of the first version of her story is reduced in Charron's narrative to nothing more than despair. Jeanne, like Pierre, is miserable. His story of her, recounted in Book Four and entitled "Pierre Charron," becomes *his* story in more ways than one.

No external focalizer arrives after this narrative to frame its value. We are left with two constructions of meaning in the histories of Jeanne Le Ber: one socially contextualized and triumphant, the other personally framed and despairing. To valorize either reading, however, would be to misread the text. Again we confront and must be content to remain within if not an anacoluthic shift, then at least an anacoluthic sensibility. For the text incorporates two different constructions of narration (externally focalized through Cécile's remembrance and character focalized through Pierre), two antithetical interpretations of the value of Jeanne's life, and two different claims of authority within historical narrative (one passed down as a shared tradition, the other reported as private and privileged knowledge). There is no way, ultimately, to identify either as right or wrong.

Pierre Charron's revision of the Jeanne Le Ber story, however, signals an abrupt shift in the content of *Shadows on the Rock*. With the beginning of his story in Book Four, the varieties of tale-telling that have heretofore composed the narrative recede to some degree; the narrative devotes less time to the spinning out of these tales and they appear with less frequency.[26]

What begins to happen instead is the foregrounding of another story, one envisioned through history and plotted within historical (causal) time.[27] After the arrival of Pierre Charron in the novel, repetition is discarded as the primary narrative structure, and a plot moved through the quick succession of specific events takes over (the return of French ships, the Auclairs' preparations for leaving, the count's death, Pierre's fortuitous return). More important though, this plot begins with and is centered in Cécile's transformation from a young girl to a woman. The stories of and as *Shadows on the Rock* give way to the story of Cécile's growth and maturation; the histories re-created as the text are reformed (in the dual sense of this word). What the novel seems to want to become in its second half is a bildungsroman. It adopts the story of Cécile's training, development, and fashioning as a figure for the cultivation, growth, and formation of Canadian culture. The sense of history as narration is revised (just as Charron revises Jeanne Le Ber's story) to become instead a narration of history. In this narrowing of its focus, *Shadows on the Rock* attempts to become, not entirely successfully, both a conventional novel and a culminating, rather than a cumulative, history.

A reader is not exactly unprepared for Cécile's rise in predominance within the narrative, however, because she is the character who most consistently tells stories, is told them, or has them focalized through her. Moreover, up to this point in the narrative, Cécile's gradually blossoming maturity has been conceived in an anacoluthic shift between two different and alternating traditions to which she may or may not adhere. One is the tale-telling tradition about the nuns which Cécile recalls as stories throughout the first half of the narrative. This tradition valorizes self-fulfillment and the dominance of one's desires, often in opposition to paternal wishes. The other tradition is that of the absent mother, also recalled in Cécile's memory, a tradition that stresses order, stability, and submission. These two strains of absent role models appear randomly throughout Books One through Three. Cécile seems drawn to both, and again the text refuses to assign either as the "meaning" toward which her fate will be directed.

The tradition of the nuns which Cécile recalls as stories throughout the narrative is significant, since it is one of two versions of appropriate adult female behavior she witnesses. Though Mother Juschereau is convinced that Cécile "has certainly no vocation" (39) for the church, she does read "admiration and rapture . . . in the girl's face, but . . . not the rapture of self-abnegation" (40). A telling difference, for though Cécile seems to admire and feel intensely these legends, the inference is that she will not imitate them. Indeed, both the stories of Mother de Saint-Augustin and Jeanne Le Ber appear in the text when Cécile is alone and falls "to musing" (40) or "abandons herself to her thoughts" (130). Her remembrance of the tales is strangely similar; both are conceived as stories plotted through the struggle to achieve that which is denied. In the tale of Mother Catherine, for instance, the young saint's "bold imagination" is "fired" from reading "letters and *Relations* of the Jesuit missionaries" (40). She vows to go to Canada, though "her superiors discouraged her and forbade her to cherish this desire" (40). Refusing to be dissuaded, Catherine one day inscribes in blood her hope: "*Je mourrai au Canada/Soeur Saint-Augustin*" (41). This text becomes her life; though the young girl is denied permission from her father, "her Bishop and superiors" (41), her compelling desires are "brought to the attention of the Queen Mother, Anne of Austria" (41). The queen intercedes for the devout girl, and she finally becomes Mother Superior of Quebec at a young age. Like the story of Jeanne Le Ber, this tale is one of female power. By desire and determination, and through the aid of other powerful women, the saints follow a destiny of their own mapping. They achieve a kind of autonomy, are endowed with considerable religious authority, and, ultimately, are the authors of their own fates. Mother Catherine's bloody inscription is synonymous with Jeanne Le Ber's statement: "*I will be that lamp; that shall be my life*" (131).[28] Both fates are inscribed within their narratives and within the text itself; they write themselves into being. If these stories have a meaning, it may be that desire and authority are possible for women to attain. One possible outcome of female action and female fate has been passed down to Cécile within the storytelling tradition.

The alternate tradition Cécile also inherits comes from her mother, who has died before the narrative begins. Madame Auclair bequeaths to her daughter "the sense of 'our way'" (25), the domestic rituals and traditions that create civilization out of a wilderness. Conceived in the novel more as an influential idea than as an actual character, Madame Auclair figures as a crucial absent presence in Cécile's development.[29] What Cécile inherits chiefly from her mother is an utter devotion to domesticity as the mainstay of her father's security and peace of mind. The ordering of the house, the well-prepared meals, the caretaking of innocents like Blinker and Jacques are all traditions passed down to Cécile by her mother. They are also valorized by the external focalizer in the narrative: "The individuality, the character of M. Auclair's house, though it appeared to be made up of wood and cloth and glass and a little silver, was really made up of very fine moral qualities in two women: the mother's unswerving fidelity to certain traditions, and the daughter's loyalty to her mother's wish" (25–26). Submission of the self to the needs and wants of others is the lesson Cécile has learned, and one to which she adheres rigorously throughout the novel. The mother's tradition is primarily one of sacrifice. Though she never discusses "her approaching death" (24) with her daughter, she does counsel about her proper role in the house and in life: "You will perhaps find it fatiguing to do all these things alone, over and over. But in time you will come to love your duties, as I do. You will see that your father's whole happiness depends on order and regularity, and you will come to feel a pride in it" (24). The antithesis, in many respects, to the plots of desire rewarded in the stories of female saints, the lesson here is sublimation of the will in the service of others, and the injunction, to wait patiently for the love and pride one will learn sometime in the future.

These two plots of female fate and experience are held in tension throughout the text until the arrival of Pierre into the narrative and his revision of Jeanne Le Ber's story. Immediately following the final rejection of Pierre as a potential lover for Jeanne Le Ber (since, in his account, she has become a crone, though they are approximately the same age), Cécile packs "her mother's bag" (185) and is taken on a journey to the Ile d'Orléans, a place that earlier in the narrative she had expressed a desire to see (109). This journey is the only one of its kind taken by any women in the novel, and for Cécile it is nothing less than an initiation into womanhood. Not insignificantly, it is Pierre, sporting "a white linen shirt and . . . a new red silk neckerchief" (186), who serves as her guide on this maiden voyage.

It is during her visit to the Harnois family that Cécile first experiences the pain of separation from her father, an experience directly related to her maturation since Pierre has now been substituted as her companion and protector. It is also at the Harnois' house that Cécile is introduced, albeit vaguely, to the suggestion of sex, the only time any such reference appears in the narrative: "When they showed her the pigs and geese and tame rabbits, they kept telling her about peculiarities of animal behavior which she thought it better taste to ignore. They called things by very unattractive names, too" (190). As evening falls, Cécile begins to feel "uneasy and afraid of something" (191). She sits up all night thinking about her father and "a great deal about her mother, too . . . how her mother had always made everything at home beautiful, just as here everything about cooking, eating, sleeping, living, seemed repulsive" (192). One obvious reading elicited by the narrative in this comparison is that of bourgeois sensibility set against country vulgarity, with the conviction that civilization is more wholesome than undomesticated nature. Yet this is not the only reading. For, while the external focalizer never explains what the "meaning" of Cécile's experience is, the journey motif lends this experience a kind of fairy-tale quality. Abandoned by and bereft of her parents, if only in her own psyche, Cécile seems to undergo a ritualized and nightmarish suffering, the day after which she awakens feeling "unreal, indeed, as if she were someone else" (193). Pierre too notices that "Cécile did not look at all like herself" (194), and takes her home where "the story" ends happily.

The "happy ending" to Cécile's journey is significant for a number of reasons. In one respect, it marks the place where Cécile's story draws together the two, alternating traditions of female fate between which she has been suspended throughout the early part of the narrative. The first reference echoes the story Cécile remembers about how when Sister Catherine reached Quebec, "she fell upon her knees and kissed the earth where she first stepped upon it" (41). Cécile recalls Sister Catherine's story when she and Pierre land, although she feels she cannot, under the circumstances, imitate it: "When she stepped upon the shore, Cécile remembered how Sister Catherine de Saint-Augustin, when she landed with her companions, had knelt down and kissed the earth. Had she been alone, she would have loved to do just that" (197). But she doesn't. What she feels instead is "as if she had grown at least two years older in the nights she had been away" (197), and she enters her father's house, fully recognizing for the first time that it is her own house too, as well as a profound expression of her self: "These coppers, big and little, these brooms and clouts and brushes, were tools; and with them one made, not shoes or cabinet-work, but life itself. One made a climate within a climate; one made the days,—the complexion, the special flavour, the special happiness of each day as it is passed; one made life" (198).

Cécile's discovery of self, however, must be read in relation to Pierre Charron's revision of Jeanne Le Ber's story. Though the text balances the two versions of Jeanne's story without signaling the truth, historical or otherwise, of either, at the end of Cécile's coming-of-age journey, narrative logic and placement elicit a comparison of Cécile and Jeanne as women whose stories are contained within and read in relation to the book entitled "Pierre Charron," and they elicit a reading of historical and sexual progression from Jeanne's story to Cécile's. The externally focalized narrative of Cécile's maturation, in fact, seems to collude with (and thus give authority to) Pierre Charron's narration of Jeanne's story, placing these two stories in a chiastic configuration within the narrative. In Pierre's version, Jeanne begins as a young, attractive, sexual woman and ends as a bitter, old, celibate one. Cécile's story, however, charts a reverse path; she matures from a child to a woman, from being completely innocent to having an awareness of sexuality, or, at least, of one's proper gender role. There is a sense too of historical progression, of moving forward toward the Canadian future and away from the French past. Cécile will not remain exiled, like Jeanne Le Ber, within her own country; she becomes it. In this light, her urge to imitate Sister Catherine's kissing of Canadian soil signals her true arrival into the narrative as a Canadienne. No longer held in suspension as a series of tales, the narrative shifts to fall in step with the march of historical time. Though related to the previous tradition of her foremothers, both her own mother and the religious female founders of her society, Cécile's own fate, her own narrative line, radically revises what has come before. She moves the narrative toward, and she at last becomes, the future.

This radical revision within the narrative has the effect of making one's experience of reading the text far less radical and experimental than when it first begins. Authority becomes the final dictate of the narrative as it submits to its own conventional ending. Everything at the close of this novel, in fact, submits to a higher authority: Cécile to her father, Auclair to the count, the count to death. In Count Frontenac's final struggle, however, the narrative embeds a figure for the submission to authority that the text demands of itself. Count Frontenac awakens from "a curious dream" (243) and recalls it within the narrative, as a narrative.

He had been awakened by fright, a sense that some danger threatened him. He got up and in his bare feet stole to the door leading to the garden, which was ajar. Outside, in the darkness, stood a very tall man in a plumed hat and large boots—a giant, in fact; the little boy's head did not come up to his boot-tops. He had no idea who the enormous man might be, but he knew that he must not come in, that everything depended on his being kept out. (244)

Read as part of the narrative text of *Shadows on the Rock,* the giant figure looming over a small boy recalls the count's own introduction into the narrative as a figure in Auclair's reminiscence about his childhood: "I was pulled out from under the counter where I had hidden, and presented to him. I was frightened because he was wearing his uniform and such big boots" (19). The narrative, in this way, links itself historically; as the count has entered the novel, so shall he exit it. A continuity of imagery is established within the narrative. It makes itself comprehensible, chronological, and readable.

One might also interpret the looming giant in the count's dream as death, especially because when the count wakes, his first act is to make a will. This act portends the closure of the count's life and of the text simultaneously. Each gives way to some logic of authority, of inevitable cessation, of closure.

Cécile too struggles against a submission to authority at the end of the narrative. Before the count's death, there is the very real threat of a return to France with her father, which seems to be her destiny. Cécile rebels mutely against the paternal authority to which she must submit. She speaks, for example, "almost defiantly" (227) to her father, though he doesn't notice her tone. The language of desire, introduced in the stories of female saints, resurfaces in the narrative: "Cécile *wished* that she could be left and scattered" (228, emphasis added) like the furniture of her home that will be given to neighbors, and she realizes that only "after she grew up, she would come back to Canada again, and do all those things she *longed* to do" (234, emphasis added). She fantasizes about journeying to "the very places where the martyrs died" (234), but must ultimately martyr herself to the authority and desires of her father, who himself desires to follow the count back to France in order to remain under his protection.

Pierre Charron, however, again becomes a figure whose presence in the narrative and whose book instigate the turn from anacoluthon to authority as the prevailing narrative construction in this text. After the count dies, both Cécile and her father become singularly displaced. Auclair feels himself to be "a helpless exile, in a strange land" (263), while she abandons the order of the house and has "no wish to set things right" (264). While the absence of the mother was able to be tolerated, the absence of patriarchal authority destroys the very safety of their lives; Cécile feels "as if a strong roof over their heads had been swept away" (259).

Enter Charron to fill fortuitously the gap in their lives and to chart the course of the narrative. For Pierre returns as authority [re]incarnate. He enters the narrative at first unrecognized by us as readers. We view "the outline of a man with a gun strapped to his back" (264) whom Cécile recognizes immediately by "the set of his shoulders" (264). Cécile's rush to embrace him here signals the redirection of female desire toward Pierre as the secular savior of the narrative. Though Cécile has, like the female saints, felt rebellion against her father *and* achieved her desire to stay in Canada, she must ultimately, also like the saints, submit to a higher authority, the difference being that this submission is one *she* desires. Jeanne Le Ber rejects rule by male authority on earth in order to become the bride of Christ. It is a union of her own choosing. Cécile too places herself within the protection of a higher authority, a man who will restore hope to their lives and who will give them "once more that feeling of security" (265). In a final paean to Pierre with which the narrative proper of the novel ends, Cécile rests happily in her assurance that "he had authority, and a power which came from knowledge of the country and its people; from knowledge, and from a kind of passion" (268). In one sense, Pierre and his authority are both the reason for and the meaning of the turn toward convention and away from anacoluthon in the novel. He possesses a new and different authority than his predecessor, Count Frontenac. For the authority Pierre brings to the text is essentially Canadian, "a power which came from knowledge of the country and its people." His authority has redirected a disparate tradition of tale-telling into an interpretable history; Canadian histories may now be rewritten as the history of Canada. The supple discontinuity of anacoluthon has become a conventional narrative; narrative histories are now a historical novel. Authority has, paradoxically, both displaced and enacted an anacoluthic shift one final time.

In noting the transformations from anacoluthon to authority, however, I do not wish to claim that these are entirely oppositional and impermeable categories. Though a noticeable shift from repetition to emplotment does occur when Pierre Charron enters the narrative in Book Four, *Shadows on the Rock* remains, finally, poised within and between *seeming* opposites and different constructions of narrative telling. Nowhere is this better demonstrated than in the Epilogue to the novel, in which the strands of fiction and history are tangled together into a complex knot one last time.

Set in 1713, fifteen years after the count's death, the Epilogue does provide a kind of closure (after-history) in its disclosure of what has happened to the main characters of the narrative. It also links itself to the beginning of the text. We again gaze down upon the harbor through the perspective of the external focalizer; the ships are arriving in Quebec one final time, coming completely full circle from the departure we witnessed on the opening page. In this sense, the Epilogue unifies the design of the narrative. No loose threads are left hanging; plot and time lines are neatly tied together.

Yet there is also a way in which this epilogue is separate from the narrative, especially in its shift of orientation. It seems almost to be an extended musing on the idea and the fact of change, what I believe is *the* central concern, both formal and thematic, of this text. Discussing King Louis's emotional disturbance at the advent of autumn, Saint-Vallier remarks to Auclair:

> "That seemed to me to indicate a change."
> "Yes," said Auclair, "that tells a story." (277)

Auclair's reply to Saint-Vallier is itself the short story told in this epilogue. King Louis's distress at hearing the autumn winds and seeing the leaves fall is a reaction against change itself, against the inevitable transformation of one thing into another which the text embeds in its own anacoluthic structure. In the brief dialectic about change with which the epilogue closes then, what we read is nothing less than a discussion by the text about itself.

The fact of change as an inevitable event of time passing is embodied in Auclair's "shocked" (270) recognition of both the physical and the spiritual changes wrought by time on Saint-Vallier. The willful bishop has learned a moral lesson made manifest in his appearance: "The narrow, restless shoulders were fat and bent; the Bishop carried his head like a man broken to the yoke" (270). In his conversation with Auclair, the "sobered and saddened" (271) bishop recounts the history of an equally aged and saddened French court rife with malice and murder; the duc d'Orléans has been accused of poisoning the king's son and daughter-in-law, putting into jeopardy the future of the monarchical bloodline. Saint-Vallier's own history, beginning with "Politics intervened" (271), is summarized by the external focalizer as one telegraphic sweep of events. France is changing for the worse in Saint-Vallier's vision; the future remains uncertain. Against this fact of change he posits what he sees as Canada's continuous present. "At home the old age is dying, but the new is still hidden. . . . The changes in the nations are all those of growing older. You have done well to remain here where nothing changes. Here with you I find everything the same" (277). This difference between the old and new countries *is* both supported and undercut by the narrative. We are told, for instance, that whereas Saint-Vallier has greatly aged, Auclair has "scarcely changed at all" (272). This difference is interesting, especially when one considers that the character of the bishop is a re-creation of a historical figure while Auclair is a purely fictive creation. Yet the equation is not as simple as the historical past seen in opposition to the continuous present of fiction. For things *have* changed in this fictive Canada. Cécile, for instance, has married Pierre Charron and "is bringing up four little boys, the Canadians of the future" (278). Jacques Gaux, meanwhile, has become a sailor. What is perhaps most telling though, occurs in the last paragraph of the text when Auclair closes his apothecary shop, for so long the center stage of tale-telling in the novel, so that he can "go up to his daughter's house" (279) and relate to her his conversation with the bishop. Things *have* altered in the fictional world of Quebec as we have experienced it, and though Auclair believes "he was indeed fortunate to spend his old age here where nothing changed" (279–80), we can be neither so certain nor so sanguine.

There is, finally, no way to decide for or against either side of the dialectic on change, because the text keeps changing its mind about the fact and the denial of change itself. This essential contradiction in and of the text can, however, be articulated. For in one respect, the text preserves by textualizing both the histories and the history of Canada. History will remain unchanged within the text; the text itself then will be an artifact not from, but about, seventeenth-century French Quebec. What this textual artifact preserves, conversely, is a sense of historical narrative as an ever-changing, distorting, altering tradition of telling.

The continuous present of every narrative is necessarily changed into a text that inevitably becomes, if not historical, then at least historicized. *Shadows on the Rock* is a text that takes as its subject and its form the transformation of fiction into history and of history into fiction. It is a text about perpetual transformation in narrative, though its physical textuality (its printed words on the page) will not change. The text then, casting *Shadows on the Rock* and cast as *Shadows on the Rock,* is essential contradiction, and there can be, ultimately, no way to reduce this to *a* clear meaning.

Shadows on the Rock then, becomes a palimpsest, a manuscript in which we can discover earlier erased writings. The text at once preserves and erases the oral tradition by altering it into a written text. In addition to the contradictions inherent in the anacoluthic shifts that occur between narratives, narrations, and even those contradictions that occur within the narrative text itself, *Shadows on the Rock* contains and holds in suspension a multiplicity of tales, histories, tellings, and meanings. The tradition of telling bequeathed to us by the elusive and shadowy rock, this text, is indeed an entire world, and a complex history, within itself.

Obscuring Destinies: Threading the Narrative of "Old Mrs. Harris"

One realizes that human relationships are the tragic necessity of human life; that they can never be wholly satisfactory, that every ego is half the time greedily seeking them, and half the time pulling away from them. In those simple relationships of loving husband and wife, affectionate sisters, children and grandmother, there are innumerable shades of sweetness and anguish which make up the pattern of our lives day by day, though they are not down in the list of subjects from which the conventional novelist works.

—WILLA CATHER, "Katherine Mansfield" (1936)

"Old Mrs. Harris," the centerpiece of Cather's 1932 collection of three stories entitled *Obscure Destinies,* is an unconventional text that demonstrates "the value of literalness in the novel"[1] at the same time that it undermines a too literal reading. Originally titled "Three Women" when it appeared in serial form in the 1932 *Ladies Home Journal,*[2] "Old Mrs. Harris" concerns the life of the Templeton family, specifically its three generations of women (Grandmother Harris, Victoria Templeton, and Vickie Templeton) and their relations among themselves and with their neighbors, the Rosens. Externally focalized in a nonchronological narrative that intersperses past memories with present action, the plot of the story is developed both through the grandmother's last months of life and through the attempt of the granddaughter, Vickie, to get into college.

This difference in literalness, which I read both as what the text values and as the way it asks to be read, is properly located in its narrative telling. Cather herself had a few words to say on the subject of the literal in "The Novel Démeublé," and not all of them good. Not surprisingly, in an essay about "unfurnished" fiction, Cather records her distaste for and distrust of Balzac's accumulation of "material accessories" and Wagner's "scenic literalness in the music drama." Yet when discussing Tolstoy, Cather notes what she calls a "determining difference" in his presentation of materiality in the novel. Things in Tolstoy's fiction, according to Cather, "are always so much a part of the people that they are perfectly synthesized; they seem to exist, not so much in the author's mind, as in the emotional penumbra of the characters themselves. When it is fused like this, literalness ceases to be literalness—it is merely part of the experience."[3] What Cather seems to be describing here is a synthesis between the telling and what is told, between narration and the narrative text. "Old Mrs. Harris," much like *Shadows on the Rock,* is a narrative that relies upon the description of material objects to convey a sense of life and character. It is a text in which things create character. Moreover, the narrative of "Old Mrs. Harris" employs an external focalizer which engages in free indirect discourse throughout, literally giving over the narrative to the characters' sensibilities and scope. In simple, unadorned, and lucid prose, the text of "Old Mrs. Harris" transcends literalness as Cather describes it, by being as plain, unembellished and prosaic as its subject—by being literal. What such a fusion of content and narrative creates, in Cather's own admission, is an "emotional penumbra," literally, a marginal region of partial obscurity. Obscurity itself, then, is the value and function of the literal in "Old Mrs. Harris" and returns us inevitably to the title of the collection and its relation to this particular work.

Obscure Destinies has a special relevance for "Old Mrs. Harris" located in its plurality of "destinies." "Destinies" in the plural conjures the "Three Women" of the original title and suggests an allusion to the three female Fates: Clotho (spinner of the thread of human life), Lachisis (the one who determines the length of the thread), and Atropos (the one who cuts the thread).[4] The three Fates function equally as figures for the three narratives, or destinies, of the "Three Women" in this story. But as the title also suggests, these destinies are ultimately obscured—dimmed, concealed, kept secret, made indistinct, or undefined. It remains unclear throughout the text, for example, whether the triad of "Three Women" signifies Mrs. Harris, Mrs. Templeton, and Mrs. Rosen as literally *the* three *women* in and of the text, or whether "Three Women" denotes the matrilineal line of Mrs. Harris, Victoria Templeton, and Vickie Templeton. Even more important, "Old Mrs. Harris" obscures these destinies or narrative threads by entangling them in a pattern of interrelated difference. The significantly differing stories and characters of the three women in the text can only be read together; they share a common narrative. As Roland Barthes has suggested, understanding "narrative is not merely to follow the unfolding of the story, it is also to recognize its construction in 'storeys,' to project the horizontal concatenations of the narrative 'thread' on to an implicitly vertical axis; . . . to move from one level to the next."[5] The spatial configuration Barthes describes results in chiasmas or, as the narrative of "Old Mrs. Harris" phrases it, in a pattern of "cross-stitch."[6] We read horizontally to see whether a particular destiny will eventuate in either death or fortune; we read vertically to intuit how these destinies themselves are intertwined within the familial bonds that Cather characterized as "the tragic necessity of human life."[7] Narrative threads and threads of fate are woven together and create the pattern in, and of, the text.

The narrative of "Old Mrs. Harris" is one marked by constant motion between characters and their stories, and by constant movement backward and forward in time.[8] It is a text obsessed with what characters, and readers, see but don't fully understand. And, as Susan J. Rosowski has argued, "by shifting point of view from character to character, Cather maintains this rhythm between outside and inside, expectation and reality."[9] "Old Mrs. Harris" then explores the necessary limitations of vision and judgment enacted every time a reader or a character attempts interpretation. Its shifting stories, chronology, and focalizer throw off balance the literal reading we may wish to apply. To read in this text is not necessarily to understand, and moreover, our understanding is always obscured and imperfectly apprehended. What we are left to disentangle is the messy and tangled underside of cross-stitching, where there is, in fact, no pattern at all, only a labyrinth of thread.[10]

The text of "Old Mrs. Harris" operates on a principle of partial and obscure knowledge. Concealment and secrecy are its predominant themes and appear initially in its chronology. As one reads from one chapter to the next, layers of revelation are peeled away. Details, information, even contradictions accumulate within the narrative, and the complexity of what and how one is asked to read expands in concentric circles. Similarly, any judgments about the characters one may be tempted to make are either undermined or overturned by what is encountered in later chapters; the text, seemingly, disallows the possibility of clear and categorical understanding. The reading process then is one of continuous and reflexive revision. One confronts throughout the text the

imperfection in and of apprehension; reading and understanding remain veiled in obscurity.

This partial understanding of the text comes from Cather's fluid and
subtle use of the external focalizer. Our directed vision of the material—
what we think we see and understand—is oriented through and within
the characters (character-bound focalization). What they know, suspect,
misread, and fail to comprehend of each other is essentially synonymous
with what we are able to know as we read, with what the narrative allows
us to see. Mrs. Rosen's desire "to get past the others to the real Grandmother" (83), for example, determines and selects the focus of reading
early in the text, and Mrs. Rosen is the character through whom the
curiosity and perspective of reading are figured. Because she occupies an
outsider's position relative to the Templeton family and its story, it is
primarily through Mrs. Rosen that readers initially approach and ap-
prehend the basic concerns within "Old Mrs. Harris."

The opening words of the narrative—"Mrs. David Rosen, cross-stitch
in hand, sat looking out of the window across her green lawn to the
ragged, sunburned back yard of her neighbours on the right" (75)—
inscribe both difference and the demarcations of perspective that will be
at play throughout the novella. The figure of cross-stitch, a sewing pattern composed of Xs, suggests any number of things at the beginning of
this work and is, significantly, associated exclusively with Mrs. Rosen (75,
106, 107). It could, in one sense, represent a metaphor for this text, because "Old Mrs. Harris" concerns the intersecting lives of three women
and because sewing is an activity commonly defined as women's work.
Cross-stitch could allude as well to fate and to narrative, both of which
are spun out as threads. This passage also frames the text in its placement
of Mrs. Rosen and, by extension, the reader, as one whose framed gaze
("looking out of the window") is necessarily directed "*across* her own
green lawn to the ragged, sunburned back yard of her neighbours"
(emphasis added). Her vision of the Templetons, and our envisioning of
them through her, is shaped as, and by, the figure of chiasmas. To posit
one line of sight in this text necessitates an intersecting line that either
crosses, doubles, or double-crosses it. Our reading is not, and cannot be,
strictly linear. For though Mrs. Rosen's interpretive desires and under-
standings will determine our reading at the beginning of the text, we will
soon discover that she is neither the only reader nor the only spinner of
narrative in this work.

Mrs. Rosen's prominence as *the* focalizing consciousness at the beginning of the narrative engages the reader in an overdetermined literalness. The narrative employs two subtly different approaches to its focalized interpretation. The first seemingly sees Grandma Harris through the eyes and adjectives of Mrs. Rosen.

> The old lady was always impressive, Mrs. Rosen was thinking,—one could not say why. Perhaps it was the way she held her head,—so simply, unprotesting and unprotected; or the gravity of her large, deep-set brown eyes, a warm, reddish brown, though their look, always direct, seemed to ask nothing and hope for nothing. They were not cold, but inscrutable, with no kindling gleam of intercourse in them. There was the kind of nobility about her head that there is about an old lion's: an absence of self-consciousness, vanity, preoccupation—something absolute. Her grey hair was parted in the middle, wound in two little horns over her ears, and done in a little flat knot behind. Her mouth was large and composed,—resigned, the corners drooping. Mrs. Rosen had very seldom heard her laugh (and then it was a gentle, polite laugh which meant only politeness). But she had observed that whenever Mrs. Harris's grandchildren were about, tumbling all over her, asking for cookies, teasing her to read to them, the old lady looked happy. (81–82)

This passage signals that it will view Grandma Harris as subject through Mrs. Rosen's consciousness since it begins with her "thinking" and ends with her observation. Sight and interpretation merge in the passage as well. The narrative records certain purely physical descriptions, such as Mrs. Harris's "grey hair." Yet it also notes other physical traits like her "large and composed mouth," and then affixes an interpretation, in this case, resignation. A similar reading of the grandmother's "large, deep-set brown eyes" occurs, interpreting them both as grave and as eyes that "ask nothing and hope for nothing." We are seduced into a literal reading of— and at—face value. Nothing in this early part of the narrative questions Mrs. Rosen's reading or interpretation and one is tempted to accept unquestioningly such assertions as "it was a gentle, polite laugh which meant only politeness." In a narrative that begins as a self-styled mystery, when the detecting character confers meaning, a reader is inclined not only to accept it but, moreover, to desire its reliability as well.

Such passages as the one quoted above erase the difference between the external focalizer and Mrs. Rosen, and suggest that she is, indeed, a credible reader. Her internalized description and interpretation of Mrs. Harris mirror the language, attitude, and perspective of the external focalizer toward the old woman, which appears in a passage three pages earlier. In this passage, the reader's gaze is directed by and through the external focalizer at Grandma Harris. Mrs. Rosen's vision of her replicates, or at least reiterates, the essential diction of this passage, a repetition that is not at all insignificant.

> Mrs. Harris sat down in her black wooden rocking-chair with curved arms and a faded cretonne pillow on the wooden seat. It stood in the corner beside a narrow spindle-frame lounge. She looked on silently while Mrs. Rosen uncovered the cake and delicately broke it with her plump, smooth, dusky-red hands. The old lady did not seem pleased,—seemed uncertain and apprehensive, indeed. But she was not fussy or fidgety. She had the kind of quiet, intensely quiet, dignity that comes from complete resignation to the chances of life. She watched Mrs. Rosen's deft hands out of grave, steady brown eyes. (78)

Several things invite attention in this passage, the first being the angle(s) of vision at work. Mrs. Harris watches Mrs. Rosen, and yet Mrs. Rosen is not the subject or the object of this gaze. Rather, the narrative composes a tableau of Mrs. Harris resting in her rocker served by the "plump, smooth, dusky-red hands" of Mrs. Rosen. The reader occupies the position of interpreting spectator located outside of the scene and peering in, not unlike Mrs. Rosen's focalizing position relative to Grandma Harris in the later passage. Equally striking is the repetition of diction between the two passages. Externally focalized, the passage above notes Grandma Harris's resignation "to the chances of life," the gravity of her "steady brown eyes," and what it terms her "dignity," reiterated in Mrs. Rosen's description of eyes that "ask nothing and hope for nothing," "the gravity of her large, deep-set brown eyes," and the "nobility" that characterizes Mrs. Rosen's vision of her. When we arrive at the passage in which Mrs. Rosen describes and interprets Grandma Harris in language that reverberates from this earlier paragraph, we naturally and even unthinkingly bestow authority on her as both a reader and as a narrator. This narrative sleight of hand woos us into reading literally. Veiled difference is easily read as no difference at all.

The authority that the narrative seems to confer on Mrs. Rosen shapes a reading of and response to the early part of "Old Mrs. Harris." We do not think to question Mrs. Rosen's ability to make presumptions about Vickie's feelings by reading her voice (108), nor do we doubt her interpretation of Mrs. Harris's "tone," which indicates to her "that Grandma really wished her to leave before Victoria returned" (87). When we read Mrs. Rosen literally, moreover, we are easily susceptible to becoming swayed by her judgments about other characters. During her afternoon visit to Grandma Harris, for instance, Mrs. Rosen mutters internalized asides to which we are privy and perhaps by which we are unduly influenced. When she pronounces, "Dat Vickie is her mother over again" (84), in one fell swoop she casts both Vickie and Victoria as antagonists of the grandmother. Having only this one reading, we are not likely to disagree. We encounter not only her sarcasm ("Mrs. Rosen was glad to hear that Vickie was good for something" [86]), but also her presumed authority as one who has a knowledge about the Templeton family which informs our understanding: "Mrs. Rosen had brought Grandma Harris coffee-cake time and again, but she knew that Grandma merely tasted it and saved it for her daughter Victoria, who was as fond of sweets as her own children, and jealous about them, moreover,—couldn't bear that special dainties should come into the house for anyone but herself" (79). What Mrs. Rosen *knows* about the Templeton family is, ultimately, all that we know as well. The effect of this is to instill a prejudice in the reader toward characters whom we have not yet glimpsed. Victoria has been introduced to us as spoilt and selfish, Vickie as lazy and like her mother. Though these judgments will be undermined later in the narrative, thus far in "Old Mrs. Harris" one experiences the safety and illusion of a single, authoritative reading.

Having been primed to make certain judgments through Mrs. Rosen's role as chief character focalizer, the reader finds facts and details that have been narrated dispassionately by an external focalizer and which acquire meaning. In "Old Mrs Harris" reading is determined by the subtle accumulation and juxtaposition of information read as factual.[11] When we are told that "there was an understood rule that Grandmother was not to receive visitors alone" (88), we want not only to know why this rule exists, but we might also be likely to attribute it to what Mrs. Rosen intimates is Victoria's oppression of the old woman. A similar reaction occurs when the external focalizer describes Mrs. Harris's cramped and depressing living conditions in the house.

> Grandmother's room, between the kitchen and the dining-room, was rather like a passage-way; but now that the children were upstairs and Victoria was off enjoying herself somewhere, Mrs. Harris could be sure of enough privacy to undress. (92)

> She left nothing lying about. . . . Her towel was hung on its special nail
> behind the curtain. Her soap she kept in a tin tobacco-box; the children's
> soap was in a crocker saucer. If her soap or towel got mixed up with the
> children's, Victoria was always sharp about it. The little rented house was
> much too small for the family, and Mrs. Harris and her "things" were
> almost required to be invisible. (98)

This litany of details offers no clue as to whether we should read with
disapproval the fact that Grandma's room resembles "a passage-way" or
that she and her things are "almost required to be invisible." The early
twentieth-century American critic T. K. Whipple argues that Cather
consistently "stirs the reader chiefly by means of the detail charged with
meaning, the implication which creates a brief flash and a sharp, poi-
gnant instant."[12] This reading applies to the way one experiences these
passages in "Old Mrs. Harris," yet what remains unclear is not the
sharpness or poignancy of the details, for they certainly have this effect,
but rather the meaning with which these details are charged, what it is *we*
read into them. Chronology and focalization have thus far been the
determining factors in the creation of meaning; we understand only
what exists in the relation between Mrs. Rosen's personal vision and the
"facts" narrated by the external focalizer.

The text, however, soon complicates matters by revealing another
model of interpretation, the consciousness of Mrs. Harris herself. At
select moments in chapter two, the external focalizer will shift into the
grandmother's remembrances and knowledge. Combined with the details of her life, what the narrative focalizes through Mrs. Harris's consciousness underscores, in a way, a reading focused on her impoverished
and powerless condition. We are encouraged to read her as a victim. This
occurs especially when Mrs. Harris links her knowledge explicitly to Mrs.
Rosen's, as in: "She knew Mrs. Rosen understood how it was; that
Victoria couldn't bear to have anything come into the house that was not
for her to dispose of" (95). Again Victoria appears as the blocking figure,
a secret Mrs. Harris and Mrs. Rosen share, much like the concealed cast-
off sweater Mrs. Rosen gives to the grandmother which becomes "the
dearest of . . . her few possessions. It was kinder to her, she used to
think . . . than any of her own children had been" (95). The simple
accumulation of such provocative judgments on the parts of both Mrs.
Harris and Mrs. Rosen, coupled with details that, in context, can be read
as damning, inevitably elicit sympathy from the reader about the grand-

mother's perceived plight. The information with which we have been supplied by the narrative directs our reading toward a judgment based on what we think we understand.

Yet also contained within Mrs. Harris's focalized narration is the first significant and profound contradiction within the narrative about the reading it has elicited. For just when we think we have arrived at the "real" grandmother's resentment toward her living conditions, the narrative overturns all our expectations with the statement: "She didn't want Mrs. Rosen to think that she was 'put upon,' that there was anything unusual in her lot" (97). Mrs. Harris does not wish Mrs. Rosen to think "that there was anything unusual in her lot" because she herself does not think there is. The secret victimization that we have been poised to discover has been contradicted. Even more confusing is the grandmother's contention that "Victoria had a good heart" (98–99), a claim about which we have only antithetical evidence so far. Nothing in our experience of the narrative has prepared us for such irreconcilably different readings, and we are forced to retreat from any sure stance we may have taken toward the nature of the Templeton family and toward the condition of the "real" grandmother. Understanding has been disrupted; the desire to affix meaning underwritten.

This contradiction inaugurates a turn in the narrative toward foregrounding the limits of interpretation. For what soon follows Mrs. Harris's history is a curious instance of misreading, which the text assigns to Mrs. Rosen. As she muses about the oddity of the Templeton family whose "feelings were so much finer than their way of living" (110), Mrs. Rosen acknowledges that she does not bother to distinguish between the Templeton twins who bring her milk: "Whichever boy brought it, she always called him Albert—she thought Adelbert a silly, Southern name" (110). In disavowing difference, Mrs. Rosen reduces the boys to a single name and a single identity, not entirely unlike the way the narrative initially encourages a reading seemingly oriented within a single, unifying vision. Nor is her interpretation of "Albert's" behavior any less questionable. Reproving him that the cookies she sends over "are for Grandma, remember, not for your mother or Vickie" (111), the focalization shifts to her reading of his reaction: "When she turned to give him the pail, she saw two full crystal globes in the little boy's eyes, just ready to break. She watched him go softly down the path and dash those tears away with the back of his hand. She was sorry. She hadn't thought the little boys realized that their household was somehow a queer one" (111).

At no time does the text again allude to or confirm the boys' realization of their household's queer nature. Mrs. Rosen's interpretation is the sole mention and claim of it in the novella. One might also regard with some reservation her explanation of why "Albert" cries. It seems just as possible that the severity of her admonishment brings tears to his eyes, or that he feels rejected and denied because he will be the bearer of the cookies without being allowed to taste a single one. The narrative offers no comment or clue as to whether Mrs. Rosen has given a right reading or simply a biased one to this incident. The text seems, however, to signal a caution against making a too precipitous placement of authority into a single voice or a single reading.

This caution is emphasized when the narrative ventures two years into the past where, in the middle of chapter three, we meet in Mrs. Rosen's memory a Victoria whom she both likes and views sympathetically: "She had to admit that her new neighbor was an attractive woman, and that there was something warm and genuine about her. . . . She was high-spirited and direct; a trifle imperious, but with a shade of diffidence, too, as if she were trying to adjust herself to a new group of people and to do the right thing" (113–14). The appearance of a likable Victoria whose attitudes Mrs. Rosen seems able to understand, coming after the disapproval we have encountered early in the narrative, is confusing at best. Discerning that Mrs. Rosen's grousings on the subject of Victoria are by no means the *only* story about the relations between the two women, one is forced to reevaluate the accuracy of a reading that has been based on the possibility of locating "the real" in a text marked by double blinds and by constant transformation in its narrative line(s).

This discovery also precedes and, in a way, introduces the chapter in which multiple focalization, perception, and judgment are at work simultaneously. Chapter four of "Old Mrs. Harris" expands its scope in its rendering of an ice cream social attended by the entire society of Skyline. This chapter exhibits the most activity and transformation of the focalizer in the text, totaling fifteen shifts in perception through seven different character-bound focalizations. Such a multiplicity of perspectives results in the suspension of judgment and the holding in abeyance of any meaning one may wish to read into the scene. Being shown how "various characters view the same facts," Meike Bal has argued, results "in neutrality towards all the characters."[13] What is perhaps most interesting about this chapter is its sympathetic presentation of Victoria Templeton as the focus of this diverse focalization, especially because it follows closely Mrs. Rosen's sympathetic remembrance of her. Though, as Bal claims, we may feel "neutrality towards all the characters" who view Victoria from different angles, the effect of the chapter is to neutralize any remaining prejudices we may hold against her as well. We are not allowed to make judgments and are even strongly discouraged from doing so in this chapter.

The spectacle of the Methodist ice cream social begins under the gaze of the Rosens, again represented as benevolent outsiders who, though "they belonged to no church, contributed to the support of all" (120). Such a stance is important, for the Rosens somehow transcend the petty squabbles of Skyline society and can therefore offer a more objective view of its workings. As they near the lighted yard of the social, the narrative begins to be focalized through their vision. What they notice specifically are the "poor Maude children" (122), the bastard outcasts of Skyline, championed subtly and graciously by a Victoria Templeton never before seen in the narrative: "I expect you children forgot your dimes, now didn't you? Never mind, here's a dime for each of you, so come along and have your ice-cream" (122). This exchange demonstrates the deftness with which Victoria Templeton preserves the children's fragile dignity. Her insistence that they climb over the fence that borders the yard and take their places inside, at her own children's table, evokes a sense of her modest and matter-of-fact generosity that anticipates no praise and expects no reward.

When the focalization shifts to the Templeton children, the narrative articulates, for the first time, praise for what has heretofore been represented as Victoria's shallowness and self-preoccupation: "They were glad to see their mother go to Mr. Rosen's table, and noticed how nicely he placed a chair for her and insisted upon putting a scarf about her shoulders. . . . As the twins watched her over their spoons, they thought how much prettier their mother was than any of the other women and how becoming her new dress was. The children got as much satisfaction as Mrs. Harris out of Victoria's good looks" (125). In the children's minds, at least, the pampering of this woman has a particular value and signifies something important for the children about themselves. They possess the prettiest mother; her specialness exalts their small place in the world. She represents the Templeton family. The narrative also voices the approval of the cultivated and gentle Mr. Rosen, who is "well pleased with Mrs. Templeton and her new dress, and with her kindness to the little Maudes. He thought her manner with them just right,—warm, spontaneous, without anything patronizing" (125). The amassing of such details and reactions elicits a reading of Victoria in an entirely different, and much more complex, light. It is not so much that Mrs. Rosen's early criticisms have been nullified as that they have been incorporated and even revised into a more puzzling and problematic portrait of this infinitely selfish and infinitely generous woman.

As the scene continues, the narrative emphasizes the paradoxical reading of Victoria Templeton by juxtaposing unqualified and loving approval with social ostracism and small-minded meanness. This appears in the character of Mrs. Jackson, a prying and petty "neighbour who didn't like the Templetons" (125). Offering a second helping of cake, Mrs. Jackson again raises the issue of the freedoms Victoria enjoys at the expense of Mrs. Harris. " 'Well,' she remarked with a chuckle that really sounded amiable, 'I don't know but I'd like my cakes, if I kept somebody in the kitchen to bake them for me. . . . I tell Mr. Jackson that my idea of coming up in the world would be to forget I had a cook-stove, like Mrs. Templeton. But we can't all be lucky' " (126–27). Though it is easy to recognize Mrs. Jackson's malice and dismiss her, the thrust of her comments is quite close to those focalized through Mrs. Rosen in chapter one of the text. The world of difference and sympathy that separates these two women makes the matter both curious and troublesome. The text, it seems, will not tip its scales in favor or in disfavor of Victoria. It holds the contradictions in her character and the consequences of her behavior in uncomfortable tension, especially as they apply to Mrs. Harris. The narrative will balance both sides of the dilemma, but it absolutely refuses any resolution of it.

The difficulty of knowing or, more properly, of not knowing how to interpret Victoria and the opposing representations of her is dramatized through what becomes an increasingly decentralized focalization. Sudden and abrupt shifts between characters who themselves are confused about the situation predominate. Mr. Rosen responds first and provides the most thoughtful, though partial, interpretation of Mrs. Jackson: "Mr. Rosen could not tell how much was malice and how much was stupidity. What he chiefly detected was self-satisfaction; the craftiness of the coarse-fibred country girl putting catch questions to the teacher. Yes, he decided, the woman was merely showing off,—she regarded it as an accomplishment to make people uncomfortable" (127). The very structure of this passage charts the process of interpretation. It moves from Mr. Rosen's inability to "tell" the difference between malice and stupidity, to his detection of a dominant emotion ("self-satisfaction"), to his decision that Mrs. Jackson has made these remarks in order to show off. Given the reasonableness of his logic and his sympathetic portrayal in the text, one has no reason to doubt his reading of the incident. But the multiple focalizations within this chapter underscore the fact that more than one reading exists and affects the course of the narrative. Mr. Rosen's interpretation, for example, is juxtaposed against Victoria's own processing of the attack. She does not, at first, "take it in" (127), and she feels "hurt without knowing just why" (127). We then witness the direction of her logic, which ends, ultimately, with her own mother as the reason and the cause of this criticism: "all evening it kept growing clearer to her that this was another of those thrusts from the outside which she couldn't understand. The neighbours were sure to take sides against her, apparently, if they came often to see her mother" (127–28). Though Mr. Rosen's explanation appears to be more objective and perhaps even closer to the truth given how the external focalizer describes Mrs. Jackson's petty and grasping character (125), the chapter ends with a paragraph ostensibly placed within the remembrance of Mrs. Harris, who assumes the same cause for this discord as her daughter.

> She knew, as well as if she had been at the social, what kind of thing had happened. Some of those prying ladies of the Women's Relief Corps, or the Women's Christian Temperance Union, had been intimating to Victoria that her mother was "put upon." Nothing ever made Victoria cross but criticism. She was jealous of small attentions paid to Mrs. Harris, because she felt they were paid "behind her back" or "over her head," in a way that implied reproach to her. Victoria had been a belle in their own town in Tennessee, but here she was not very popular, no matter how many pretty dresses she wore, and she couldn't bear it. She felt as if her mother and Mr. Templeton must be somehow to blame; at least they ought to protect her from whatever was disagreeable—they always had! (128–29)

This passage contains a curious combination of an explanation for and a partial indictment of Victoria's behavior. It is difficult to note within it exactly where the focalization resides and where it shifts. It seems as if Mrs. Harris's sensibility about the difference between southern and midwestern values shapes the major part of it, while the external focalizer appears in the last sentence, voicing Victoria's complaint with "She felt." Again the narrative refuses to answer the puzzle, eliciting a sympathy with Victoria's rejection and perhaps even an understanding of her intense desire to be accepted. Yet the passage also incorporates the infantilization of her character in its last sentence, as she demands protection from her husband and mother and assigns blame to them because of societal attitudes. She is represented as both victim and victimizer, and the text offers no direction as to how one ought to read this. As the narrative of "Old Mrs. Harris" unfolds, reading becomes vastly more difficult and profoundly less clear.

Nor is reading made any easier or further clarified in the following chapters, which introduce what seems to be the thesis of the novella, the argument that Mrs. Harris's "place in the family was not exceptional, but perfectly regular" (129–30). Chapter five also reiterates and expands the earlier "history" Mrs. Harris recalls about what she misses in the South and why she has followed her family westward (96–97). This repetition of telling within the narrative accomplishes a seeming clarification of what has been the story's most enduring mystery, namely, *why* Mrs. Harris's position is *what* it *seems* to be. On the most accessible level of reading, the external focalizer mines Mrs. Harris's memory to recall and elaborate the foreign condition of social and familial behavior in the South. Her position in the Templeton household is presented in the text by being placed in relation to regional, cultural, and historical difference.

Yet *within* the language of this narrated history lurks both a diction and a description that will throw into question the simple explanation which difference between cultures and regions offers as one construction of meaning. The external focalizer inscribes a difference *within* its narration of the difference *between* two societies. One manifestation of this difference within the narrative can be located in the presentation of women's economic and social conditions, focalized uncritically as historical facts.

> That was the great difference; in Tennessee there had been plenty of helpers. There was old Miss Sadie Crummer, who came to the house to spin and sew and mend; old Mrs. Smith, who always arrived to help at butchering- and preserving-time; Lizzie, the coloured girl, who did the washing and who ran in every day to help Mandy. There were plenty more, who came whenever one of Lizzie's barefoot boys ran to fetch them. The hills were full of solitary old women, or women but slightly attached to some household, who were glad to come to Miz' Harris's for good food and a warm bed, and the little present that either Mrs. Harris or Victoria slipped into their carpet-sack when they went away.

To be sure, Mrs. Harris, and the other women of her age who managed their daughter's house, kept in the background; but it was their own background and they ruled it jealously. They left the front porch and the parlour to the young married couple and their young friends; the old women spent most of their lives in the kitchen and pantries and back dining-room. But there they ordered life to their own taste, entertained their friends, dispensed charity, and heard the troubles of the poor. Moreover, back there it was Grandmother's own house they lived in. (130–31)

Though the narrative does not lean toward or otherwise elicit any judgment about the role of women in this society, two aspects of its history cannot be ignored. The first is the fundamental difference between what power Mrs. Harris possessed as the "owner" of both her house and, as the text phrases it, her "own background" which she "ruled . . . jealously," and her pronounced disempowerment in the present. The power of activity dramatized by the verbs within the passage—to manage, direct, order, entertain, dispense, and hear—no longer characterizes her function or her status in Skyline. The second aspect of narration that calls attention to itself is the difficult life of the "helpers," and the hardship of their social position as economic nomads. Though southern society has found a way to incorporate them into its network, the precariousness of their fate ultimately depends upon the generosity and interest of women like Mrs. Harris and Victoria Templeton. Such "facts" make more confusing the act of interpretation. We are directed to read simultaneously Mrs. Harris's power and her loss of it. We also, perhaps, recognize the inevitable hierarchy and servitude within a social scheme which accords some people (Mrs. Harris) power or status at the expense of others ("the helpers"), a situation replicated, respectively, by Victoria and Mrs. Harris in the narrative present. This objective and externally focalized narration of history, then, actually inscribes ambivalence into its telling and into our reading.

Ambivalence reappears within the narration's diction as well, in a curiously comparative passage among the more obscure within the entire text. "Here in Skyline, [Grandmother] had all her accustomed responsibilities, and no helper but Mandy. Mrs. Harris was no longer living in a feudal society, where there were plenty of landless people glad to render service to the more fortunate, but in a snappy little Western democracy, where every man was as good as his neighbour and out to prove it" (133). What are we to make of this? The diction of the passage tends to suggest that the external focalizer valorizes the feudal society in which the "landless" are genuinely "glad to render service to the more fortunate," to the benefit of both, as if this is a social construction of places assigned by fate or by nature. The "snappy little Western democracy, where every man was as good as his neighbour and out to prove it," conversely conveys a sense of defensive competition which fosters the attitudes of the Mrs. Jacksons in the world. When compared, feudalism bests democracy hands down. Yet no matter how much better the values of feudal society seem to be when compared to the aggressive, self-assertion of small town democracy, the dominance of the privileged classes is exactly what oppresses Mrs. Harris in Mrs. Rosen's eyes. Since the text *seems* to argue that such "feudal" arrangements are simply misplaced in the West, we are perhaps directed to understand that Skyline's reading of Grandma Harris as oppressed is based on the denial of difference and a misapprehension of cultural attitudes and standards. Yet as the narrative has represented Grandma Harris's life so far, especially in chapter two, we have witnessed primarily the unhappy effects of the privileging of some over others. We have felt the futility of Mrs. Harris's life because of her adherence to the codes of feudal society.

Yet what follows this externally focalized description of historical and cultural difference is the shift of focalization into Mrs. Harris's own reading and interpretation of difference. We seem, at last, to have reached the "real Grandmother." And what we discover is nothing less than the solution to the riddle of relations as it has been posed in the text.

> Grandmother knew that these meddlesome "Northerners" said things that made Victoria suspicious and unlike herself; made her unwilling that Mrs. Harris should receive visitors alone, or accept marks of attention that seemed offered in compassion for her state.
>
> These women who belonged to clubs and Relief Corps lived differently, Mrs. Harris knew, but she herself didn't like the way they lived. She believed that somebody ought to be in the parlour, and somebody in the kitchen. (134)

It is difficult not to imbue the grandmother's reading with authority. Her intimate knowledge of Victoria answers the charge of cruelty implied early in the text; outside criticism makes "Victoria suspicious and unlike herself." What we have seen, the passage suggests, is behavior altered because of stress. We learn too that Mrs. Harris herself *prefers* the feudal arrangement of "somebody . . . in the parlour, and somebody in the kitchen." The narrative also focalizes what is essentially Mrs. Harris's complicity in Victoria's selfishness, her all-consuming desire to keep her daughter different from the small-town housekeepers of Skyline whose attire of "a short gingham dress, with bare arms, and a dust-cap on [their] head to hide the curling kids" (134), she finds distasteful and which she reads as an emblem of their downtrodden condition.

> To Mrs. Harris that would have meant real poverty, coming down in the world so far that one could no longer keep up appearances. Her life was hard now, to be sure, since the family went on increasing and Mr. Templeton's means went on decreasing; but she certainly valued respectability above personal comfort, and she would go on a good way yet if they always had a cool pleasant parlour, with Victoria properly dressed to receive visitors. To keep Victoria different from these "ordinary" women meant everything to Mrs. Harris. (134–35)

Mrs. Harris's interpretation in this passage is predicated on difference and, specifically, on what Victoria's difference from other women in Skyline "means." Victoria, in one respect, functions for Grandma Harris as a signifier of social status and of the "respectability" she values "above personal comfort." What we have read sympathetically heretofore as the grandmother's powerlessness and marginal position within the family is actually a choice she has consciously made to ensure the maintenance of her daughter's difference and power. The narrative ultimately proffers an explanation of the "real" grandmother who, it concludes, has "ceased to be an individual, an old woman with aching feet," and who has instead become "part of a group, . . . a relationship" (136–37). Defined this way, the reader can now understand "why it was worth while" (136) for the grandmother to live as she does.

Juxtaposed to this seeming clear chapter, however, is its successor in which the *displacement* of resentment is foregrounded as the central object and focus of our reading. Chapter six, in fact, reinscribes the grandmother's resentment about displacement as an actual subject of the text, and then displaces it onto her cat, Blue Boy. Its plot concerns the cat's death due to "distemper" (138), which brings on the most sustained and outwardly expressed bout of the grandmother's own distemper in the text. The narrative records not only a new and unheard harshness in her voice over the cat's death (138), but it illustrates subtly the relation between these two figures. When we are initially introduced to the cat in chapter one, as it purrs contentedly in Mrs. Harris's lap, Mrs. Rosen notes the resemblance between the two of them: "it struck her that he held his head in just the way Grandmother held hers. And Grandmother now became more alive, as if some missing part of herself were restored" (84).[14] This relation is recalled when the grandmother becomes "indignant . . . gloomy and silent" (144) at Victoria's suggestion that the dead cat be thrown in with the trash, destined for "a gully out in the sagebrush" (144). Mrs. Harris's protestations to the twins about this outrage are frightening because of "the anger and bitterness in her tone" (144), and the narrative notes also that the boys "had seldom seen such resentment in their grandmother" (145). It is the displacement of the cat that Mrs. Harris resents chiefly, the fact that it does not merit, in Victoria's consideration, a proper grave. The twins, after burying the cat as their grandmother has demanded, recall another, to them, curious and incomprehensible occasion of their grandmother's resentment, which reinscribes the issue of placement and displacement in the narrative.

> They knew their grandmother got put out about strange things, anyhow. A few months ago it was because their mother hadn't asked one of the visiting preachers who came to the church conference to stay with them. There was no place for the preacher to sleep except on the folding lounge in the parlour, and no place for him to wash—he would have been very uncomfortable, and so would all the household. But Mrs. Harris was terribly upset that there should be a conference in the town, and they not keeping a preacher! She was quite bitter about it. (147)

Since she no longer owns her own capacious house, Mrs. Harris has no say about the inability to perform what she reads as a necessary social form. The preacher is literally crowded out of the house with its redirected function and priorities; he is displaced, as are the grandmother's desires. The burial of Blue Boy and the displacement of the preacher are details that, when read together, reintroduce the marginal and powerless condition of Grandma Harris in the Templeton family. The clear meaning at which we think we have arrived in chapter five is itself displaced by the subject of displacement in chapters six and seven. The text of "Old Mrs. Harris" continues to place the reader upon a seesaw of shifting loyalties and of consistently redirected or revised understanding. It encourages the free play of multiple and contradictory interpretations, and it absolutely refuses to assign a *single* meaning to itself.

One other revealing instance of displacement occurs within the frame of those two chapters focused on the grandmother's bitterness. At the end of chapter seven, the external focalizer relates a past story, set in "last summer" (151), about Vickie Templeton. Significantly, in the narrative it follows Grandmother Harris's exit from the parlor where she, Victoria, and Mrs. Rosen have been chatting about the permutations or, as Victoria sees it, the profound absence, of "romance" in Vickie. The story focalized introduces the possibility of Vickie's attending college (the University of Michigan) which will become *the* dominant subject of the narrative for the next three chapters. It remains connected as well to the previous imagery by returning to the act of burial: "They [a professor, his male students, and Vickie] had a splendid summer,—found a great bed of fossil elephant bones, where a whole herd must once have perished. Later on they came upon the bones of a new kind of elephant, scarcely larger than a pig. They were greatly excited about their finds, and so was Vickie" (152). What is it exactly that we "find" in this curious passage wholly unrelated to anything else in the narrative? One could, on one level, locate coherence within its imagery, beginning with the desire for burial and ending with excavation. Mrs. Harris wishes to bury her cat, but ends up effectively burying her outrage; it is discussed specifically as "resentment" and "bitterness," two expressions of repressed and unvoiced anger. The effect of the two chapters is to excavate and relocate this anger within the narrative, to balance *and* to contradict repression with the narrative itself voicing Mrs. Harris's reaction because actually she says "nothing" (145).

Yet we also discover a displacement in this passage which is essentially narrative in effect when it addresses the scientific "fact" of evolution. The "fossil elephant bones" of an older past have evolved and given way to "the bones of a new kind of elephant, scarcely larger than a pig." Evolution itself is an example of displacement; one species crowds out and supplants another. Similarly, Vickie's prominence in the narrative, her narrative line, and her fate, will occupy the space left by Mrs. Harris as she advances toward her death at the end of the text. Mrs. Harris's narrative line has not ended in meaning, but will remain suspended in ambivalence until her death, which will, ultimately, be the only solution or resolution that the text offers to the mystery of her character and situation. Her destiny remains obscure. This displacement also functions as a figure of chiasmas. The grandmother declines toward death, her destiny, while Vickie progresses out of Skyline toward a kind of educational upward mobility. The point where both their fates and the two lines of narrative development meet forms the pattern of cross-stitch with which the text began. Left with only contradiction and obscurity in Mrs.

Harris's story, the relation of Vickie to her family and specifically to her grandmother redirects our reading toward the more expansive pattern of cross-stitching that composes a family (what Cather, in her essay on Katherine Anne Porter, calls those "innumerable shades of sweetness and anguish"), or what we might more properly term the family pattern.[15]

The incident of excavation, though, does not mark the first, sustained appearance of Vickie in the text, for she appears also in the first half of chapter three. What links chapters three and seven, and why perhaps Vickie figures in both of them, is the juxtaposition each incorporates between the young girl and the "three women" (Mrs. Harris, Mrs. Rosen, and Mrs. Templeton) in the text. Vickie's role, on both occasions, is that of an outsider; in chapter seven, for example, she becomes the subject of conversation and debate between the three married women. Discussing Vickie's newfound interest in education, Mrs. Rosen surmises that there is "something very personal in Vickie's admiration for Professor Chalmers," to be countered by Victoria that "There ain't a particle of romance in Vickie" (150), stressing the difference between mother and daughter. Mrs. Rosen finally "solves" the altercation about Vickie's sexuality, noting: "There are several kinds of romance, Mrs. Templeton. She may not have your kind" (150). Such notations of Vickie's "difference," especially about the issue of ambiguous sexuality, represent yet another example of Cather's play of sexual signification throughout her fiction. Appearing here simply as a resistance to the mother's heterosexuality, Vickie's actual sexual orientation remains unsignified and obscure throughout the text.[16]

This conversation about a nascent sexuality recalls a previous conversation in chapter three between the three women on the subject of babies. Significantly, this is also the chapter in which Mrs. Rosen begins to see Victoria as likable and, in some ways, like herself, or like the self she would wish to be. The childless Mrs. Rosen envies and rejoices in Victoria's motherhood which she witnesses when the latter appears in the Templeton parlor to nurse her baby in "a white challis négligée" (115), the picture both of the madonna and of the eternal feminine. The tableau, moreover, suggests those undercurrents of sexuality, which produces babies and transforms women into mothers. Sexuality is the unspoken subtext of the mother and child configuration, and the narrative inscribes this in a highly eroticized passage on nursing: "She reappeared with the baby, who was not crying, exactly, but making eager, passionate, grasping entreaties,—faster and faster, tenser and tenser . . . Hughie . . . fell to work so fiercely that beads of sweat came out all over his flushed forehead. . . . When he was changed to the other [side], Hughie resented the interruption a little; but after a time he became soft and bland, as smooth as oil, indeed" (115–16). The act of consummation characterizes this language; this is not only maternity, but the world of sexual experience as well. And in passing the baby Hughie among themselves, the three women affirm their bonds in a kind of maternal and marital communion. Vickie is, tellingly, placed outside *both* of these conversations and outside the tripartite grouping of the "three women" as well. Her fate, or narrative line, seems signified as markedly different from the three women, especially concerning the issue of sexual choice and destiny.

Vickie's difference within the text of "Old Mrs. Harris" is inscribed as primarily a textual one. In chapter three, Vickie comes into contact with three textually embedded texts. The first allusion is to *Wilhelm Meister,* which Vickie returns to the Rosens having read and, she says vaguely, having liked. Including the apex in the male tradition of the bildungs-roman, *Wilhelm Meister,* in a text centered on female relations and experience, calls a certain attention to the work. In this male tradition, protagonists undertake an expedition of individuation. They journey out into the world in order to discover themselves and to secure a respected place within society at large. Though it has not yet been introduced as a textual fact, this same desire to undertake a journey beyond her familial and female sphere will be Vickie's. The thread of her fate, the trajectory of her desire, and the line of her narrative all point out of the text. The education she will receive and the destiny she will follow transgresses the demarcations of story line in "Old Mrs. Harris." Vickie appears definitively in this allusion as an other within the frame of the narrative and as outside of it as well.

The second of these allusive texts is Goethe's *Faust,* which Vickie stumbles upon in "the very German picture of Gretchen entering the church, with Faustus gazing at her from behind a rose tree, Mephisto at his shoulder" (106). Certain parameters of interpretation frame this picture. The story of *Faust,* in its various manifestations, is primarily a story about obsessive and transgressive ambition. Yet what draws Vickie's attention to this text is the figure of Gretchen, which alludes to certain choices confronting Vickie in the narrative. In the context of *Faust,* the

picture of Gretchen's entrance into the church comes at the point in the
poem when she most desires to repress her desires, to escape from a
sexuality that has become all-consuming and that will, in fact, be responsible for the murder of her mother, of her child, and finally, of herself.
Since it occurs in a chapter that will later celebrate the maternal, it is not
only ironic, but perhaps also signifies a fate in which Vickie will not
share, since her textual encounters stand in contrast to the grouping of
three women around the baby and in contrast to the scene late in the text
in which Victoria, pregnant again, curses her femaleness and her fate
(178–79). Gretchen then appears as a figure of dangerous limitation to
Vickie since she embodies the principle of the eternal feminine, of
Vickie's mother. Ultimately, these texts seem to provide two troubling
alternatives: dangerous ambition or self-destructive femininity.[17] The
correct choice for Vickie remains obscure.

There is a third text that Vickie discovers though, the *Dies Irae*
inserted "between the first and second parts in this edition" (106) of
Faust. Curiously enough, in standard editions of *Faust,* the *Dies Irae* is
the hymn Gretchen hears when she enters the church in part one, and its
message of moral condemnation increases her desperation. In "Old Mrs.
Harris," however, it is moved from its original placement to "between"
the two parts of *Faust.* This displacement suggests its pivotal and balancing function between two other texts, *Wilhelm Meister* and *Faust.* As the
last of the three texts, the *Dies Irae* casts an apocalyptic light upon the
presentation of an ambition which is valorized and an ambition which
results in tragedy. Moreover, the *Dies Irae,* as a song of judgment and
death, foreshadows the literal end of "Old Mrs. Harris."

> Day of wrath, upon that day
> The world to ashes melts away,
> As David and the Sybil say. (107)

But who and what are we being asked to judge here? Vickie? Mrs. Harris?
The text itself? No indications are forthcoming. The narrative records
only that "Vickie went on stumbling through the Latin verses" (107),
though their content remains suppressed and left out of the text. This
omission is both telling and confusing, for the succeeding stanzas of the
Dies Irae make explicit what the text may be trying to accomplish, at the
same time that they defer precisely the kind of moral judgment the hymn
suggests.

Then shall, with universal dread,
The sacred mystic book be read,
To try the living and the dead.

The judge ascends his awful throne,
He makes each secret sin be known,
And all with shame confers their own.[18]

Read in relation to "Old Mrs. Harris," what we arrive at in these stanzas suggests both the argument for and the impossibility of interpretation, which is the essential paradox of this text. "Old Mrs. Harris," the "sacred mystic book" about familial relations, structures itself so that we are constantly asked to render judgment, to take sides, to read sympathetically and critically. As readers of the text, we are its judge. Yet the text also questions any judgment we are incited to make by undermining what we think we understand through the introduction of new information, narrative contradictions, or a more capacious perspective. Guilt in this narrative is shared by each and every character; since "all with shame confers their own," we, as judges of this text, are hard pressed to enact any sort of judgment. Such implications profoundly affect our omniscient, and yet limited, role as readers. Even when we are presented with two opposing views of ambition in two different texts, the culminating third text, explicitly judgmental and presumably clarifying, calls into question the very act of judgment itself. We will, it seems, both desire Vickie's success and witness its hurtful effect on her family simultaneously. Moreover, our own role as fallible and revisionary readers of this text renders all judgments and interpretations partial and ambivalent at best. The experience of trying to decipher the difference between two textual versions of ambition, only to be confronted by a third text, which relocates this difference within the act and process of our reading, mirrors the experience of reading "Old Mrs. Harris" itself.

Vickie's story line then, seems to have been designated by the text(s) as different from that of her mother and grandmother because it is centered in ambition, and yet similar in that it is presented ambivalently within the narrative.[19] This ambivalence tellingly records itself in Vickie's self-punishment for the desire to leave her family. She waits in agonized impatience and fear for the letter that will free her and upon which she believes her life depends: "There was no alternative. If she didn't get it, then everything was over" (154). Yet into her anticipation creeps unconscious guilt, with the result that "she managed to cut her finger and get ink into the cut," giving herself "a badly infected hand" that has to be carried in a sling (154–55). It is the hand that must be disempowered in this context, the hand that wrote the application, the hand that scripts her desires, the hand that is, somehow, infected and sick. Her forward movement into the world, one of the primary lines of plot development in the text, is also an act with consequences. The consequences themselves are nothing less than differences from her mother and grandmother, and the separation of the narrative into two separate and even contradictory lines or strands of plot. Vickie's difference surfaces subtly when she receives her letter of acceptance to college: "The strange thing was that, one morning a letter came" (155). What is strange about this comment is that there is, seemingly, nothing strange about this at all; the letter is what Vickie has been waiting for in order to discover what direction her fate will take. What is, however, strange about the letter is its enforcing of difference in Vickie's character and destiny. With its reception arrives a necessary distancing of Vickie and her family. She becomes reserved and even somewhat alien and alienated in her difference, as her narrative line veers off and out of the novella.

The line of Vickie's fate and narrative is addressed by Mr. Rosen when he translates an aphorism and bestows it upon Vickie at her celebration dinner: " '*Le but n'est rien, le chemin, c'est tout.*' That means: The end is nothing, the road is all" (158). The narrative imbues this comment with a kind of prophetic authority and signified difference by noting that there is "something *strange* and presageful in his voice" (158, emphasis added). Mr. Rosen, in fact, literally translates Vickie's difference into the text by inscribing the road that will lead her out of the narrative entitled "Old Mrs. Harris." Vickie's destiny, unlike her mother's and her grandmother's, will be neither circumscribed nor constricted as the text winds down. Her destiny is left open-ended and unsignified, seemingly different from the other women's in the text. Yet the very last paragraph of the novella erases any and all difference between its narrative lines by asserting the same, unified ending for all its characters and their threads of fate. What we have been directed to read as Vickie's difference will ultimately be resolved as and reduced to no difference at all. *This* configuration of cross-stitch, the advance and withdrawal of meaning as apprehensible in the narrative, will constitute the text's essentially ambivalent pattern as it tries to create closure for itself.

Grandma Harris's death ends in obscurity, although there are a number of allusions that repeat motifs from the narrative. This combination of obscurity and repetition provides a sense of closure and narrative integration, at the same time that it still obscures the answer of what constitutes the "real" grandmother. On the afternoon of her death, Mrs. Harris is attended by the twins (181), a replication, of a sort, of Blue Boy's death in the barn where the grandmother and the two little boys sit with the suffering cat. Again Vickie appears, heedless to the suffering of others and oblivious to her grandmother. Her ironic grumbling that she can get no attention when her "whole life hangs by a thread" (186) reveals the narrative's self-consciousness about itself, its closure, and its need for continuity. We also are asked again, for example, to read the difference between two texts. The grandmother's narrative does not end with *Joe's Luck,* the "boy's book" of fortune and advancement that Bert reads to her before her death (183), but with her preferred text, the second part of *Pilgrim's Progress* "where Christiana and her band come to the arbour on the Hill of Difficulty" (184). Like the stanzas quoted from the *Dies Irae,* the narrative here incorporates another text on death and, in this instance, benevolent judgment: "*Then said Mercy, how sweet is rest to them that labour*" (184). Later in this chapter, the narrative will seemingly once more elicit a judgment from the reader when it summarizes, one final time, the litany of "Grandmother's little secrets: how hard her bed was, that she had no proper place to wash, and kept her comb in her pocket; that her nightgowns were patched and darned" (187–88). Since these grievances are focalized through Mrs. Harris's consciousness, it is difficult to know exactly how to read them. Is this meant to signify the *last* and *final* criticism about the grandmother's life, or is it rather one last turn, one more cross-stitch in the pattern of contradiction so prevalent in this narrative? It is, ultimately, impossible to tell. The narration of Mrs. Harris's death enforces this fallacy of interpretation, in fact, by asserting that even those dying are apt to misread: "Old Mrs. Harris did not really die that night, but she believed she did" (189). Even the fact of death is merely a matter of interpretation according to the narrative, and, more important, is presented essentially as incorrect. Despite the drawing together of its threads and motifs, the narrative line of Mrs. Harris does not come to an apprehensible point. It ends in what can never be known, in the literal obscurity of death.

It is only in the very last paragraph of the text that we seem, at last, to receive some kind of answer or meaning to the problems this narrative has raised. At first glance though, the final paragraph of "Old Mrs. Harris" may strike the reader as not even part of the narrative proper, so foreign and revised is its focalization.

> Thus Mrs. Harris slipped out of the Templeton's story; but Victoria and Vickie had still to go on, to follow the long road that leads through things unguessed at and unforeseeable. When they are old, they will come closer and closer to Grandma Harris. They will think a great deal about her, and remember things they never noticed; and their lot will be more or less like hers. They will regret that they heeded her so little; but they, too, will look into the eager, unseeing eyes of young people and feel themselves alone. They will say to themselves: "I was heartless, because I was young and strong and wanted things so much. But now I know." (190)

No longer is the narrative in the consciousness of characters or even, it seems, within a recognizable focalization. The external focalizer in this paragraph is authoritative, omniscient, judgmental, and metatextual. Instead of being focalized through an outsider looking for answers, the narrative ends with a disembodied voice proclaiming *the* meaning of the text. Verbally denoted in a fixed and fated future tense, the focalizer claims that though the grandmother has escaped the narrative, Victoria and Vickie are still in it, "had still to go on, to follow the long road that leads through things unguessed at and unforeseeable." This version of the text envisions a linear narrative that ends only in death, the fate of all humankind. In a litany of future certainty, "They will think. . . . They will regret. . . . [they] will look. . . . They will say," the narrative reads fate in general as nothing more than the inevitable process of aging and increasing isolation. Read literally, the passage interprets the story of "Old Mrs. Harris" as the story of all humankind. Everything ends in death; "their lot will be more or less like hers."

In one respect, the ending of "Old Mrs. Harris" attempts to disavow the unconventional within itself. On a thematic level, the difference we have been directed to read between the fates of Vickie and Mrs. Harris, and even, to an extent, between Vickie and Victoria as well, is utterly erased. Their narrative lines are drawn together into the same "long road," and the "freedoms" that Vickie and Victoria enjoy, for which Mrs. Harris has sacrificed herself, are merely illusory because their fates "will be more or less like" the grandmother's. In terms of the text's narrative as well, this final paragraph enforces a meaning that the rest of the text has either obscured or deferred. An omniscient authority frames the narrative as a tale told ("Thus Mrs. Harris slipped out of the Templeton's story") that is also imbued with a didactic meaning ("They will regret that they heeded her so little"). This external focalizer's interpretation valorizes the literal, and in refuting the multiplicity of readings within its own narrative it ruptures itself from within. This final paragraph tries to rewrite our reading of the narrative entire, and much as in *My Mortal Enemy,* what remains is textual disjunction. It is, ultimately, impossible to make this final interpretation cohere with a text that dramatizes the fallacy of interpretation. If we accept what this closing paragraph argues, then we are forced to read the text against itself.

Or perhaps we aren't. For an alternative interpretation could read this closing paragraph as simply one more and the final contradiction in the pattern of the text. In this reading, the end of the story is what J. Hillis Miller terms "the retrospective revelation of the law of the whole," the obscure destiny that is death itself, the final double X in the eyes, the ultimate unknowable secret.[20] Both the narrative proper and this closing paragraph conform to a teleology of mortality that ends in death. Though the text, read this way, seems to close off "Old Mrs. Harris" with one meaning, it instead opens it up with none. Death remains the ultimate meaning that resists any meaning, making this ending consistent with what has come before. Perhaps most tellingly, this paragraph ends by focalizing what Vickie and Victoria "will say to themselves" at the end of their lives in an abstract future beyond the text. Its claim to "know" rests within quotations, within individual interpretation which we have experienced as precarious and partial at best. This is not contradiction but confirmation. The pattern of cross-stitching in the text is summed up in one final, uninterpretable X; all lines of fate and of narrative are drawn together into death. Somewhere, and perhaps nowhere, in between, lies not truth, but the convergence of these lines in a text that remains, indeed can never be anything else but, obscure.

5

Lucy Gayheart:
The Bildungsroman as Grecian Urn

A book is made with one's own flesh and blood of years. It is cremated youth. It is all yours—no one gave it to you.

—WILLA CATHER, 1921

Thus Nature spake—the work was done—
How soon my Lucy's race was run!
She died, and left to me
This heath, this calm, and quiet scene;
The memory of what has been,
And never more will be.

—WILLIAM WORDSWORTH,
"Three Years She Grew" (1799)

Lucy Gayheart (1935) is *the* Cather novel critics love to hate. And no wonder, because it is the strangest hybrid among all her works. David Stouck describes it as her "most complex novel philosophically," conveyed in "the commonest of narrative forms—the love story" and containing, uncharacteristically, "all the elements of a dime-store 'romance.'"[1] Yet few people have ever heard of *Lucy Gayheart,* and even fewer have read it, so disparaged and displaced is it within the critical canon. As Bernice Slote has observed, both *Lucy Gayheart* and Cather's last novel, *Sapphira and the Slave Girl* (1940), "have been viewed secondhand; that is, the most familiar Cather themes from the earlier books were imposed on them: for *Lucy Gayheart,* it was the theme of the struggling artist."[2] Thus, the common perception of the novel is that it "is reminiscent of *The Song of the Lark,*" though as an inferior and ultimately earthbound replication. In the critical litany, it stands as "curiously lifeless," "hardly up to

116

the standard of" previous Cather fiction, "mawkishly sentimental," and "more conventional in tone and quality than any novel Miss Cather had yet written."[3] Clearly, the critical summation of both the novel and Cather is that "the story she has to tell in this present instance is neither new in matter nor treatment."[4]

Yet this last pronouncement comes from Cather herself in an 1899 review of Kate Chopin's *The Awakening,* written when Cather was still cutting her literary teeth. And her apprenticeship shows. For the review is at once declamatory, defensive, condescending, and, for the most part, wrong. Cather's reading of *The Awakening* is so curious, in fact, that something else entirely seems to be the subject of, and at stake in, this review. That something is Cather's ambivalence about what constitutes the proper stance a writer should and can take toward the novelistic tradition of *Madame Bovary, Anna Karenina,* and, marginally, *The Awakening,* in which female heroines inevitably and tragically take their own lives.[5] The thorn in Cather's young flesh seems to be the question of whether to lay responsibility at society's door or at the feet of the women themselves.

Cather begins the review by revealing the paradoxical position she occupies as a male-identified writer who happens to be a woman: an author's choice of themes is frequently as inexplicable as his choice of a wife. It is governed by some innate temperamental bias that cannot be diagrammed. This is particularly so in women who write" (697). The remainder of Cather's review discusses Chopin's "temperamental bias" toward the "trite and sordid theme" of self-obsessive female passion, while it simultaneously distances the reviewer herself from participation in, or even sympathy for, this "temperamental bias," which she locates "particularly" in women.[6] Her chief criticism of the female characters in texts like *The Awakening* is that they behave in limited, and perhaps even feminine, ways.

> Edna Pontellier and Emma Bovary are studies in the same feminine type; one a finished and complete portrayal, the other a hasty sketch, but the theme is essentially the same. Both women belong to a class, not large, but forever clamoring in our ears, that demands more romance out of life than God put into it. The unfortunate feature of their disease is that it attacks only women of brains, at least of rudimentary brains, but whose development is one-sided; women of strong and fine intuitions, but without the faculty of observation, comparison, reasoning about things. (698)

The connections Cather creates within her diction are telling about her own antifeminine bias. To her identification of a "feminine type," she appends "romance," "disease," "one-sided" development, and "intuition." What they lack, she concludes, are the faculties of "observation, comparison," and reason, traits commonly associated with, and even *as*, male authority. Cather also compares "this passion . . . against Shakespeare, Balzac, Wagner, [and] Raphael" (699), and, not surprisingly, finds it lacking. Yet what remains most striking about this review is Cather's conflation of Chopin with these female protagonists. Much like the "women of brains . . . whose development is one-sided; women of strong and fine intuitions," Cather despairs over the fact that "Miss Chopin has devoted so exquisite and sensitive, well-governed a style to so trite and sordid a theme" (697). While Cather does not confuse Flaubert and Tolstoy with their heroines, Chopin, as a female author who has committed the cardinal sin of creating this "feminine type," is not so lucky.

> *These people* really expect the passion of love to fill and gratify every need of life, whereas nature only intended that it should meet one of many demands. *They insist* upon making it stand for all the emotional pleasures of life and art; expecting an individual and self-limited passion to yield infinite variety, pleasure, and distraction, to contribute to their lives what the arts and the pleasurable exercise of the intellect gives to less limited and less intense idealists. (698–99, emphasis added)

This is both a textual and an authorial critique; effect and intent are read as one and the same. What Cather advocates here is an author who will not "awaken" her heroine exclusively to passion, but to "what the arts and the pleasurable exercise of the intellect" can endow life with, an awakening to life itself. Cather seems to want not a more moral, but a "less limited" awakening for these heroines. And this is precisely what she attempts to provide in *Lucy Gayheart*.

Lucy Gayheart is a novel of arrested motion. Not only does the book enclose its heroine in what Cather calls "that singular brightness of young beauty"[7] between the frozen winters that frame the work, but the novel itself is frozen on the brink of possibility, seizing the young part of the heroine's life before it climaxes and then declines, something that Cather wished she had done in her earlier novel *The Song of the Lark* (1915).[8] Yet the text also conforms to the pattern of arrest that characterizes many "awakening" novels both in its bringing to a standstill the progress of its heroine's growth and in its seizure of her newfound independence by authority of custom or of law.[9] *Lucy Gayheart,* in fact, incorporates many of those same failings that Cather singles out for scorn in Chopin's novel. When, for instance, one reads Cather's comment that Edna Pontellier, "like Emma Bovary, had been in love with innumerable dream heroes before she was out of short skirts" (697), one cannot help comparing her own comment about *Lucy Gayheart:* "She had intended to show youth's tendency to hero-worship which somehow 'seems a little ridiculous . . . though it is a natural feeling in all ardent young people.' "[10] Also striking is the parallel between Cather's characterization of Edna's "vague and visionary passion for a tragedian whose unresponsive picture she used to kiss" (697), and the unresponsive tragedian of *Lucy Gayheart,* Clement Sebastian, whose picture in a "tarnished silver frame" (231) is one of the last images in the novel. Lucy Gayheart meets her end from the same causes, according to Cather, that result in the deaths of Emma Bovary, Anna Karenina, and Edna Pontellier: "They have driven the blood until it will drive no further, they have played their nerves up to the point where any relaxation short of absolute annihilation is impossible" (699). Lucy Gayheart's annihilation, similarly, occurs when "such a storm of pain and anger boiled up in her that she felt strong enough to walk into the next county. Her blood was racing, and she was no longer conscious of the cold. She forgot to look where she put her feet; they took care of themselves" (197). Like Edna Pontellier's swimming, the physical activity of skating which symbolizes Lucy's desire for advancement and movement also brings about her death. In her idealization about love, her awakening to life through a romantic attachment, and the intensity of her obsession which ultimately destroys her, Lucy Gayheart is the quintessence of the fate, in Cather's own words, "to which unbalanced idealism not infrequently leads" (699).

Lucy Gayheart, however, is not an awakening novel. It is a self-conscious revision of an awakening novel. This revisionary difference lies at that point where Cather believes " 'the awakening' comes. . . . Sometimes [the awakening] comes in the form of arsenic, as it came to Emma Bovary, sometimes it is carbolic acid taken covertly in the police station . . ." (699). Cather not only misreads when "the awakening" occurs in Chopin's novel, but her identification of it *as* death absolutely contradicts the way most feminist critics read the chronology and the development of "awakening" in novels by women, where the "movement is inward, toward greater self-knowledge and the nature of the world" which, inevitably, results in "an awakening to limitations" imposed by society on female conduct, potential, and aspirations.[11] Unlike Chopin's novel, in which the heroine awakens to a sexual passion that dramatizes the insufficiency of her life, Cather's novel begins by teaching her heroine a lesson about what "the passion of love" can and cannot fulfill in a life. Only when Lucy Gayheart finally understands and accepts what the narrative argues is the insufficiency of *love,* does she "awaken"—into death. Both of these schemes involve the protagonists' learning a lesson of sorts. But in Chopin this "lesson" is a recognition of the way society limits female choice and female development, whereas for Cather, the lesson Lucy learns is one about the proper expectations for and limits of her own passion.

Lucy Gayheart, however, never once conceives the desire to be an artist, separating her both from Edna Pontellier and, closer to home, from *the* successful woman artist in Cather's novels, Thea Kronberg. In revising a scheme she disparages, Cather displaces an awakening to sexual passion by replacing it with Lucy's awakening to art through her romantic, and unconsummated, passion for the great artist and singer, Clement Sebastian. Lucy aspires throughout the novel to be nothing more than Clement's apprentice, literally as his accompanist and spiritually as a devotée to what art offers through him. Passion in *Lucy Gayheart* is subordinate to art, or rather, Lucy awakens fully to a passion for and an appreciation of art through her partial awakening to romantic passion.

Cather's melding of art and passion into the same desire in *Lucy Gayheart* has some curious effects. The text seems to point Lucy Gayheart toward the apprehension of an "art of living" that Susan Rosowski associates with male protagonists of the bildungsroman, but it kills her off just as she seems ready to grasp it.[12] It is as if Cather wants to amalgamate her "awakening" novel with the bildungsroman, but cannot because of the limited, "one-sided" awakening heroine she has created. Cather, then, has both revised and replicated her own reading of the pattern in novels of female awakening, and in doing so she has written a text that aspires to enter both the awakening and the bildungsroman genres, and that fails in both accordingly. Cather has not, like Chopin, written a novel about a tragic heroine who awakens to the socially enforced limitations of her life as a woman. Nor has she written an apprenticeship novel in which the protagonist learns *and* then conquers "the art of living." She has instead, in *Lucy Gayheart*, written a novel about a limited and potentially tragic heroine who awakens to, but does not *master*, "the art of living." Cather's own sex-stereotyped language in her review enforces David Stouck's categorization of the novel as at once "philosophical" and as a "dime-store 'romance.'" In addressing how one receives sustenance in life through art it is as "philosophical" and reasonable as Cather wishes awakening novels to be. Yet in submerging this theme within a novel about a young woman's passion for a married man old enough to be her father, it teeters toward the "dime-store 'romance,'" or, as Cather called it more darkly, toward that "goal to which unbalanced idealism not infrequently leads." It is both and neither at once.

There is a way, though, that *Lucy Gayheart* does acknowledge the problems inherent in the desire to script a female story into a bildungsroman, and that is through its narrative. For *Lucy Gayheart* begins as an artifact already intact, as a story that has been fashioned into folk myth by society.[13]

> In Haverford on the Platte the townspeople still talk of Lucy Gayheart. They do not talk of her a great deal, to be sure; life goes on and we live in the present. But when they do mention her name it is with a gentle glow in the face or the voice, a confidential glance which says: "Yes, you, too, remember?" They still see her as a slight figure always in motion; dancing or skating, or walking swiftly with intense direction, like a bird flying home. (3)

Lucy Gayheart first appears in the text as a memory, one whose story is finished before it has even begun—the antithesis of the expected trajectory in a bildungsroman. The abundance of present participles in this description—dancing, skating, walking, flying—locates Lucy Gayheart within the continuous present of fiction. Her constant and, in the novel, characteristic motion is literally arrested at the very beginning of text, exactly the same way that her frozen footsteps will represent its final image. Cather's choice of both title and image here recalls Wordsworth's 1799 poem, "Lucy Gray, Or Solitude." Like *Lucy Gayheart*, "Lucy Gray" is the story of a young girl who drowns when she loses her way during a snowstorm. Wordsworth's poem also begins as a story that has been recounted to the narrator, who then recites it for us: "Oft I had heard of Lucy Gray." The subtitle, "Or Solitude," moreover, is the primary lesson to be learned in *Lucy Gayheart*; one must find something to sustain the self since human relationships are essentially ephemeral and subject to change. Art is all that remains. And, like Lucy Gayheart, little Lucy Gray is both identified *and* lost by her footprints.

> —When in the snow the mother spied
> The print of Lucy's feet.
> . . . .
> They followed from the snowy bank
> Those footmarks, one by one,
> Into the middle of the plank;
> And further there were none! (Lines 43–56)

It seems possible that in appropriating certain motifs of Wordsworth's "Lucy," Cather is consciously alluding to a western literary tradition in which women cannot be artists, but can become art through death. Lucy Gayheart's awakening to art is represented as her transformation into art, which is especially suggestive since the novel ends with Harry Gordon's (Lucy's rejected suitor) narration of her life and what she means to him, a stance akin to that of the narrator in Wordsworth's other "Lucy" poems.[14] Like *Anna Karenina* and *Madame Bovary,* moreover, *Lucy Gayheart* is a text that is signified by its heroine's name; the woman *is* the text, and vice versa. There seems to be a way, then, that Cather is self-consciously aware of the differences between a story of female apprenticeship and one of male maturity and advancement. The former exists within a tradition that represents it as finished before it has even begun.

The first two indirect discourses of Lucy's consciousness underscore the conflict between the autonomy and ambition that the text wants Lucy to achieve, and the romantic passion and limitation that will lead to her inevitable death. Indeed, the novel seems poised "between a plot that charts development and a plot that unravels it."[15] Lucy Gayheart's introduction into the narrative as a character rather than a memory occurs in the novel's second chapter. She is at a skating party on "her last afternoon" (7) before she departs for the city, moving gracefully and athletically over the frozen river in which she will drown at the end of Book two. Overtaken by Harry Gordon, who desires "a turn with Lucy before the sun goes down" (8), she skates until she is near exhaustion. Harry then adopts the role of her chivalric protector, and she becomes completely passive beneath his benevolent power: "He guided her in to the shore at some distance from his sleigh, knelt down and took off her skating shoes, changed his own, and with a sudden movement swung her up in his arms and carried her over the trampled snow to his cutter. As he tucked her under the buffalo robes she thanked him" (11). Lucy's sudden shift from activity to passivity, from moving with "intense direction" (3) to being moved as if she were an infant (guided, carried, tucked), is ritually reenacted throughout the narrative. Each time we are alerted to her autonomy or progress, we read it in conjunction with a successive instance of her incapacity. Lucy seems forever to be taking two steps forward and three steps back.

Yet even within this chapter the cycle of advance and withdrawal is not complete. As Lucy sits snugly in Harry's sleigh, her inner yearnings take shape in an epiphany, another significant feature of awakening novels.[16]

> The sleigh was such a tiny moving spot on that still white country settling into shadow and silence. Suddenly Lucy started and struggled under the tight blankets. In the darkening sky she had seen the first star come out; it brought her heart into her throat. That point of silver light spoke to her like a signal, released another kind of life and feeling which did not belong here. It overpowered her. With a mere thought she had reached that star and it had answered, recognition had flashed between. Something knew, then, in the unknowing waste: something had always known, forever! (11–12)

This first epiphany seems to represent for Lucy some kind of illumination about herself, since "that point of silver light" reiterates or reflects the light within her own name. Her response is to free herself from "the tight blankets" Harry has bound protectively about her. And though the epiphany's meaning seems to reside in the "recognition" between Lucy and the star, it is impossible to perceive clearly what the diction of this passage signifies. We know only that the star speaks to Lucy "like a signal," that "something" knows something about her, and that this something releases "another kind of life and feeling which did not belong here." "Here," in this context, seems to be ambiguously localized. It suggests not only "here" in Haverford, but "here" in Harry's sled as well. Lucy may be reacting against small town restrictions upon her ambitions and advancement, or against the marriage which we soon learn Harry has in mind, or both. Equally elusive is the allusion to stars, which recurs in the narrative with close proximity to this passage. Not only is Lucy's father an amateur astronomer (16), but her first memory of Clement Sebastian recorded in the narrative also centers upon his rendition of a song about a Greek sailor who has "steered his little boat by [the stars'] mild, protecting light" (29). Lucy's father studies the stars, Clement

Sebastian (himself an established artist or "star") sings about them, and
the young Greek sails by them. What we encounter within the imagery of
this epiphany is a heroine who has ambitions, or, more accurately, vague
yearnings and aspirations toward something, and yet that "something"
seems to exist solely within a male realm of possibility. If the "true
nature" of Lucy's situation is that her ambitions will find no safe or
secure port in which to dock, then the "mild, protecting light" which the
stars offer to the sailor may be "something" entirely beyond her grasp.

Again, as in the preceding skating scene, the suggestion of female
autonomy is subsumed within a masculine ethos. For the abstract "flash
of understanding" that Lucy has momentarily apprehended is, for her,
"too bright and too sharp. It hurt, and made one feel small and lost" (12).
Confused, she reverts to a superior and already established male power:
"Lucy shut her eyes and leaned on Harry's shoulder to escape from what
she had gone so far to snatch" (12). Lucy's own desire for a movement
into the larger world is balanced by her, seemingly, equally strong desire
to shield herself from that world within a safe, masculine presence. As
early as the second chapter then, the contradictory elements within
Lucy's character render her confusing to read, and they make it difficult
to anticipate her decidedly "untraditional" development, since she seems
to straddle both the bildungsroman and the awakening traditions at
once.

The text's peculiarly precarious position between these two traditions
appears as well in its representation of sexuality. In trying to revise the
convention of awakening novels, Cather must necessarily introduce her
protagonist to romantic passion, then find some way to move her
beyond it into another, broader definition of self. This second movement
is more characteristic of the bildungsroman, in which male protagonists
frequently indulge in romantic and sexual attachments, yet ultimately
transcend them by the novel's end to acquire the proper partner in
marriage. The female heroine in the awakening novel, however, never
seems able to survive this initial attachment, as if romantic and sexual
attachment are so transgressive for women in the first place that death is
the only possible result. In *Lucy Gayheart* two different and, essentially,
gendered configurations of sexuality appear and, again, elicit a reading
sensitive to traditional representations of male and female patterns of
development. As Lucy leaves Haverford for Chicago, for example, the
narrative records the connection between her pleasure at being alone
and sexual release: "Lucy undressed quickly, got into her berth, and

turned off the lights. At last she was alone, lying still in the dark, and could give herself up to the vibration of the train,—a rhythm that had to do with escape, change, chance, with life hurrying forward. That sense of release and surrender went all over her body; she seemed to lie as if in a warm bath" (23–24). Sexuality in this passage is conceived both through Lucy's sense of autonomy and adventure in the world and through a sense of self-containment. Only when "alone" does she, paradoxically, "give herself up to" the vibrations of the train and of life; she releases and surrenders herself to her anticipations and desires. Similarly, when she arrives in Chicago the narrative emphasizes her exhilaration over the fact that "for the first time in her life she could come and go *like a boy;* no one fussing about, no one hovering over her" (26, emphasis added). Freedom is explicitly related to gender here. Lucy feels as well a heightened sense of self-possession. She is "glad as never before to be back with her own things and her own will" (27), and rejoices that, alone in her own room, "she seemed to find herself again" (27). One could perhaps assume at this point that Lucy's ambivalence and retreat may have arisen out of her panic at being in Haverford when, she believes, "she had scarcely been herself at all" (27). The repetitive emphases on autonomy, self-possession, and movement all would seem to indicate that Lucy Gayheart is now properly charted on her own developmental course. So seemingly self-possessed, she leads us to assume that she will be able to make her own way in Chicago.

Yet even as the narrative elicits our belief in Lucy's individual wholeness, it presents evidence that throws off course any and all expectations we may wish to entertain about what kind of development and story hers will be. For Lucy, we learn, revels not in her aloneness or in her individuality, but in the romantic fantasies in which she can indulge when alone. She does not rejoice, for instance, in the room of her own because it is her unique space, but rather because the "four walls held all her thoughts and feelings about him" (27). We also discover that Lucy does not think of Chicago as a landscape that beckons her to explore and experience it. She instead "carried in her mind a very individual map of Chicago" (24) whose geography is marked exclusively by those places where she has glimpsed Clement Sebastian: "a high building on Michigan Avenue where Sebastian had his studio—the stretch of park where he sometimes walked in the afternoon—the Cathedral door out of which she had seen him come one morning—the concert hall where she first heard him sing" (24). Most significant about her reaction is that it is entirely internalized. While on the one hand this self-containment seems to represent a kind of direction and purpose, on the other it is exposed as a retreat from the world and a desire to live in fantasy. Lucy's "greatest fault" (34) is, according to her music teacher, Auerbach, her lack of ambition. Despite her excitement about living in Chicago, she can only imagine her future as "teaching piano to the neighbours' children in Haverford" (64). She behaves in the world with an exaggerated reticence; even when Auerbach encourages her to be Sebastian's practice accompanist, she decides initially to "decline the risk" (34). The focus of Lucy Gayheart's energies, so it seems, will be on a romanticized relation with a man she has met only once. "Sebastian's personality had *aroused her*" (28), the narrative suggestively declares, and it seems apparent that we are reading a novel in which the heroine will "awaken" to sexual and emotional passion through her over-idealized involvement with a man she cannot, and does not, really possess.

Because the novel begins Lucy's life in Chicago by stressing her attraction to and infatuation with a male figure, some critics have envisioned heterosexual romance as the *proper* focus of the novel.[17] But *Lucy Gayheart* remains a meditation on what it means to write a woman's story outside the conventions of the bildungsroman, the *kunstleroman*, the awakening novel, and even the popular novel of romance. Cather's novel, especially in its ambiguous representation of sexuality, displays an authorial awareness of writing around, and even of writing in opposition to, the conventions of heterosexual relationships and heterosexual romance that frequently determine how one tells a woman's story.[18] Not only is sexuality displaced from Lucy Gayheart onto other characters, but the novel is the one text in Cather's oeuvre that deals most directly with homosexuality in the characters of James Mockford and Clement Sebastian. *Lucy Gayheart,* in fact, occupies the curious position of being the most explicitly and strangely sexual of Cather's works *because* it disperses the sexual component of awakening novels away from its heroine and onto other characters so that Lucy can experience an artistic, rather than a sexual, awakening.

Early in the novel, before Lucy even leaves Haverford, the reader encounters one of the most unusual female creations in Cather's fiction, the small-town vamp, Fairy Blair. Fairy has little fondness for Lucy, whom she finds "frightfully stuffy and girly-girly" (15). Yet she, like Lucy, behaves with more life and physical energy than do the other girls in

Haverford, and also like Lucy, she is represented in the narrative through that activity.

> She ripped off her grey fur coat, threw it into the air for the boys to catch, and ran down the platform in her travelling suit—a black velvet jacket and scarlet waistcoat with a skirt very short indeed for the fashion of that time. . . . She caught two boys by the elbow, and between these stiffly overcoated figures raced out into the silent street, swaying from left to right, pushing the boys as if she were shaking two saplings, and doing an occasional shuffle with her feet. She had a pretty, common little face and her eyes were so lit-up and reckless that one might have thought she had been drinking. Her fresh little mouth, without being ugly, was really very naughty. She couldn't push the boys fast enough; suddenly she sprang from between the two rigid figures as if she had been snapped out of a sling-shot and ran up the street with the whole troop at her heels. They were all a little crazy, but as she was the craziest, they followed her. (13–14)

This extraordinary passage contains more sexual allusions than one usually finds in an entire Cather novel. "Crazy" Fairy Blair, in fact, is the incarnation of carnality in this text, as the various meanings of the adjective suggest—wild, eager, distracted by desire, erratic, infatuated, and obsessed. Her description not only begins with a discarding of clothes, but it also catalogs any number of traits commonly associated with *female* promiscuity: a skirt provocatively too short, a "common" face, "reckless eyes" that make her appear as if "she had been drinking," and a "fresh little mouth [that] was really very naughty." There is also some sort of phallic connotation in the rigid and stiff figures of her two male companions, though Fairy herself seems to be the active sexual agent since it is "she [who] couldn't push the boys fast enough."[19] The narrative adds one final touch to her hypersexuality when it describes her laugh as "curious, . . . like a bleat, which had the effect of an indecent gesture" (17). Like a goat she symbolizes, in this highly sexualized and condensed description, the very essence of lust. Fairy Blair mirrors Lucy Gayheart's distinguishing physical energy and power; all the explicitly sexual feelings and behavior, which the narrative will not associate with Lucy, it factors out to her. She embodies one side of Lucy that the novel represses for the sake of a revisionary awakening.

Another female character who also possesses traits not belonging to Lucy follows closely upon the heels of the remarkable Fairy Blair. Harriet

Arkwright, a woman to whom Harry Gordon is unofficially engaged and will eventually marry, is an example of a vaguely threatening female power in the text. The twin of Harry's self-possessed assurance (Harry/Harriet), and focalized through his consciousness, the description of Harriet makes clear what the acceptable limits of female power and authority are, in Harry's terms, and what masculine expectations demand a woman to be.

> If she was twenty-six years old and still unmarried, it was not from lack of suitors. She had been in no hurry to tie herself up. She managed her own property very successfully, travelled a good deal, liked her independence. A woman of the world, Harry considered her; good style, always at her ease, had a kind of authority that money and social position give. But she was plain, confound it! She looked like the men of her family. And she had a hard, matter-of-fact voice, which never kindled with anything; slightly nasal. Whatever she spoke of, she divested of charm. If she thanked him for his gorgeous roses, her tone deflowered the flowers. (21–22)

The acceptable authority Harriet possesses is of "money and social position." Far less acceptable is her implicitly threatening sexual authority. Not only plain, she resembles "the men of her family" and like Fairy Blair she appropriates, at least metaphorically, the same phallic power associated with men—she can deflower the flowers. But if Fairy is hyper-feminine sexuality made carnal, Harriet Arkwright is too competent and, at least to Harry's mind, not feminine enough. She not only has no need for men, since she manages "her own property very successfully" and likes her independence," but she also has chosen, the narrative implies, not to marry: "She had been in no hurry to tie herself up." This colloquial expression parallels Lucy's feelings about marriage to Harry and their life together in Haverford as one of restriction and even bondage. Yet Harriet actually possesses what Lucy only *thinks* she aspires to—independence, self-sufficiency, autonomy. She is a second version of what Lucy is not, and of what she will not become. Harriet Arkwright seems to be the "strong" heroine Cather did not write about in this novel. She is even, perhaps, the character a feminist critic might wish Lucy to be.

Yet the character who manifests the most complex and troubling relation to Lucy is James Mockford. He is, in fact, her doppelgänger. Lucy's first description of Mockford betrays a number of subtle and implicit connections between them which the novel adopts as one of its leitmotifs.

There was something uncanny in that young man's short, insinuating fingers. She admired him, but she did not like him. . . . something in his physical personality set her on edge a little. He was picturesque—too picturesque. He had the very white skin that sometimes goes with red hair, and tonight, as he sat against an olive-green velvet curtain, his features seemed to disappear altogether. His face looked like a handful of flour thrown against velvet. . . . for some reason she didn't like the way he moved across the stage. His lameness gave him a weak, undulating walk, "like a rag walking," she thought. . . . How strange it was that James Mockford's bad hip should bring about the most important thing that had ever happened to her! (38–39)

Mockford is, in this passage, the agent of Lucy's relationship with Clement Sebastian, because she herself believes him to be inadvertently responsible for "the most important thing that had ever happened to her." Yet Lucy perceives Mockford to be a sort of rival. Not only is he the real accompanist and she merely the replacement, but she knows that Sebastian is "attached to James Mockford" (52) in a way that makes her profoundly uncomfortable; at one point she looks into a mirror and glimpses Mockford's reflection in place of her own, gazing back at her with "a strange smile flickering over his face; as if he had a safe card up his sleeve" (63).

What exactly Mockford's "safe card" is, the text never explains, though the narrative does hint time and time again at his homosexuality. Lucy describes him as somehow "too picturesque," and is repelled by his "short, insinuating fingers" and his "weak, undulating walk." Sebastian even characterizes him as "this queer, talented, tricky boy" (92), and though this is more a comment about his strange nature than about his sexual preference, "queer" was, at the time during which Cather both set (1901) and wrote (1935) the novel, a slang expression for homosexuality.[20] Mockford does occupy some kind of privileged relation with Sebastian as accompanist and companion, a position that Lucy envies and in which she desires to place herself.

The darker reverberations of his reflection however, are embodied in his name. Though Mockford's lameness seems to be the antithesis of Lucy's characteristic walk, the physical fact of his impaired progress "mocks" or parodies her own arrested development, which was so much the subject of Book one. Mockford arrests Lucy's development in yet another way. His arms are the ones wrapped around Sebastian's neck, causing them both to drown; without Sebastian's star to guide her, Lucy is plunged into a directionless despair. Mockford is, ultimately, the destructive doppelgänger for both Sebastian *and* Lucy.

When Lucy recalls first hearing Sebastian sing, accompanied by Mockford, one of his Schubert pieces is "Der Doppelgänger," a doppelgänger being the ghostly double of a live person who haunts him through life and is visible only to him. Certainly Sebastian sees a side of Mockford no one else does and appreciates him for things the narrative refuses to discuss. But it is Lucy who is haunted by his too white pallor (38, 90–91). She cannot, in fact, "get his white face out of her mind" (60). And what Lucy realizes about Mockford, which she alone knows and which she alone can see, is his inexplicable power of destruction: "Why had she never told Sebastian she knew this man was destined to destroy him? Why hadn't she thrown herself at his feet and pleaded with him to beware of Mockford, that he was cowardly, envious, treacherous, and she knew it!" (158). The reason Lucy "knows" Mockford so well is because he is one of the dark meanings she reads in Sebastian's singing, "a revelation of love as a tragic force, not a melting mood, of passion that drowns like black water" (31). In the death embrace between Mockford and Sebastian that drowns them both lies Lucy's understanding of love. Mockford is what she might become if the novel expressed her relationship with Sebastian in sexual terms.

In Mockford's name itself is the prefiguring of Lucy's own death by drowning as well; he is, *literally,* her own ghostly and destructive double. "Mockford" by definition, combines the verb, "to mock" with "ford," a noun. A ford, the shallow and usually narrow part of a river that may be crossed by wading, is the part of the Platte River on which Lucy thinks she is skating before the ice gives way beneath her and she is pulled down into its icy, rushing water. But the river has changed course while Lucy has been in Chicago, and it "now flowed where the shallow arm used to be" (194). It is, by another name, a "mockford," a deception of where the safe and shallow arm of the river actually lies. Perhaps most tellingly though, the "mockford" is Lucy's own mistake, her own delusion, since her sister, Pauline, believes that "anyone could see" (194) how the river has changed. In this final, allusive irony, Lucy and her supposed nemesis, Mockford, become one.

The nature of Lucy's relationship with the middle-aged opera star, Clement Sebastian, is and remains ambiguous and unconsummated in even the tamest physical sense because Sebastian's own sexuality is fairly ambiguous. The most definitive thing one can say about it is that his life seems to be structured homosocially. His constant companions are Mockford and Giuseppe, his devoted valet. The few "facts" we learn though Lucy draw the portrait of a man who always speaks "of his wife in a very chivalrous way, and admiringly" (52), although he is estranged from her because of a jealousy "not of the usual sort" (78). The text soon reveals that Sebastian's wife is jealous of *his* attentions to a "charming" and "talented" young boy (79) whom Sebastian takes into his house when he learns that the child has been orphaned. He also, suggestively, reads Lucy's infatuation as "rather boyish" and "more like a chivalrous loyalty than a young passion" (80). And when Sebastian muses to himself about what constitutes "the most satisfying tie men can have," his answer is provocative: "Friendships? Larry was the man he had cared for most. Among women? There was little for sweet reflection in that chapter" (78). Not only does Sebastian recall men first, but he can choose *a* man, where with women no individuals stand out in his memory. Sebastian also confesses to Lucy that part of her attraction for him lies in remembrance; he admits that in her he has found the same "young ardour, [and] young fire" of the "nice boy" whom he had taken into his house and who had become the object of his wife's suspicions (88). There is perhaps a reason then why Sebastian stutters when Lucy asks him if he has ever gotten "any pleasure out of being in love" (69). His response, "N-n-no, not much" (69), is the only incidence of impairment in his otherwise mellifluous speech throughout the novel.

In revising the focus of an awakening novel, *Lucy Gayheart* necessarily deemphasizes its sexual catalyst and supplants the abstract categories of "art," "wisdom," and "sadness" as better, or perhaps, more practical aspects of life that one can and should awaken to. Thus the text's presentation of Lucy and Sebastian's relationship has to be ambiguously physical; it retains a suggestion of the sensual elements in an awakening at the same time that it proffers and, in fact, prefers a more substantial foundation (art, wisdom) upon which to grow. Yet Lucy cannot grow too much. She cannot develop as do the protagonists of a bildungsroman precisely because she is part of a female tradition in which a limited but passionate heroine awakens to her limitations. Whether one, like Cather, locates these limitations in the heroines themselves, or, like Chopin, interprets them as social restrictions enforced upon women, is not the point. The fact remains that *Lucy Gayheart* can neither advance its heroine successfully in the world nor delineate her rapid decline into a morass of sexual excess and transgressive social behavior. Lucy Gayheart, for another hundred pages at least, will remain suspended in frustrating contradiction and agonizing inactivity between these two teleologies.

As Cather was finishing the manuscript of *Lucy Gayheart,* "she wrote Zoë Atkins that she had lost patience with her silly young heroine,"[21] a reaction that will not surprise any reader of the novel. For after Sebastian allows Lucy to become intimate with him, the narrative focalizes *her* interpretation of what it means to live in a state of heightened sensitivity where "everything [is] so still about her, everything *so wide awake* within her" (135, emphasis added). Lucy believes herself to be directed toward a goal, and her language reiterates this: "She had never had such a piano at her command, or so definite a purpose to direct her" (131–32).

What makes her self-satisfied narration so annoying to read though is the fact that it is so elaborate and even ironic a self-deception. Lucy's direction is not self-motivated, nor is it directed toward her own goal: "She was not always struggling against something, she was going with something much stronger than herself" (136). Again, as when Harry Gordon carries her to the sled and tucks her in, she is being acted upon rather than acting. For her "nothing else mattered when all was going well with Sebastian" (114); *his* success "was the important thing" (114). Lucy, in fact, begins to live her life through Sebastian entirely. She spends her days hunting through newspapers for news of him (96), and seems totally unfazed by Auerbach's warning that she must find something to do because "for the platform they always have a man" (133), so she will not be able to continue indefinitely as his practice accompanist. She is perfectly content "to choose one's master and serve him in one's own way" (86). She has become *his* fantasy wife, *his* devotée, *his* humble servant. So it comes as no surprise that his departure to Europe throws her into a state of intensified passivity. She cannot muster even "the faintest stirring of any wish or desire" (118–19) and feels as if "an enormous emptiness had opened on all sides of her" (116) in his absence. What Sebastian has bequeathed to Lucy is an incapacitating dependence. She has "awakened" to romance, though she has learned nothing.

Though it is true that Lucy's inability to exist independently from her relation with Sebastian begins to grate on the reader's nerves, it is also true that Lucy's "feelings" convey most of what the text seems to present as its "meaning." Significantly, the philosophical impact of Lucy's feelings occurs when Harry Gordon returns to the narrative in Book one, ready to ask Lucy to marry him. The repetition of her "feelings" emphasizes the unbridgeable differences between them, since Harry believes that "facts are at the bottom of everything" (101), and it suggests what Lucy has actually learned from Sebastian. As she sits with Harry listening to an opera, the narrative voices two separate but similar feelings she experiences, signalling through repetition the potential significance of her perception: "The music kept bringing back things she used to feel in Sebastian's studio; belief in an invisible, inviolable world. . . . She sat through the rest of the opera feeling that nothing had really vanished, everything would come back" (104–5). The "world" of Sebastian's studio is, quite simply, the world of art, a world that cannot be destroyed by change and that cannot, significantly, be defined because it is intangible. Though one cannot see it, one can experience it through recall. It will either "come back" or be brought back through memory. Art cannot be lost because it is permanent. Cather described this belief explicitly in terms of literature when she wrote a preface to Sarah Orne Jewett's stories. The special nature of Jewett's art she characterizes as "a quality which one can remember without the volume at hand, can experience over and over again in the mind but can never absolutely define, as one can experience in memory a melody." Art, according to Cather, leaves "in the mind of the sensitive reader an intangible residuum of pleasure; a cadence, a quality of voice,"[22] the very thing Lucy Gayheart experiences when she remembers life through music. Her conviction that the essence of her relationship with Sebastian *will* return to her ("nothing had really vanished, everything would come back"), is upheld in the second book, even after Sebastian has died, when Lucy truly "awakens."

Yet this essence, this quality, defies expression in language. It can only be "felt on the page without being specifically named there."[23] *Lucy Gayheart* literally demonstrates how words can have more than just a "direct meaning" through a telling narrational embedding. In the Chicago Art Museum, Lucy and Harry quarrel about modes of representation as they stand before an exhibit of French Impressionists. Outraged, Harry "began pointing out figures that were not correctly drawn" (101). Lucy, however, reads the paintings with more flexibility and humility: "I don't know anything about pictures, but I think some are meant to represent objects, and others are meant to express a kind of feeling merely, and then accuracy doesn't matter" (101). What Lucy discusses is the artistic and philosophical basis of impressionism, perhaps best exemplified in the Impressionists' painting the same scene as a series, representing the way time alters and transforms everything in life, though each individual painting captures light and life in a moment before it

becomes subject to change. One can "read" an Impressionist painting
moreover, only by standing some distance from it. The painting's subject
and essence are visible only from "a long distance . . . a long perspective"
(38), that position Lucy feels Sebastian adopts toward his songs, his art.
One reads best, in other words, through the recall of memory. Throughout the novel, in fact, distance from a person allows one to read that
person fairly: Sebastian understands his failed relationships in Book one;
Lucy realizes the meaning of Sebastian's life in Book two, and Harry
remembers Lucy's best self without recrimination in Book three. The
narrative suggests this relation between remembrance and correct interpretation when Lucy hears Sebastian sing for the first time: "She kept
feeling that this was not an interpretation, this was the thing itself" (38).
One apprehends truth (the thing itself) through feeling, and this truth is
best conveyed when once removed, when it has become fixed in the
memory or created as a text. Yet truth cannot, paradoxically, be defined
in language. It exists within the "invisible, inviolable world" of memory
and of feeling: "Sebastian was listening not to what she said, but to the
rush of feeling in her warm young voice. There is no way to define that
ring of truth in a voice, he was thinking, and no mistaking it (85). Truth
may be inexplicable and ambiguous, as the text claims, but it also
undeniably exists; there is "no mistaking it." When Lucy realizes that
words can have more value than "their direct meaning" (95), it is not so
much an indirect, as it is an inexpressible and "inviolable," meaning that
we, as readers, are directed to accept. *Lucy Gayheart* demands that we
recognize its "truth" and its "meaning" about art, memory, and relationships, though it refuses resolutely to define either.

Because "truth" in this novel is a "felt" rather than an articulated
concept, it becomes especially difficult to create a "true" reading of Lucy
and to locate Lucy's "true" reading of herself. As the lesson of her
awakening through Sebastian grows increasingly abstract, so too does
her language. Near the end of Book one and throughout Book two, her
feelings are conveyed obscurely and ambivalently by a floating signifier
that confounds the reader's ability to assign meaning altogether.

> That happiness she had so lately found, where was *it?* Everything threat-
> ened *it,* the way of the world was against *it. It* had escaped her. She had lost
> *it* as one can lose a ravishing melody, remembering the mood of *it,* the
> kind of joy *it* gave, but unable to recall precisely the air itself. And she
> couldn't breathe in *this other kind of life. It* stifled her, woke in her a frantic

fear—the fear of falling back into *it* forever. If only one could lose one's life and one's body and be nothing but one's desire; if the rest could melt away, and *that* could float with the gulls, out yonder where the blue and green *were changing!* (102, emphasis added)

This passage begins with a tangible "happiness" and ends with dissolution ("were changing"), moving from the apprehensible to the abstract. And this inability to accept change is Lucy's main problem. As her happiness dissolves throughout the passage—turning from a relationship she has "lately found," to a relationship that has "escaped her" and that she has "lost," to a remembrance of its "mood" and "the kind of joy it gave," to a horror of living without it perpetually, to death ("If only one could lose one's life") and, finally, to disembodied reduction as desire itself—so too does "it" become more variable in its meaning, signifying transcendence and terror simultaneously. Because Lucy cannot have what "it" originally signifies ("That happiness"), she becomes subject to such a profound loss of "meaning" that she herself desires to die and be transformed into her own floating signifier, an essence "that could float with the gulls, out yonder, where the blue and green were changing." The passage's transparent allusion to Chopin's *The Awakening* in its last sentence suggests how far Lucy has come, and how far she still has to go. Like Edna Pontellier, Lucy envisions death as the culmination of her desire because "the way of the world was against it." The difference, however, is that Lucy desires this death before she really awakens in the second book to the realization that "remembering the mood of it, the kind of joy it gave" is all one can reasonably expect in life. And although the text will arrive at its heroine's understanding and acceptance of desire itself as a floating and abstract signifier ("the mood of *it*"), the novel will also transform her into the figure of itself as a text. While Lucy Gayheart may learn a different lesson than Edna Pontellier, her end remains the same. She too awakens into death, even as her death is rendered as life transformed into art.

The end of Book one and the beginning of Book two increase the reader's distance from Lucy by exaggerating the spectatorial nature of reading. We do not, for instance, witness or experience Lucy's reactions to and feelings about Sebastian's death; she, like him, simply slips out of the narrative and is presented in absentia, "as if she were a memory" already (38). Instead, the Auerbachs happen upon the story of Sebastian's death in a newspaper (137–38); they will then tell Lucy about the story they have read, which is itself an eye-witness account narrated by the sole survivor of the accident, the Belgian violinist, Gustave Wierta. The narrative constructs a double or even triple distancing from those reactions that would augment our sense of Lucy as a character. She is already, to some degree, turning into the fixed symbol into which she will be transformed at the end of the text.

When Book two begins, the novel returns to an externally focalized narration that describes Haverford life in 1902. Some details of no consequence, such as the fact that "cloth tailored suits" (143) have come into fashion, are juxtaposed against more allusive and portentous comments like: "rainfall had been scant and the corn burned in the tassel" (143). While the narrative hints at the tragedy to come, Lucy is again framed, literally from the perspective of Mrs. Alec Ramsay, who watches her out the window. To her, Lucy appears as a "diminishing figure" (146) who now walks not "as if she were hurrying toward something delightful" but "as if she were running away from something, or walking merely to tire herself out" (146). The distinguishing difference in her characteristic walk is the first narrative signal that something has happened to her. By the end of the text her walk is all that will remain. Lucy Gayheart has already begun her reduction and petrification into symbol.

Much of the action of the second book is Lucy's obsessive desire to make some kind of connection with Harry Gordon, who treats her politely but with exaggerated reserve and distance. Lucy dogs his footsteps around Haverford much the same way she shadowed Sebastian in Chicago before she knew him, believing that Harry is the "one person in Haverford [who] could help her" (148). While it is not exactly clear what Lucy wants from Harry, two assumptions seem close to the matter. First, Lucy wants to repair their friendship for she realizes that "she ha[s] lost an old friend" (130), something that Sebastian had warned her about earlier: "things happen to our friendships; that's the worst about living. Young people can't know what it means" (83). Feeling herself bereft and completely alone, Lucy now tries to rekindle some kind of intimacy with Harry on her own terms: "It would be enough if he would stop on the street-corner occasionally and tell her a funny story in his real voice, which very few people ever heard, and look at her with real kindness that used to be like a code sign between them whenever they met" (150). This "code sign," however, has become confused by different desires and interpretations. In refusing Harry's rather boorish offer of marriage— "And now isn't it about time we got down to business?" (108)—Lucy has ruptured their usually unvoiced communication system. She can no longer have access to Harry's "real voice" or "real kindness" because she has frustrated his desires and he has withdrawn himself out of pride and the desire to punish her. Because their separate desires can find no common ground on which to meet, Harry's friendship remains yet another relationship irrevocably lost for Lucy.

If one is struck by what appears to be Lucy's denseness, her selfish inability to understand why things can't go back to being the same with Harry, equally disturbing is Lucy's diction when she voices these desires to herself.

> Perhaps it was because he was big and strong, and a little hard. He knew the world better than anyone else here, he had some imagination. He rose and fell, he was alive, he moved. He was not anchored, he was not lazy, he was not a sheep. Conceited and canny he was most days of the month; but on occasion something flashed out of him. There was a man underneath all those layers of caution; he wasn't tame at the core. If he should put his hand on her, or look directly into her eyes and flash the old signal, she believed it would waken something and start the machinery going to carry her along. (175)

Lucy yearns for the vitality Harry embodies; he has imagination, life, movement, flashes of decisive action. What she desires in him is that same reactivating life force Sebastian saw in her. Lucy, in short, wants Harry to give her reasons to live again. Yet to this revivifying power Lucy connects Harry's virility; it is male authority and perhaps even a suggestion of phallic power that she thinks will "make something and start the machinery going to carry her along." Harry is "big and strong, and a little hard"; he "rose and fell"; he is a "man" who isn't "tame at the core." Most suggestive though is Lucy's fantasy of the way Harry will "waken" her; she conceives it almost as a benediction of male authority, as if Harry possesses the healing power of Christ: "If he should put his hand on her . . . she believed." Although Lucy's language explicitly signals the awakening to come, it is still an awakening enacted through men. She and the narrative have not yet abandoned the tradition that the novel will, finally, attempt to revise.

The most salient feature of Lucy's awakening is not its activation by or through a man, but rather its origin in the music of a woman. Taken by her father to the opera one night, Lucy hears an aging soprano infuse life into art: "Her voice was worn, to be sure, like her face, and there was not

much physical sweetness left in it. But there was another kind of sweetness; a sympathy, a tolerant understanding. She gave the old songs, even
the most hackneyed, their full value" (181). Most telling about Lucy's
development in this passage is the shift from "physical sweetness"—
sexuality, romance—to a more abstract and vague sweetness, an approach to life from a perspective of "sympathy" and "tolerant understanding" much like the way Sebastian himself lived: "His manner, when
she was with him, was that of a man who has an easy, if somewhat
tolerant, enjoyment of life" (52). Equally striking is Lucy's internalization
of this knowledge.

> The wandering singer had struck something in her that went on vibrating;
> something that was like a purpose forming, and she could not stop it.
> When she awoke in the morning, it was still there, beating like another
> heart. Day after day it kept up in her. She could give her attention to other
> things, but it was always there. She felt as if she were standing on the edge
> of something, about to take some plunge or departure. (181–82)

In this passage, Lucy is no longer merely acted upon; it marks the first
real time that she begins to change from within. This time the abstract
and floating signifiers (it, something) become synthesized as part of her
person ("it was still there, beating like another heart") rather than as
disembodied desire. Lucy too is no longer waiting for something to carry
her; she is "standing on the edge of something, about to take some
plunge or departure," the two options that, the text seems to signal,
constitute the possible plot lines for this kind of story.

Lucy reaches her apotheosis of understanding on Christmas Eve,
undergoing a kind of figurative rebirth. Again the narrative veils in
oblique language and refuses to signify what "it" is Lucy has finally
grasped. It reveals only that "Clement Sebastian had made the fugitive
gleam an actual possession" (183) and that with him Lucy has "learned
that those flashes of promise could come true, that they could be the
important things in one's life" (183–84). Of special significance in this
moment is Lucy's release from the desire to possess Sebastian himself.
She realizes that "he was, in his own person, the door and the way to that
knowledge" (184). The complete refusal of the narrative to signify gleam,
promise, or knowledge is the central, and problematic, revisionary moment in this text. For Lucy cannot reshape her desire for Sebastian into
an acceptance of his symbolic import if her "awakening" relies upon
sexuality and romantic love. What she awakens to must be necessarily

abstract so that when she asks herself: "How could she go on, alone?" (184), she can make the required transference from dependence on men to an acceptance of life: "What if—what if Life itself were the sweetheart? . . . Oh, now she knew! She must have it, she couldn't run away from it. She must go back into the world and get all she could of everything that had made him what he was" (184). The floating signifier "it" has finally become something not beyond Lucy's grasp or something she is at the mercy of (102), or even something undefined growing inside her (182). "It" is now something she believes herself capable of possessing. And when her "awakening" chapter ends with *the* definitive assertion of self-control and self-possession—"She must look out for herself from now on, and she would do it" (186)—Lucy seems at last to be under her own power. It is almost possible to believe she will depart rather than plunge to her death.

Lucy Gayheart remains, however, a failed attempt to revise what Cather complained was the chief failure of awakening novels, that is, the debilitating limitations of their female protagonists. Cather's text does revise the kind of awakening its heroine will have, and then it blithely marches her off to a version of the suicide with which these novels end. This essential ambivalence of *Lucy Gayheart*, its simultaneous revision of and rigid adherence to a novelistic tradition of female failure, is one of its more interesting problems. After Lucy's awakening the narrative immediately undercuts her newfound sense of self and purpose. The text contradicts itself, for instance, when after her awakening Lucy reverts to a longing for Harry's masculine power.

> If only she could have that strength behind her instead of against her! It was more than physical strength; it was something that could keep up to the bitter end, that could take hold and never let go. She was so without any such power that even to think of it heartened her a little. . . . He was full of that energy which moves quietly, but always moves. It might get a man almost anywhere, she thought. And the people who hadn't it, even those with nice tastes, like her father, never got anywhere. (189)

Is this simple regression? Has Lucy's awakening been an elaborate narrative ruse? Perhaps not entirely. There is a way to place this passage within the scheme of Lucy's awakening, and that way is through juxtaposition and comparison. Lucy longs for Harry's power and energy not for its own sake, but almost out of envy because it "moves" one so effortlessly: "It might get a man almost anywhere, she thought." There seems to be some allusion to traditions contained within this passage. Harry has the character to be a character in a bildungsroman, a character who has the power to move and to rise in the world. Lucy, by implicit comparison, does not. Harry's energy allows him to be a figure who "always moves"; Lucy will end up as a figure reduced to and held in static tension as three remaining footsteps going nowhere forever. Thus it becomes especially sardonic that Lucy's goal is to rent Sebastian's studio, because she has absolutely no conception of how she can earn money in order to make her own way (190). Lucy Gayheart has only male figures on whom to model herself; their power and potential success are not available to her as examples that she can follow. The real tragedy of *Lucy Gayheart* is that even while the heroine escapes one avenue of limited and delusive awakening, the text is unable to negotiate her entrance into the "social script" of a world that cannot place her in anything other than a love relation.[24]

The most immediately accessible woman on whom Lucy might possibly model herself is her older sister, Pauline, introduced in the second book as "a much more complex person than" Lucy (168). Much of the narrative of Book two centers on Pauline, and her prominence suggests an explicit textual comparison between the kind of life each sister finds herself in. For Lucy and Pauline are caught in a family drama where the split between female aspiration and female sacrifice affects both in equally limiting ways. Pauline has not only raised Lucy after their mother's death, she has also occupied in Haverford the role of Lucy's effaced and forgotten mother.

> It was not until Lucy was old enough to go to high school that Pauline began to be jealous of her. Then she realized that everyone, even the Lutheran pastor and the Frau Pastor, had one manner with her and another with Lucy. Mrs. Ramsay and Harry Gordon's mother were always sending for Lucy on one pretext or another. Pauline was asked to their houses only when they gave a church supper, or a benefit for the firemen. And Lucy's father spoiled her; that was Pauline's sorest jealousy. If at breakfast she told Lucy to come directly home after school and help her with the ironing, Mr. Gayheart was very apt to say that she must stop first at the shop and do her practising. (169–70)

Focalized through Pauline's consciousness, the narrative lists her painful snubs and very real grievances. Although Lucy has not "the least idea of what Pauline was really like—never considered it" (171–72), it is difficult for a reader to ignore the suggestion that Pauline's dull and unrewarding life is what Lucy's life could have become had not Pauline's hard work made it possible for her father to insist that Lucy "grow up at the piano" (170). Lucy's and Pauline's lives are two halves of one whole, knotted most tightly through economics: "Lucy had earned nothing during her first two winters in Chicago. Mr. Gayheart paid for her lessons and her living expenses. That was why he was always short of money, and why Pauline had to raise onions" (172). Pauline *must* raise onions so Lucy, who "earned nothing," can continue with her music in an exciting world far beyond Pauline's most suppressed desires or imaginings. One goes *because* the other stays. And herein lies another salient difference between the awakening and the bildungsroman traditions. Most male protagonists go out into the world and earn their own living. They do not live well at first and usually sacrifice a number of things as the price they must pay to secure a position in the world. Lucy cannot and will not make the same sacrifices. The implication in her earlier conversation about professions with Auerbach is that it is even difficult for "women with great talent and great ambition" to make their own way in the world, much less for Lucy (134). This seems to be a dark comment on the cost of any female ambition in a world that will not allow women to pay their own way. Yet Lucy has no desire even to do this. When Pauline complains that "more than sixteen hundred dollars you cost us in those first three years. . . . You might have sent back just a little after you began to earn something, to show good intentions" (191), Lucy replies with complete unconcern: "I thought of it, but I bought clothes instead" (192). Pauline is not only an antimodel for Lucy—what she fears her life will become if she stays in Haverford—but also an ironic signal for the reader to realize that Pauline has become what she is *because* of Lucy's life. Hers is the other story in *Lucy Gayheart,* and in featuring her prominently in Book two, the text continues to chart ambivalently its evocation of Lucy's awakening. Sebastian's music may allow Lucy to overreach herself, but Pauline is the one who foots the bills.

Lucy Gayheart's death is rendered no less ambivalently than her life. Quarreling with Pauline because she refuses to take piano pupils and earn some money while in Haverford, Lucy storms out of the house intent on skating. Lucy's direction, however, is regressive; she heads west instead of east toward her anticipated new life in Chicago. The snowstorm outside balances the rage she feels inside, and yet nature soon wins out. Cold and depressed, Lucy longs to return home. When Harry

Gordon happens by in his cutter, Lucy asks for a lift and is politely refused. Outraged by his spite, Lucy reacts in a way that demonstrates her newfound authority at the same time that it undermines it: "Lucy sent just one cry after him, angry and imperious, 'Harry!' as if she had the right to call him back" (197). Though her "imperious" anger evinces more power than she has heretofore displayed, the narrative seems to question subtly her "right to call him back," as if Lucy has less right to this authority than she might think. Maddened by both Harry and Pauline, Lucy reverts to simple physical sensation: "she forgot to look where she put her feet; they took care of themselves" (197). Since her feet lead her to her death, are we directed to read "they took care of themselves" as an indication of Lucy's responsibility for her own violent death? In keeping with the contradiction so prevalent in this novel, yes and no seem to be the appropriate answer. When Lucy begins to be dominated by her passion—a revisionary passion of feeling rather than of sexuality—she becomes incapable of reason: "Her blood was racing, and she was no longer conscious of the cold . . . she saw nothing (198). It is because of her unthinking, passionate response that when her feet take "care of themselves" they lead her to her death. Lucy, like other awakening heroines, is at the last too given over to emotion and not ruled enough by reason, and this one-sidedness brings about her inevitable destruction.

Yet even at the moment of her death, the text does not allow us to dismiss Lucy's fate as entirely and unambivalently inevitable. We are, I believe, encouraged by the narrative to hope that she might survive.

> Lucy was more stimulated than frightened; she had got herself into a predicament, and she must keep her wits about her. The water couldn't be very deep. She still had both elbows on the ice; as soon as she touched bottom she could manage. (It never occurred to her that this was the river itself.) She was groping cautiously with her feet when she felt herself gripped from underneath. Her skate had caught in the fork of a submerged tree, half-buried in sand by the spring flood. The ice cake slipped from under her arms and let her down. (199)

There is virtually no way to read this passage without recognizing Lucy's development as a self-sufficient character. At the moment of danger she becomes reasonable, calm, and self-possessed. No longer acting blindly, she "gropes cautiously" with her feet and keeps "her wits about her." And though Lucy's feet may have inadvertently delivered her into this predicament, she dies because something inanimate pulls her down: "she felt herself gripped by something underneath." Lucy's final movement in the novel epitomizes her predicament throughout; she struggles upward while something unseen beneath makes it impossible for her to free herself. Caught in this tenuous position, she neither gives up nor conquers. As she has been carried or swept along throughout most of the novel, here too she becomes more a pawn than a person. Lucy Gayheart is, finally, given over to death. She never fully possesses any power or choice.

Lucy's final enclosure in one of the "wagons crawling along the frozen land" (201) suggests that the novel has itself reached closure; *Lucy Gayheart* the text will end with the death of Lucy Gayheart, the protagonist. This neat structure is underscored by a seemingly tidy imagery. Lucy, still in motion, is transported back into Haverford rather than away from it for good, and she will be buried in the town she sought to escape at the beginning of the novel. This death procession has a sense of waste, of tragic irony, of climax. It has the sense of an ending.

Yet curiously the novel does not end. Lucy Gayheart, both the character and the novel which we have come to identify as *her* story, becomes entombed within the third book of the novel, a book that constitutes a kind of overplot to the story of her awakening. This third book is Harry Gordon's story: literally what has happened to him twenty-five years after her death, and fictionally, since the selectively omniscient narrative voice here is located in his consciousness. Cather herself "suggested that the novel doesn't pull together until one reads the last part,"[25] and most critics have tended to agree with this assessment, believing the third book to be an integral part of the structure proper that "ties up ends and underlines meaning."[26] Yet there remains something profoundly unsettling about giving over the narrative to the man who has just inadvertently brought about the death of the novel's heroine. Even more troubling is the fact that Harry Gordon inherits not only narrative authority, but the physical possessions of Lucy Gayheart and her family as well. He has not only the last word, but also the last artifacts of her existence. Ultimately these two are crucially linked. The memories of Lucy Gayheart which Gordon muses over in this third book are events we have already encountered in the novel. Thus Harry becomes a reader of the text already represented, an interpreter not only of Lucy's life, but also of her death. And, significantly, these memories he mulls over during an evening are a piece of writing as well. They have a certain order. They present Lucy in a certain light. They attempt to capture her as a fiction. In this way, Harry scripts the final picture of Lucy; he possesses her imaginatively as surely as he possesses her dresses, her music, her picture of Sebastian, and her father's house. His is the final voice we hear. His version of her is the one with which we are left. The question is: Ought we to be content with this? Can we read it literally?

The narrative presents two different readings of Lucy's story before we encounter Harry's longer one. They have the effect of highlighting an awareness of the different stories Lucy has now become, and they elicit a reading of Harry's version as simply that, another story about Lucy Gayheart. The first allusion suggests how *Lucy Gayheart* has deviated from the usual marriage plot conventions of tales about growing young women: "And now the story was finished: no grandchildren, complete oblivion" (207). Society does, however, recall Lucy as a tragic figure, suggested by its memory of her as "a bird being shot when it rises in its morning flight toward the sun" (207), a metaphor that echoes imagery used to describe Edna Pontellier in *The Awakening*.[27] These two different scripts of Lucy's story reinforce an ironic perspective that underlies Book three. And though the narrative directs us to read Harry Gordon with a "tolerant sympathy" because "he has much to bear" (208), we are nonetheless aware of the difference between Harry's position as *the* subject and focalizer of the last book, and Lucy's position as *the* textual subject of *his* focalization and interpretation.

Harry Gordon supplants Lucy, both in the text as her story becomes the subject of his narration, and in her family as he develops a relationship with Mr. Gayheart that is "like a son's regard, indeed" (210). Yet Harry Gordon's relationship with Mr. Gayheart involves not only an inheritance of property, but, characteristically, repayment as well. For if Harry's "friendship with Mr. Gayheart had been a solace," it is also "like an act of retribution" (222). It is an act of atonement for Lucy's death whose recipient is her father. Ironically, Lucy becomes the catalyst for a masculine network of textual and familial relations.

In one respect, Harry's own life story is the bildungsroman Lucy Gayheart's story could never be. Although he evaluates his present life as utterly different "from the life young Harry Gordon planned" (209), he has nonetheless achieved social and financial success. He owns "the first car in the county" and "his farms were scattered far and wide" (221). He is also president of the Haverford bank, and in his youth he went abroad "with an ambulance unit which he had helped to finance" to aid in the allied struggle of World War I (210). Harry's life is, however, "dull" and "empty." He has attained the worldly success that eluded Lucy's grasp, yet he suffers from an emotional impoverishment that she never felt. Both, ironically, embody attributes that the other lacks. Each of their stories within their respective traditions remains incomplete in some significant way.

One character who seems to have bridged this gendered gap is Harriet Arkwright. She reappears in Book three as the complement of Lucy and as an indication of what Lucy's story might have, and perhaps even should have, become. Harriet, in many ways the ambitious female twin of Harry, not only takes "his place as president of the bank and manager of all his business interests" (210) while he is in Europe but also, the narrative informs us, finds unique fulfillment in this active role: "That was probably the happiest period of her life" (210). Harriet's inclusion both in this chapter and in the novel entire is more than as a romantic foil to Lucy, more than simply the other choice Harry has with regard to wives. For here, as in Book one, Harriet's presence reiterates both female activity and female power; she has discovered a way of life that allows her to exercise her own power successfully. Her marriage to Harry, however, is not as successful. It remains a cordial but contractual agreement rather than a marriage of sympathy. The narrative seems to suggest that Harriet has attained what Lucy could not because she marries Harry Gordon, while it also describes the emotional inadequacy of their relationship because they are too similar, too much alike. Lucy seems to be suggested as the character who would be Harry's proper partner. One implication is that marriage to Harry might have really been the *right* ending to Lucy's story. Yet Harriet's brief history at the end of the novel also raises implicitly the issue of gendered scripts generally. Beyond Lucy and the question of "awakening," the stories of both Harry and Harriet underscore the ways in which conventional, societal expectations determine the scripts within which men and women struggle to be the authors of their own identities.[28]

Harry Gordon's narration in chapter three, though, necessarily forces the reader to question whether marriage would have, or indeed could have, been the correct solution to Lucy's dilemma. Although his focalization does adhere to the pattern of memory in which Sebastian and Lucy also participate, it does incite questions about both what and how Harry remembers. The chapter begins in Harry's memory: "Tonight was an occasion for remembering; he felt it coming on" (214). The narrative

occasion here is the filling in of Book two's absent story, the answer to
why Gordon behaves as he does to Lucy. Harry's memory, as it composes
the narrative of the chapter, moves from regret, to desire, to anger, to
reconciliation with what has been lost, and finally to artistic distance.

Initially, the narrative records Harry's honest assessment of his behavior through the clarifying lens of hindsight: "In looking back over his
life . . . he had begun to understand it a little better" (214). The narrative
touches on his regret over his "hasty marriage" (214) to Harriet, his
knowledge that Lucy "wanted him to help her" (216), his confusion, his
bitterness at being rejected ("she deserved to be punished" [216]), and
his "contrary conviction [that] . . . after they had both been punished
enough, something would happen . . . he and Lucy would be together
again" (217).

Harry's remembered projection of what the conclusion of his relationship with Lucy will be is presented ironically in the narrative: "A
man who is young and strong looks forward. If he has been a fool
and thwarted his own will—that is temporary" (217). Yet the language
through which he remembers these desires is more than a little disquiet-
ing. Harry's articulation in this passage essentially is derived from a
diction of dominance. He not only "knows he is going to have his own
way" (217), but "the certainty of his ultimate mastery stirred in him like
something alive. When the hour struck, nothing could stop him" (217).
He, in his own way, is as much a romantic as Lucy, believing that if only
he could have "walked home with Lucy" the night he sees her at Mrs.
Ramsay's, "everything would have come out right" (217). What Harry
wants, however, even if it is recalled as a past longing, nonetheless
remains the antithesis of what Lucy claims she wants. The "nice house
and garden in a little town, with money enough not to worry, a family"
(134) that Auerbach envisions as the only future "for a girl like you, Lucy"
(134), she compares to being buried alive: "It's being planted in the earth,
like one of your carrots there. I'd rather be pulled up and thrown away"
(134). And while Lucy's words are truer than she realizes, it isn't clear that
marriage to Harry, or even romantic escape from Haverford with him,
would have been better. The simple fact that "Harry had never doubted
what the end would be" (217) bodes ill for a female heroine trying to
locate and define the self. Harry, it seems, would have ended Lucy's story
with marriage, while Lucy, ironically, wants to begin creating the self
alone at that moment. There can be no reconciliation between the two;

Lucy neither marries nor matures. Death constitutes the only possible ending to her story.

Harry's narration begins to turn Lucy's story into art, to endow her death with some kind of meaning. Harry is, at this moment, both a spokesman for Cather's own transformation of her subject into text (from Lucy Gayheart to *Lucy Gayheart*), and its ambivalent advocate. For even as Harry narrates Lucy into art, the reader is forced to question nothing less than her own complicity in dismantling Lucy's story. If we accept the diminution of her suffering compared to Harry's ("Lucy had suffered for a few hours, a few weeks at most. But with him it was there to stay" [221]), if we accept him as not only the contiguous but also the continuous narrative voice of the novel, then we, by implication, agree with him about Lucy that "perhaps it was no great loss to have missed two thirds of her life, if she had the best third, and had been so young,— so heedlessly young" (222). This is difficult to do since within Harry's narrative we discover violent evidence of Lucy's struggle to stay alive inscribed even into her flesh: "The cuts on her wrists and hands showed that she had struggled to cling to the ice" (219).

Once Lucy's life has been assessed and her death rationalized, the narrative begins the process of abstracting Lucy into both memory and muse: "In spite of all the misery he had been through on her account, Lucy was the best thing he had to remember. When he looked back into the past, there was just one face, one figure, that was mysteriously lovely" (223). What most characterizes this passage is the metamorphosis of Lucy the person into Lucy the objet d'art. Harry's stance toward this Lucy—"the best *thing* he had to remember"—recalls another Lucy transformed into art, the "Lucy" of Wordsworth's poems who also "seemed a thing that could not feel / The touch of earthly years."[29] In Harry's memory "Lucy Gayheart is no longer a despairing little creature standing in the icy wind and lifting beseeching eyes to him" (224), though this too is a recollection rewritten by Harry's need for ultimate mastery since Lucy's last stance with him is actually "angry and imperious" (197). Instead she has been transformed through his memory into art and into abstraction: "She has receded to the far horizon line, along with all the fine things of youth, which do not change" (224). Lucy becomes a memory, a touchstone for Harry's lost youth and, by the novel's end, art itself. In other words, she has become all those things that the narrative values as best and most sustaining in life. Yet to become these "things"

Lucy has had to be killed off; she dies into art. And, as Susan J. Rosowski has persuasively argued, the reader both knows and feels acutely the contradiction inherent in this ending. Writing about the conclusions to both *Lucy Gayheart* and *Sapphira and the Slave Girl*, Rosowski contends that "Cather used the endings of these novels to remind her reader of culturally mandated conventions. . . . By their conventionality, these endings would erase the fictions that preceded them. . . . In each, the traditional elements of strong endings evoke an immediate sense of satisfaction. Yet each evokes also an aftereffect with the realization that dark questions remain unresolved."[30] It is, finally, this tension between Cather's fiction of failed female development and the narrative's progressive development of Lucy into a fiction that will be inscribed into the novel as that ambivalent sign of arrested motion, those three cement footsteps fleeing and frozen, that constitutes the final reductive riddle of the text itself.

These three footsteps couple the story of Lucy's awakening with the text's self-conscious representation of itself as art. They embody "the straight, slender foot of a girl of thirteen, delicately and clearly stamped in the grey-white composition" (226). Lucy's assertion of self and her inclination toward impulse are preserved in stone, just as her story is preserved as the novel itself.

> He noticed a slip of a girl in boy's overalls, barefoot, running about the flower garden, watering it with a length of rubber hose. . . . She had not seen him. Suddenly she dropped the hose, glanced back at the house to make sure no one was observing her, and darted forward. She cleared the mason's cord and ran over those wet slabs—one, two, three steps, then out into the weeds beside the road, almost in front of Harry. She looked up at him and laughed. (225–26)

This passage encodes the potential for self-assertion and self-possession that Lucy has not been able to live up to in the novel, and about which, at least in this instance, the novel seems to express a kind of regret. Lucy here is no longer a child but not yet a woman, acting out her defiance at social conventions, purposefully ignoring areas forbidden to her. Significantly, she is attired in "boy's overalls," is barefoot, wields "a length of rubber hose," and as usual, is in motion, "running about the flower garden." Her act of darting forward, clearing the mason's cord, and leaving three running footsteps attests to her desire to escape, to leap beyond the possibilities, or lack of them, which the small town contains.

The sidewalk itself is the novel in miniature. Although the three footsteps signify Lucy's desire for life, they are both abbreviated and held in check the same way that the novel itself encloses her development in its three books. They suggest movement, but remain fixed. Like "this very side-walk which was never to go any further" (225), Lucy's desires, the possibilities her awakening suggests, and her progress into the world are arrested within the novel of awakening. The text itself is a "grey-white composition," capturing "some baffling suggestion of quick motion in those impressions" (227). *This* female novel of development, the text seems to suggest, must arrest its heroine into art since no other plot will express or contain her contradictions adequately. The three footsteps, in "very low relief" become a symbol for Lucy's revised but still ambivalent awakening (226). They are, finally, the only marks that Lucy Gayheart will ever make in the world.

This disjunctive and deconstructive tension "between a plot that charts development and a plot that unravels it"[31] is what renders *Lucy Gayheart* the novel as enigmatic and undecipherable as the three foot-steps, frozen in flight, which stand as the final reduction from language to artifact. It is Cather's most ambivalent text about how one tells the stories of women who are neither as powerful nor as provocative as novelistic conventions dictate. The novel remains vivid and even poi-gnant as a philosophical fiction concerned with the imaginative transfor-mation of life into memory and, finally, into art. Lucy Gayheart the character is revivified as a text, much the same way that the narrator of "Lucy Gray" insists: "—Yet some maintain that to this day / She is a living child" (ll. 57–58). Yet *Lucy Gayheart* is also a bleak look at the failure inherent within fictions of female development. Though perceived to be Cather's most failed novel, it is, in the end, too good at capturing life, at arresting those three footsteps in flight, when what we really want, though it is impossible, is for those feet to keep running, to find an avenue of escape both in life and within the fiction itself.

6

Enslaved by History:
The Burden of the Past and
Cather's Last Novel

The nigger boy who plays by ear on his fiddle airs from *Traviata*
without knowing what he is playing, or why he likes it, has more
real understanding of Italian art than these aesthetic creatures [club
women] with a head and a larynx, and no organs that they get any
use of, who reel you off the life of Leonardo da Vinci.
                                                    —WILLA CATHER, 1921

A stereotype is an already read text.
                            —BARBARA JOHNSON, *A World of Difference*

There is a story about Willa Cather's early life in Virginia, a tale recounted by her biographers,[1] that usually appears to demonstrate Cather's plain, stubborn willfulness and her refusal to accede to the "feminine" codes of behavior dictated both by her family and by the rural
Virginia society in which she was raised. At the age of three, Cather was
summoned to the parlor to meet an aged and imposing southern judge,
and instructed to say "Hello" or "Howdy-do, pleased to meet you"; this
might perhaps have been followed by a curtsey. Instead, Cather planted
herself before the old man and declared "I'se a dangerous nigger, I is,"
much to the consternation and, one suspects, repressed amusement of
her family. It is one of those tales of childhood transgressions, forgiven in
the telling, since it illustrates comically impulses that have since been
repressed and channeled into more civilized and appropriate social
behavior.

Race has frequently been an unspoken issue in criticism of Cather's
fiction because, like the offhand comment in the epigraph quoted above,

Cather's racial sensibilities are likely to strike the modern reader as less than enlightened, to say the least. As in her portrait of blues musician Blind d'Arnault in *My Antonia* (1918), African heritage for Cather frequently signifies some preternatural artistic (musical) talent. Combining gross stereotyping with a not unsympathetic description, Cather's portrait of Blind d'Arnault, for instance, employs a diction of racial difference to simultaneously praise his talent while stressing his irrevocable, and implicitly denegrating, otherness.

> It was the soft, amiable Negro voice, like those I remembered from early childhood, with the note of docile subservience in it. He had the Negro head, too; almost no head at all; nothing behind the ears but folds of neck under close-clipped wool. He would have been repulsive if his face had not been so kindly and happy. . . . He could never learn [to play the piano] like other people, never acquired any finish. He was always a Negro prodigy who played barbarously and wonderfully. As piano-playing, it was perhaps abominable, but as music it was something real, vitalized by a sense of rhythm that was stronger than his other physical senses—that not only filled his dark mind, but worried his body incessantly. To hear him, to watch him, was to see a Negro enjoying himself as only a Negro can.[2]

To dismiss Cather as a regressive racist, however, is to ignore the ways in which her novels participate in and are informed by what Bell Hooks calls "a discourse on race that interrogates whiteness," however inadvertently.[3] And nowhere is this discourse more insistently foregrounded than in Cather's cryptic and final novel, *Sapphira and the Slave Girl* (1940), whose narrative is focused not on African-American exceptionalism, but rather on the suspicions, sadism, and sexual oppression implicit within the system of antebellum slavery.

Sapphira and the Slave Girl is a text that has supported numerous biographical readings, since it is Cather's last major fiction about her earliest memories. Both Phyllis Robinson and Sharon O'Brien begin their narratives by reading the novel as a chronicle of Cather's early history in Virginia; the text for them constitutes a return to origins, a conduit to Cather's narrative genesis.[4] O'Brien, in particular, sees the novel as Cather's return, full circle, to acknowledge what she calls "the writer's debt to the women storytellers of her childhood."[5] Judith Fryer has also read the novel this way, arguing even more pointedly that "the bonding of women, is literally the story—not only the plot of the novel, but the legend told and retold as a story and remembered as the signifi-

cant event in the childhood of the storyteller."[6] This particular interpretation focuses on the Epilogue within the novel entitled "Nancy's
Return" (273–95). The Epilogue employs a first-person address, in which
the narrator situates herself as a small child in Back Creek who has
listened to and remembered stories about the characters in the novel we
have just read, *and* who witnesses the reunion of the escaped slave,
Nancy, now a grown woman, with her mother, Till. Cather herself
stressed the literal nature of this novel in letters to Viola Roseboro,
insisting that "the book is so full of old family and neighborhood tales
that it might be considered largely non-fiction."[7] Cather's self-conscious,
and for her, unusual, erasure of the difference between personal, historical "fact" and fiction makes possible O'Brien's conflation of authorial
and textual narrative with her claim "that the child—who grew up to
become the author Willa Cather—is indeed telling that story herself,
both passing on the tales she once heard in the Willow Shade kitchen and
proclaiming herself the inheritor of a tradition of female narrative."[8]

But to focus solely on Cather's inheritance of a female narrative
tradition is to ignore the brutal manifestations of power relations within
the institution of slavery—especially as practiced by Sapphira upon
Nancy—which constitute the plot and all the action of this curiously
meditative narrative. Cather herself argued that she was trying to capture
something pervasive and evil within the domestic daily life of antebellum
Virginia, something that she referred to only as "the Terrible."[9] Recently,
Elizabeth Fox-Genovese, drawing from diaries and letters, has refuted
the claim that a community of women, black and white, existed in southern plantation societies. According to Fox-Genovese, women's work and
social roles confined them to plantation households where they coex-
isted "in the explosive intimacy of a shared world but not in a women's
sphere," owing to the sometimes subtle but nonetheless established
hierarchy of race and domination. Fox-Genovese concludes that under
such circumstances it is impossible to believe that a mutually supportive
community of women could exist: "Did slave and slaveholding women
share bonds? participate in a sisterhood? The simple and inescapable
answer is no."[10]

What makes a reading of female bonding problematic in *Sapphira and
the Slave Girl* is race, especially the insistent articulation of racial difference that pervades the narrative. Despite its analysis of Sapphira Colbert's power as a slaveholder to persecute and abuse Nancy, the novel's
rhetoric of race seems entirely conceived within stereotypic utterances

about the essential nature of African Americans; numerous references to "gay darkies" (70, 102), barefoot "niggers" with conspicuous white teeth displaying "eager affection" toward their "masters" (17, 34), and the "foolish, dreamy, nigger side" of Nancy's "nature" can be found throughout the narrative (178).[11] Thornier still is the claim made in the Epilogue that these stories have been passed down to the white child-narrator by Till, Nancy's mother, an assertion that further complicates and even obscures the text's attitude toward its black characters. If this novel is, on one level, about the tradition and the art of storytelling, this art, as it is reflected in the text, needs to be examined critically rather than be uncritically embraced. For to do less is to accept or ignore the politics of racial difference embedded in this narrative.

Many critics have addressed the "problematic" nature of representation in *Sapphira and the Slave Girl,* and most agree that the narrative is ambivalent in its attitudes toward its African-American characters, as well as toward Sapphira Colbert, who it regards as, paradoxically, both monstrous and admirable.[12] Part of this ambivalence stems from Cather's shifting and ambiguous focalization throughout the narrative, a characteristic that I argue frustrates the reader's desire for narrative coherence in all her late fiction. *Sapphira and the Slave Girl* employs both external and internal focalization in its narrative, alternating between the two with such abruptness and rapidity that a reader will find it difficult to locate a consistent narrative point of view. Nor does the switch to character-bound focalization in the Epilogue clarify matters, because the child narrator represents herself as one to whom these stories have been passed down; literally, she is both narratee and narrator in the Epilogue simultaneously. Though insisting that the child narrator is Cather herself may "explain" the novel's narrative riddle, it does not, however, affect the experience of reading *Sapphira and the Salve Girl,* nor does it help to illuminate the contradictory racial attitudes embodied within the novel. Ultimately, reading *Sapphira and the Slave Girl* is an experience that the critic William Curtin, with impressive understatement, characterizes as one in which "the narrative technique does not make clear the relation of the narrator to the story."[13]

The other locus of ambivalence about both race and narrative arises from the text's status as a historical novel. According to Mildred Bennett, "*Sapphira* started as a complete history of the manners and customs of the Shenandoah Valley, and wound up with Willa cutting out all background that was not essential to her story"—by Cather's estimate, "a

good six pounds."[14] Cather's emphasis on "manners and customs" as the
primary material of history suggests the similarity of *Sapphira and the
Slave Girl* to *Shadows on the Rock,* a novel that also evokes a culture
through attention to the domestic rituals of women's lives. But whereas
about *Shadows on the Rock* Cather can declare that "really, a new society
begins with the salad dressing more than with the destruction of Indian
villages," *Sapphira and the Slave Girl* cannot support such a sanguine
view of history.[15] Though Cather may have purposefully avoided Indian
wars in her novel of French colonialism in North America, she cannot
escape the fact of slavery in any fictional representation of the antebellum South. Indeed, the plot of the novel—Sapphira's persecution of
Nancy and the latter's eventual flight to safety in Canada—is concerned
solely with the dynamic of power and powerlessness that is inherent
within the culturally and legally enforced relationship of mistress and
slave. Yet *Sapphira and the Slave Girl* is also a novel about Cather's early
childhood, and when she began the novel "memories of Virginia came
flooding back."[16] Ultimately, the novel cannot reconcile the horrors of
history with its fondly evoked memories of landscape, custom, and
character, and the failure leads to an internal division that, as Hermione
Lee argues, arises from Cather's psychological investment in the story she
tells: "The family past for which personal nostalgia was felt was the slave-
owning past; the affectionate personal retrospect could not indulge the
social organization which formed the economic basis of that pastoral.
Built into Cather's domestic history of a particular West Virginian family, in the years leading up to the Civil War, was the ambivalence about
slavery which her novel re-enacted."[17]

　　Reading *Sapphira and the Slave Girl* as a historical novel, however,
depends not only upon *what* the text designates as the material(s) of its
particular history, but perhaps even more importantly, upon *how* that
history is (re)constructed into narrative. Like *Shadows on the Rock,*
Cather's last novel conceives of history as a series of tales told, as stories
passed down orally, in this case to the implied author of *Sapphira and the
Slave Girl,* the young child in the Epilogue who may or may not actually
be Willa Cather. As a consequence, the novel is extraordinarily self-
conscious about its status as fiction (a text), and as fictions of history,
those tales remembered and transmitted as the collective memory and
cultural consciousness of a particular society within a specific historical
frame. *Sapphira and the Slave Girl* is, among Cather's oeuvre, the novel
most aware of itself as a text, and it foregrounds its own artifice not only

in the Epilogue, but throughout its narrative in numerous ways. In its opening pages, for example, after introducing Henry and Sapphira Colbert at breakfast, the narrative addresses the implied reader with the sentence: "How these two came to be living at the Mill Farm is a long story—too long for a breakfast table story" (5). The appearance of such an address is singular in Cather's fiction. The narrative not only nods to its own temporality—it cannot tell their history at this moment in the text because it would require too much narrational time within the story—but it also constitutes one of the few times within Cather's work where the external focalizer, rather than rigorously effaced and effortlessly transparent, is an actual presence in the narration.

Unlike *Shadows on the Rock,* however, *Sapphira and the Slave Girl* has difficulty in reconciling its competing claims of fiction and history. Whereas the earlier novel incorporated research about seventeenth-century French Quebec into its experimental and anacoluthic structure of tale-telling as the agent of both history in general and Cather's written fiction in particular, *Sapphira and the Slave Girl* attempts to fuse fiction with what are, for Cather, "real" memories, rather than a researched and fictionally represented history. The novel seems to be divided between competing narrative impulses: to plot a tale of suspicion, jealousy, and eventual release—to create, in other words, a formal fiction—and to re-create the historical landscape of memory and of myth by participating in a storytelling tradition specific to that region and time. And by closing with the Epilogue, the text, finally, chooses historical remembrance as its primary mode of discourse. Though the novel tries, like *Shadows on the Rock,* to demonstrate the relationship of fiction and history, its narrative is unable to amalgamate the representation of power within slavery into its nostalgic remembrance of an authorial and historical past. In other words, the novel's plot and its central fiction are ultimately subordinated to the structure of historical remembrance that shapes this experimental, ambivalent, and divided text.

Sapphira and the Slave Girl is a novel whose design is determined by narrative retrospection, a stance that dominates the first half of the work. Specifically, the opening narration of *Sapphira and the Slave Girl* orients itself within the past and is especially concerned with recounting the personal histories of its characters. There are a total of fifteen such narrated histories in the novel, technically known as *anachronies:* "specific points of disparity between the temporal order of the story sequence and that of the narration." But what characterizes these histories even more precisely is that each of them is an *analepsis,* "a textual point of retrospection, [which] reaches back to a time anterior to that being narrated."[18] In other words, virtually one half of the entire novel, Books One through Five, is composed mostly of narrated histories that are separate from the story time in which the plot of *Sapphira and the Slave Girl* is conveyed. Frequently, *analepses* are used for purposes of exposition, and they have this function in the novel since Cather was self-consciously trying to reconstruct the manners, attitudes, and stories that composed this rural community in pre–Civil War Virginia. The difference between the two halves of the novel (Books One through Five and Six through Eight), however, remains striking; in the latter half, only one *analepsis* occurs, and the dominant narrative concern is advancing the story of Sapphira's jealous persecution of Nancy through the figure of Martin Colbert, an amoral rake whom Sapphira has invited to Back Creek expressly to rape, and therefore ruin, Nancy. Henry Canby, in the *Saturday Review of Literature,* argued that Cather was "not writing a melodrama of slavery and seduction, but recreating, with subtle selection of incident, a society and a culture and a sociology."[19] In fact, the novel incorporates *both* of these impulses, in separate halves and in separate narrational times.

Sapphira and the Slave Girl is self-conscious not only about telling stories to compose its narrative, but also about telling stories from the past: the histories of the slaves at the Colbert house—Jezebel, Sampson, Till, Nancy, Tansy Dave, Tap; the history of the consummate storyteller of the region, Mrs. Ringer; the history of Rachel Blake's life in Washington, D.C., the governmental social scene, the death of her husband, and her subsequent return to Virginia; and, finally, the history of Sapphira and Henry Colbert's marriage, and her paranoid suspicions about his fidelity. Equally striking is the way these histories are narrated, as part of the collective memory of the society. At certain times the *analepsis* is focalized as individual reflection, employing a character's consciousness and colloquial phrasings, as when Rachel Blake muses: "Now, Mandy Ringer had lived a hard life, goodness knew, but misfortune and drudgery had never broken her spirit. . . . Mrs. Ringer was born interested" (118–19). At other instances, such retrospection is externally focalized and narrates simply and even elliptically the events that have transpired in the past, such as the story of the aged Jezebel's capture, transport, and enslavement. In both manifestations, the simplicity of narration in these histories evokes the sense of them as tales recounted, an essential attribute of those stories that survive and are passed down as part of a culture's history and sense of identity. These *analepses* that figure so prominently in the first half of *Sapphira and the Slave Girl* are not merely textual points of retrospection. Rather they are narrations of retrospection, models of the way we are directed to read the entire novel itself when we arrive at the Epilogue. The novel, in this way, asks to be read as the collective memory of a culture, a series of disparate tales that together compose a tapestry of mid-nineteenth-century life and sensibility in the South.

But whose life, and, more particularly, through whose sensibility? It is a question readers must ask perforce because of the novel's ambivalent and contradictory representation of race. If indeed *Sapphira and the Slave Girl* is a history of the Shenandoah Valley, then the parameters, as well as the agency, of that history must be carefully mapped. Book Three of the novel, entitled "Old Jezebel," is an illuminating capsule of the way in which race is conceived within the historical consciousness that shapes this text. Combining present story time with the tale of Jezebel's enslavement, the novel's third book demonstrates not only the equivocation about slavery itself that so informs this narrative, but also how cultural codes determine the tales a society tells about its history, and about what it selectively remembers from its past.

"Old Jezebel" is split into three sections. The first and third parts are narrated in the present story time of the novel and enclose the history of Jezebel's transport from Africa to America which forms the entire second section. As is common in Cather's narratives, these three sections are meant to be read together, in juxtaposition, so that "meaning" is approximated only by inference and interpretation. Moreover, as is also the case in Cather's fiction, the attempt to arrive at some coherent and non-contradictory meaning is an illusory goal at best.

The first part of "Old Jezebel" centers on Sapphira's visit to Jezebel's cabin, where the old woman lies bedridden and dying. Bringing syringa ("mock-oranges") from the garden, Sapphira sits with Jezebel and reminisces about the history of the Mill Farm that they share together—the planting of the garden and the "good times" of their youth (87). Their mutual recall of a common past emphasizes the subtle parallels that the narrative suggests lie between them: both are now "house-bound" with some form of illness (Jezebel with age and infirmity, Sapphira with edema) and, as Sapphira counsels the dying slave, both must "take what comes to us and be resigned" (87). Sapphira's solicitousness toward

Jezebel's comfort seems to go beyond that of mistress to aged slave; they are, the narrative implies, intimates because they share the same history. They created the landscape of Mill Farm together. They are bound by time and by memory in a way that transcends other relationships, even of family. They have, this brief section seems to suggest, a kind of equality that is deeply felt and springs from a shared humanity which supersedes the limitations of power and hierarchy inherent within their assigned roles of mistress and slave.

Yet within this section as well reside conflicting implications of white power and black otherness that necessarily disrupt the smooth surface of similarity that the narrative, on one level, seems to assert. As Sapphira gazes upon Jezebel, for example, her immediate assessment is that the old woman "looked very like a lean old grey monkey" (86). Though this comment is focalized through Sapphira, it resembles the externally focalized description of Jezebel's hand at the end of the section as a "cold grey claw" (89), aligning, implicitly, Sapphira's perspective with that of the external narration. Sapphira's dominant power is again subtly emphasized even in the way the narrative asserts the shared history of the two women. "I expect you remember those things, too," Sapphira prompts Jezebel, underscoring her expectations of what the aged slave woman ought to remember. And as if accommodating itself to the power of those expectations, the narrative not only structures Jezebel's response as unvoiced agreement, but it also fixes her within an established hierarchical relation by using her race, rather than her name, to signify her person: "The old negress looked up at her and nodded" (88). The most curious and astonishing moment of otherness, however, appears at the end of the section. Trying to cajole Jezebel into eating, Sapphira inquires if there isn't anything the old woman would especially fancy. Jezebel's response is singularly startling: "No'm, I cain't think of nothin' I could relish, lessen maybe it was a li'l pickaninny's hand" (89). A reader's response is likely to resemble Nancy's, who declares that Jezebel must be "out of her haid" (89) to say such a thing. But Sapphira's sharp retort, "I know your granny through and through. She is no more out of her head than I am" (88), bestows an aura of obscure legitimacy on Jezebel's utterance. Again, paradoxically, the narrative stresses their mutual understanding and comprehension at the same time that it leaves the strange, alienating, and even frightening request of the old woman deliberately unexplained.

The history of Jezebel's capture and enslavement, part two of "Old

Jezebel," seems to signify the riddle of flesh eating with the information that Jezebel "came from a fierce cannibal people" who could not be "broken" as easily as other Africans (91). Yet this explanation is a back-handed compliment at best, playing as it does on an ignorance of African peoples, as well as on established stereotypes of primitive, ferocious, wild, and uncivilized natives, whose blackness characterizes the state of their unenlightened souls. Contained within this second section as well, however, is a dispassionate account of the horrors of slavery, describing the murder of Jezebel's family, her march to the sea in leg irons, and the conditions aboard what the text calls "a model slaver" (92).

> The negroes were stowed between the upper and lower decks, on a platform as long and as wide as the vessel; but there was only three feet ten inches between the shelf on which they lay and the upper deck which roofed them over. The slaves made a long voyage of from two to three months in a sitting or recumbent position, on a plank floor, with very little space, if any, between their bare bodies. . . . All were kept naked throughout the voyage, and their heads and bodies shaved every fortnight. As there was no drainage of any sort, the slaves' quarters, and the creatures in them, got very foul overnight. . . . Except in rough weather, the males, ironed two and two, were allowed out on the lower deck for a few hours while their platform was being scrubbed and fumigated. At the same time, the women were turned out on the lower after deck without chains. (91–92)

This account is as close as the text comes to critiquing slavery explicitly, in part because it simply recounts historical information that is separate from the novel's plot and the family dynamics in which the story of *Sapphira and the Slave Girl* exists. Relying solely on description and allowing the "facts" to speak for themselves, these first few paragraphs of Jezebel's history are markedly different from the tale that follows, in which Jezebel's essential character is defined and explained according to the narrative expectations established when the reader initially encounters her as an old woman.

The tale contained in part two of "Old Jezebel" illustrates the conjunction of story and history into the experimental narrative of *Sapphira and the Slave Girl*. Separate both from the novel's plot—Sapphira's visit to her cabin—and from its historical narration about the middle passage, the tale which the narrative tells about Jezebel is an animating one. For the story recounted in this section is one of origins; though this is not the first encounter with Jezebel in the novel, it is the first and the only tale *recounted* about her. Moreover, because this remembered and recited tale is about Jezebel's earliest beginnings, it possesses the authority of source. It is the genesis of her history as a character within the novel. This tale also possesses an authority within the narrative, because it not only explains the unaccountable behavior that precedes it in part one, but it also is represented as an *analepsis,* a literal retelling of history that has been recalled at this particular point in the narrative. Passed down into the tale-telling tradition inherited by the child narrator in the Epilogue, Jezebel's history is recalled as a story, while the narrative, simultaneously, represents this story as the beginning of Jezebel's history.

Because it is a tale of origins in a novel composed of episodic scenes, the text signals that something essential about Jezebel's character will be revealed in this solitary narration of her history. On board the slave ship, Jezebel becomes embroiled in a fight with other African women. When the ship's mates separate her, she nearly bites off the thumb of one "like a mastiff," according to the text (93). The angry mate assures the captain that "the female gorilla . . . could never be tamed" and insists that she should be thrown overboard (93). Not inclined to dispose needlessly of his "cargo," the captain has Jezebel "brought up in heavy irons for his inspection" (93). Her subsequent description, focalized through the captain, conflates character and body in one defining assessment of Jezebel herself.

> Her naked back was seamed with welts and bloody cuts, but she carried herself with proud indifference, and there was no plea for mercy in her eyes. . . . As he walked up and down, smoking his pipe, he looked her well over. He judged this girl was worth any three of the women,—as much as the best of the men. Anatomically she was remarkable, for an African negress: tall, straight, muscular, long in the legs. The skipper had a kind of respect for a well-shaped creature; horse, cow, or woman. And he re-spected anybody who could take a flogging like that without buckling. (93–94)

Contained within this quote is what seems to be the defining element of Jezebel's character: her purposeful resistance to capture and enslave-ment. She carries herself with "proud indifference" to the pain her captors have inflicted and refuses to submit or to plea for "mercy." The passage stresses as well both the economic and dehumanizing nature of slavery. The captain not only regards her as a commodity, approximating her "worth," but he also assesses her body as he would an animal's; she is, to him, a "well-shaped creature," comparable to a horse, cow, or other form of livestock. Though the quote ends with his respect for her indomitable spirit, its effect is curiously contradictory, both defining her character and denying her humanity simultaneously.

While the passage might seem to invite both skepticism and ironic distance, owing to the captain's skewed perspective as a merchant of human beings, the story's conclusion only underscores the representation of Jezebel as a kind of animal with an assertive nature. Put on the block for sale, Jezebel is examined by a Dutchman and a doctor, who inquire about her disposition. Told that the scars on her back were put there by "the niggers who captured her," the doctor, who is both "kind and shrewd," demonstrates the old adage that sugar works better than vinegar.

> He fumbled in his pocket and brought out a deerskin pouch, from which he took two squares of maple sugar. One he put in his own mouth, and smacked his lips. The other he offered to Jezebel with a questioning smile. She opened her jaws. At this the second mate, standing by, looked the other way. The doctor put the sugar on Jezebel's tongue. She crunched it, grinned, and stuck out her tongue for more. The doctor gave his friend the deciding nod. (95–96)

The maple sugar in this disturbing passage functions as a metonym of the doctor's kindness; Jezebel is tamed as a wild animal would be, a comparison underscored in the narrative with the comment that Jezebel's "personal manners were too strong for even a Dutch farmer's household, so he lodged her in the haymow over the cow barn" (96). The implication of this story is that slavery itself does not elicit Jezebel's resistance, but rather the kind of treatment accorded her within it. Its effect is to displace and submerge the injustice of slavery within a representation of the threat Jezebel poses if not handled properly. In the passage above, a kind of comic terror is engendered by the question of whether Jezebel will bite the hand that feeds her. The dénouement of this scene—Jezebel wooed into placidity by food—reduces the woman who disdained enslavement with a "proud indifference" into a potentially dangerous, though comically defused, creature whose threatening orality defines her being. Its devolution into comedic stereotype suggests as well its link to the prevailing visual representation of African Americans characterized by wide, toothy grins and grimaces, common throughout the nineteenth and well into the twentieth century.[20]

Despite its incidental critique of slavery, this *analepsis* of Jezebel's history rationalizes her enslavement by plotting a tale of cannibalism contained and civilized. Both animalistic and infantile, the Jezebel of this remembered tale—the "female gorilla" who has bitten off a man's thumb—prefigures the "lean old grey monkey" who jokes about eating "a li'l pickaninny's hand" in the novel's present story time. Slavery becomes the means through which Jezebel is transformed from the fierce, African (equated here with cannibal) other, into the domestic(ated) servant who has served the Dodderidge family faithfully all of her life. Narrated anonymously as history, the racial politics and attitudes within Jezebel's story seem simply to exist, attributable to no single consciousness in particular. Yet the interchangeable diction between the two sections, spanning past and present, suggests that one encompassing cultural sensibility informs the narrative entire. As is common in Cather's fiction, such a sensibility can only be approximated through *how* a particular narrative is constructed, because part of the way in which this novel operates is to conflate tales from the past with present narration, and thus to obscure the authorial origin of this particular history. It is both part of the fabric of the fiction that is *Sapphira and the Slave Girl,* as well as an instance of historical remembrance that has survived generations through its transformation into a story.

The end of Jezebel's history within this section illuminates the narrative logic that informs the racial attitudes through which this fictionalization of history is constructed. Jezebel's *analepsis* concludes with a brief summation of her life at the Mill Farm where, the text indicates, she "had been in the family ever since" Sapphira was born (96). Moreover, she has risen to a position of power within the ranks of the slaves and has been "entrusted" to "oversee the gardens at the Mill Farm" (96), thus drawing her history back to the opening section of Book Three in which Sapphira brings flowers to Jezebel and the two reminisce about planting that garden together. Indeed, Jezebel not only oversees the garden work, but also has become a literal overseer of the other slaves, especially of the young boys "who did the shrubbery and shaped the hedges" (96). And it is here, in this transformation of Jezebel from rebellious slave into guardian of the slave system that the narrative most clearly demonstrates its racial politics. For not only has Jezebel progressed, in the narrative's terms, from insurgent to enforcer, but she also has evolved from a silent and dangerous orality to the language of law and order. It is her admonition to one "slack boy" which ends her history: "You ain't no call to be comf'able, you settin' down de minute a body's back's turned. I wisht I could put dock burs in yo' pants!" (96, 97). Giving Jezebel the last words of her history seems to endow her with a kind of narrative equality; she too has a *say* in her own story, much like the way Till's voice ends the novel. But like Till, what Jezebel speaks in this short passage is the language of the master; her words reiterate the stereotype of lazy slaves who must be watched constantly lest they try to shirk their assigned tasks. The force that subtly dominates and shapes the narrative of Jezebel's history is evolution: from resistance to tractability, from silence to language, from primitive to civilized, and from threat to containment. Indeed, what this story of Jezebel's past reveals more than anything else is the power of narrative to re-create history according to specific ideological needs. The narrative structure of this tale defuses the threat that enslavement poses to the oppressors by transforming Jezebel's early powerful resistance into the comic attempt of young boys to avoid hard work. Moreover, and perhaps most important, it also displaces the brief sense of injustice about slavery with which it begins onto Jezebel as a figure who "meted out justice" to other, less threatening resisters (96). Slavery civilizes the African other this story claims, and in doing so, reveals itself as a tale told, and retold in this narrative, to legitimize slavery itself. Jezebel's history then is a fiction of white slave-owning culture and functions in this narrative to underpin the prevailing racial assumptions upon which the novel's plot is ambivalently erected. Memory, in this brief tale, is transformed into the authority and "objectivity" of history.

Maxwell Geismar, an early and astute critic of Cather's fiction, suggested that "in the 'legend' of Jezebel, the fierce African tribeswoman, who is captured, examined, and sold almost purely for her value as a sexual animal, Cather defines the real background, and the basic moral issues of *Sapphira and the Slave Girl* in less than a dozen pages."[21] I would agree with Geismar that sexuality and enslavement are the "basic moral issues" in this text, but I would suggest that rather than appearing in the tale of Jezebel's history, they are raised explicitly in the third section of "Old Jezebel," when the narrative returns to present story time and recounts Jezebel's death and the preparations for her funeral. Part three of "Old Jezebel," in fact, highlights the inherent contradictions and ideological containment in the text's representation of race, slavery, and freedom that makes *Sapphira and the Slave Girl* such a troublesome text within Cather's oeuvre.

To speak of ambivalent race, and indeed racist, representation in this novel is to acknowledge the genuine sympathy and affection between masters and slaves that the text presents, as well as its rigid adherence to and belief in rank, hierarchy, and difference between black and white persons. The novel, for example, asserts that Jezebel was a valued, respected, and even beloved member of the Dodderidge's extended farm family through its careful detailing of her funeral arrangements. Sapphira insists that one of her own "embroidered nightgowns" be used to clothe the old woman in her coffin, with the added concern that "if they're yellow with lying so long, Nancy can bleach one with alum and hang it in the sun" (98). The meal prepared for Jezebel's watchers also emphasizes the respect accorded to the old slave woman. Sapphira insists not only on two kinds of meat, but that "light" bread be baked in quantity. Glossed as a footnote at the bottom of the page, the definition of "light" provided in the text has two separate functions. First, in interrupting the dialogue between Sapphira and Lizzie, the cook for the Colbert family, the presence of a footnote forces the implied reader to recognize this story as a fiction recounted by an implied storyteller, one who provides historical definitions for words and, indeed, for recipes, with which the reader may be unfamiliar. Such an occurrence appears in only one other Cather novel, *Shadows on the Rock,* and in both cases what these disruptive footnotes stress is the novel's self-consciousness of its own fictionality, its own production as a text. The difference between "light" and corn bread, however, the former made from wheat and more difficult to prepare, also signifies a demonstration of affection for Jezebel within the narrative.[22] Her value to the family will be symbolized by their tribute of a less common, more esteemed kind of bread. The narrative also suggests that death reduces all persons, regardless of rank, into a common oblivion. Though the grave plots of the Dodderidges and their slaves are divided by a "wide gravelled path," the narrative notes as well that "the mounts of masters and servants alike were covered with thick mats of myrtle" (101), obscuring any differences of rank or race in the shared shroud of earth.

Yet within this same short interlude, the care given to Jezebel's funeral is achieved through the threat of selling Lizzie's daughter, Bluebell. Sapphira controls her cook through this intimidation, ensuring only in this way that the arrangements will be to her satisfaction. "Remember this," she declares to Lizzie, "if you don't do me credit at Jezebel's wake, I will send Bluebell back to Loudoun County for good, as sure as I sit here" (100). Not only is this the antithesis of how Sapphira behaves to both Jezebel and Till, but the narrative justifies it by representing both Lizzie and Bluebell as stock racist characters. They are the lazy and shiftless "niggers" who deserve such reprimand, while Till, Jezebel, and even Nancy are the faithful and industrious "darkies" who earn the respect and the affection of their masters. This devolution into stereotype occurs throughout the novel and is perhaps best illustrated by the comment of the external focalizer in this section that "the darkies were always gay after a funeral" (102). Indeed, what becomes increasingly apparent in this novel is that the sympathy and respect accorded African-American characters is conceived solely within the parameters of racist presumptions about how loyal, patient, accommodating and hard-working slaves are *supposed* to be. What might strike the modern reader as textual ambivalence about the fact of slavery in this novel is instead a difference in treatment between those slaves who merit decency and those who do not.

Yet it is also clear that Cather did perceive something to be wrong in antebellum slave-holding society; if she had not, she would not have written to Viola Roseboro that she was trying to re-create "the Terrible" in this novel. Leaving Cather's cryptic allusions about her own prose deliberately unsignified seems the wisest course to follow, though it might be safe to say that "the Terrible" probably does not refer to slavery itself. What the novel does seem obsessed with containing and managing are the consequences of slavery upon the society it so lovingly and nostalgically re-creates. Sexuality, as the threat of miscegenation, and the desire for freedom, represented by runaway slaves, are the very issues that become the center of the novel's plot. And like the tale of Jezebel's origins, in which the figure of the rebellious slave is introduced and then defused, the relation between power and sexuality is something the novel acknowledges, and then tries to contain through a series of complex and elaborate displacements. Miscegenation is both the fact and the fear that animates Sapphira's plot against Nancy, and it is also what forces Nancy to flee against her will. Indeed, the curious contradiction within this text is its focus on the very thing that rips apart the society it also wants so fondly to remember and to re-create in its narrative.

As so often happens in Cather's late fiction, the question of sexuality is elaborated in terms of female power, specifically the power Sapphira wields to control the sexual behavior of her slaves, and her own physical disempowerment due to the edema that has swollen her feet and legs, confining her to a wheelchair and terminating any sexual relations she may have wished to have with her husband, Henry. After Jezebel's funeral in the final section of Book Three, Sapphira retires to her room to mull over a scene she has witnessed during the funeral.

> Behind the dark cedars just outside the stone wall, her husband and Nancy stood in deep conversation. The girl was in an attitude of dejection, her head hanging down, her hands clasped together, and the Master, whatever he was saying, was speaking very earnestly, with affectionate solicitude. . . . Never before had she seen him expose himself like that. Whatever he was pressing upon that girl, he was not speaking as master to servant; there was nothing to suggest that special sort of kindliness permissible under such circumstances. He was not uttering condolences. It was personal. He had forgotten himself. (103–4)

On the most obvious level, this scene suggests Henry Colbert's solicitude toward Nancy and her confusion as to why she has fallen out of favor with her mistress, a kindness that Sapphira consistently misreads throughout the novel. According to her dictates of behavior, her husband has crossed the line of proper hierarchical relations, and what must then ensue inevitably are the improper relations of a sexual nature between white and black. To forget oneself in matters of race has explicitly sexual connotations in this novel, because it erases the difference between white and black, masters and slaves, an act that ultimately threatens the social stability of slave-holding society. Believing that Nancy is not sleeping outside her door but is instead consorting with her husband at the mill, Sapphira feigns an attack, only to find both Nancy and Till attending her with "promptness and sympathy" (107). Despite this evidence of both Nancy's and her husband's fidelity, "the meaning of that intimate conversation which had gone on under her very eyes this afternoon" remains deliberately unsignified in the text (105). If the fact of a sexual liaison between master and slave woman is not immediately apparent, the threat remains, and is in fact pervasive throughout the narrative.

This threat of miscegenation is tied in the novel to male sexuality and appears as a force that is only provisionally contained. In the novel's opening pages, for instance, Nancy is discussed as Till's "yellow child," born after two of Henry Colbert's brothers had been visiting the farm (8–9), though she resembles "the portrait painter from Cuba" who had also been in residence at the farm around that time. Sapphira's reaction to Till's pregnancy is to marry Till off to Jeff, "a capon man" (43), who is unable to perform sexually, thus keeping Till free to function as Sapphira's chief servant and attendant. Yet the strain of uncontainable sexuality that runs through the men in Sapphira's extended family is not so easily dispatched. Despite the text's assertion that "although Henry was a true Colbert in nature, he had not behaved like one, and he had never been charged with a bastard" (66), his relation to Nancy remains problematic and ambiguous. For Henry Colbert romanticizes Nancy out of her humanity; she seems "to him more like an influence than a person" (192). Initially, he views her "free from care, like the flowers and the birds," and identifies "her with Mercy, Christiana's sweet companion" in Bunyan's *Pilgrim's Progress* (67).[23] Yet when forced to acknowledge her sexuality and the danger posed to her by his own nephew, Martin Colbert, Henry is revolted: "Now that he must see her as a woman, enticing to men, he shrank from seeing her at all" (193). Though he has managed heretofore to control his sexual desires, what he refers to as his "family inheritance" (192), when Martin Colbert becomes an increasing danger to Nancy, Henry feels himself beginning "to see through Martin's eyes" (209), to envision Nancy as sexually available. Henry, in other words, begins to see, if not behave, through the power of race.

The brief scene of Sapphira's seemingly groundless suspicions in Book Three then is an illuminating one, highlighting the repression and displacement operative in this novel. Though it internalizes the threat of miscegenation posed by white male sexuality, repressed in Henry and manifested in Martin, the text displaces the rape of slave women by the white masters onto the white mistress of the house. It is, after all, Sapphira's idea to invite Martin Colbert to Mill Farm for, the narrative hints, the plan of raping Nancy: "She almost believed she had urged him to come solely because she liked to have young people about" (154). And by displacing the sexual power of slave-holding men onto a physically disempowered mistress, the novel maintains that such sexual abuse is simply an aberration; *Sapphira and the Slave Girl* deflects the socially disruptive reality of miscegenation by scripting it as the misguided reaction of an unreasonably jealous and frustrated woman. Sapphira facilitates the very act she fears, creating a plot of triangular desire composed of herself, Martin Colbert, and Nancy. Outside this configuration stands Henry Colbert, exonerated by his wife's plot which becomes the primary action in the narrative. Defusing the power of the master by replacing it with the paranoia of the mistress rewrites the sexual politics of power within slavery. The threat, the novel argues paradoxically, is both within and without the family. If male sexuality constitutes an uncontrollable force ("the Colbert nature"), it nonetheless is a woman who bears ultimate responsibility for Nancy's persecution. Though the fact of miscegenation remains, attributing its agency to a woman necessarily lessens its threat, as well as its reality.

Even the scene of Martin Colbert's attempted rape of Nancy employs a diction of sensuous orality rather than phallic force. Tracking Nancy into a grove of cherry trees, Martin happens upon her in the boughs of a tree where, the text indicates, she has attempted to escape him for a short while: "Someway no troubles followed a body up there; nothing but the foolish, dreamy, nigger side of her nature climbed the tree with her" (178). Indeed, though only subtly apparent, the narrative emphasizes Nancy's racial "difference" during this brief scene, and one of its effects is to heighten the potentially transgressive tension of such behavior. Flirting with Nancy, Martin registers her "soft darky laugh" (179), and, stepping up on the chair she has used to climb the tree, he places his head between her dangling thighs, "and drew her two legs about his cheeks like a frame" (180). Nancy struggles in alarm and begs him to let her go. His response is perhaps the most sexually explicit in all of Cather's fiction: " 'Pretty soon.—This is just nice.—Something smells sweet—like May apples.' He seemed murmuring to himself, not to her, but all the time his face came closer" (181). Nancy manages to call for help, temporarily frustrating Martin's designs, though his relentless pursuit continues throughout another book (Book Seven). Yet the actual threat Martin poses to the young woman seems diminished by the sexual representation of this scene. Sensuality and seduction, rather than force and mastery, characterize their interaction. Despite Nancy's protestations and the accompanying sense of violation, the scene seems to play down the brutality of his actions, especially by its unusual evocation of oral, rather than genital, sex, since the former not only seems more consensual than the latter, but it also does not result in pregnancy and children, that unignorable evidence of the fact of miscegenation.[24] Indeed, though Martin Colbert carries the full burden of sexual villainy in the novel, the text also endeavors to contain and deflect the threat he embodies, ambiguously linking his attempted violation of Nancy with spring and regeneration (May apples and ripe cherries). The threat of miscegenation remains in the novel, however, and it is what spurs Nancy's escape in the plot. Much in the same way that the actual act of sexual intercourse between black and white is suppressed in the novel, so too is the issue of freedom. Book Three, for instance, immediately following the night scene of Sapphira's suspicions about her husband's fidelity, concludes with Henry Colbert's own musings about the justice and injustice of slavery. Though Henry Blake, like his daughter, Rachel, hates "the whole system of slavery," he nonetheless reasons that "Jezebel's life . . . seemed a strange instance of predestination. For her, certainly, her capture had been a deliverance" (108). Colbert's interpretation not only provides a sense of repetition and closure to the book's encapsulated history of Jezebel, but it also stands absolutely uncontradicted by any other information in the text itself. Colbert recalls an occasion three years past when he offered manumission and the promise of employment in Pennsylvania to Sampson, his capable and courageous "head millhand," only to hear Sampson plead to stay on at the mill with the Dodderidge family. Sampson's utter rejection of freedom confirms Colbert's belief that freeing the slaves on his farm would be "an injustice to the slaves themselves. Where would they go? How would they live? They had never learned to take care of themselves or to provide for tomorrow. They were a part of the Dodderidge property and the Dodderidge household" (108).

Seeking an answer in the Bible, Colbert discovers only a rationale for a benevolently administered slavery: "There were injunctions of kindness to slaves, mercy and tolerance. *Remember them in bonds as bound with them.* Yes, but nowhere did his Bible say that there should be no one in bonds, no one at all.—And Henry had often asked himself, were we not all in bonds? If Lizzie, the cook, was in bonds to Sapphira, was she not almost equally in bonds to Lizzie?" (110). The effect of this passage at the end of Book Three is extraordinary. For though it is focalized through Henry Colbert, it adopts a biblical authority to justify slavery, and it addresses a previous scene of power and intimidation (Sapphira's threat to sell Bluebell if Lizzie does not prepare a generous spread at Jezebel's funeral) by insisting that some kind of mutual dependence exists in the daily interactions between owners and their slaves. Indeed, Sapphira *is* dependent on Lizzie for the preparation of her meals, but in this blithe summation of reciprocal bondedness the text seems to repress the facts that Sapphira also *owns* Lizzie, her daughter, Nancy, Till, and all the other slaves on the farm, and that she has the power to protect or to ruin their lives at whim. It insists, seemingly, that hierarchical relations are more subtly constructed than the simple dichotomy of black and white, and implies that such personal relations can be equally trying for masters and mistresses, especially when dealing with a troublesome and lazy slave like Lizzie.

It would be fair to say, in fact, that *Sapphira and the Slave Girl,* like both "Old Mrs. Harris" and *Lucy Gayheart,* believes adamantly in hierarchy. Even Rachel Blake, who masterminds Nancy's flight north, contends that it is only "the *owning* that was wrong" (137) in the slave system, despite her knowledge that both her mother and her mother's slaves "believe in it" (221). The attitudes of both Rachel and her father represent the entire critique of slavery in this novel, and both, significantly, incorporate allusions to the slaves' own resistance to freedom in their internal debates. Even Nancy must be ordered by Rachel to escape, and then only because of Martin Colbert's attentions. She, like all the other African-American characters in this novel, is perfectly contented to remain enslaved on the Mill Farm. The novel finally endorses a nostalgic and fond remembrance of slavery, as in Rachel's memory of how her mother usually treats her slaves.

> There was her singular indulgence with Tansy Dave, her real affection for Till and old Jezebel, her patience with Sampson's lazy wife. Even now, from her chair, she took some part in all the celebrations that darkies love. She liked to see them happy. On Christmas morning she sat in the long hall and had all the men in the place come in to get their presents and their Christmas drink. She served each man a strong toddy in one of the big glass tumblers that had been her father's. When Tap, the mill boy, smacked his lips and said: "Miss Sappy, if my mammy's titty had a-tasted like that, I never would a-got weaned," she laughed as if she had never heard the old joke before.
>
> When the darkies were sick she doctored them, sent linen for the new babies and had them brought for her to see as soon as the mother was up and about. (220–21)

In the novel's terms, this passage represents a vision of a perfectly ordered society; the mistress cares for her slaves, and they, in turn, respond to her kindness with good will and affection. Slaves escape to the north only under extreme duress, and even then reluctantly. Freedom is not even desired by the enslaved; rather, they rest and refuse it. What the narrative arrives at, finally, is a plantation mythology, asserting that slavery had its good sides as well as its bad, especially when its ill effects are the result of *female* frustration and misinterpretation, and are safely defused in the end.

A similar equivocation occurs in the novel toward Sapphira herself. After Nancy's escape, the mistress refuses all contact with her daughter and the family seems permanently alienated. But when both of Rachel's children develop diphtheria, their grandmother swallows her pride, calls her town doctor, and assists her daughter as best she can. When one of the little girls dies, Sapphira suggests that Rachel and her remaining granddaughter move into the big house with them. This revelation of Sapphira's generosity and largess of spirit precedes her imminent death, a condition, her husband discerns, that she will meet "with that composure which he had sometimes called heartlessness, but which now seemed to him strength" (268). Facing death with dignity and resolve, Sapphira is miraculously transformed into the heroine of the novel, her persecution of Nancy seemingly forgotten. And when she admits to Henry that she might not be as inherently "good" as her daughter, his reply condones both her behavior and, seemingly, slavery itself when he concludes, "Sometimes keeping people in their place is being good to them" (268). Because the abiding alienation between Sapphira and Rachel has been over the very issue of slavery, Henry's admission confers a peculiar legitimacy upon Sapphira's actions, especially because it appears at the end both of her life and of the narrative proper.

This subtle accretion of attitude and point of view ultimately subordinates the plot of *Sapphira and the Slave Girl* within its evocation of history as the pleasures of remembrance. And nowhere is this influence more sharply demonstrated than in Book Five of the novel, "Martin Colbert," which spins the basic plot of Nancy's persecution by this predatory relative of the Colbert family. Yet within Book Five there occurs one narrative *anachrony*, which is, curiously both an *analepsis* and a *prolepsis*, a flash forward to events that have yet to occur in this narrative. Sent by Sapphira to gather laurel at the "Double S," a road making four connected loops down the side of a mountain, Nancy stops by Rachel Blake's cottage to ask for protection from Martin Colbert. Accompanying Nancy on her expedition, Rachel begins to believe the truth of Nancy's tale when they encounter Martin Colbert on horseback.

In the middle of this scene, however, is a lengthy description of the landscape in Back Creek, followed by a meditation of the "Double S" that disrupts and transcends the story time of the novel's plot.

> The road followed the ravine, climbing all the way, until at the "Double S" it swung out in four great loops round hills of solid rock; rock which the destroying armament of modern road-building has not yet succeeded in blasting away. The four loops are now denuded and ugly, but motorists, however unwillingly, must swing round them if they go on that road at all.
>
> In the old times, when Nancy and Mrs. Blake were alive, and for sixty years afterward, those now-naked hills were rich in verdure, the winding ravine was deep and green, the stream at the bottom flowed bright and soothingly vocal. A tramp pedlar from town, or a poor farmer, coming down on foot from his stony acres to sell a coonskin, stopped to rest here, or walked lingeringly. When the countrymen mentioned the place in speech, if it were but to say: "I'd jist got as fur as the Double e-S-S," their voices took on something slow and dreamy, as if recalling the place itself; the shade, the unstained loveliness, the pleasant feeling one had there. (170–71)

What makes this particular passage unique in the novel is its insistent reiteration of "now," referring not to an event yet to occur in the story sequence, but to the immediate present of the narration, the continuous present of reading the text "now." Such a purposeful fissure in the narrative underscores the text's representation of itself as a narration occurring in a specific historical moment about another historical moment antedating it by between sixty and ninety years. Nowhere else in Cather's fiction does a novel so ostentatiously reveal itself to be such a self-consciously constructed narrative. Moreover, this passage expresses a profound sense of loss about the past, when the hills were "rich in verdure," instead of being "now-naked." Indeed, the only way in which the past can be recaptured, its loveliness regained, is through memory, both that of "the countrymen who mentioned the place in speech," as well as that of the narrative itself which explicitly scripts this passage as a memory of "the old times," thus re-creating "the pleasant feeling one had there."

The "Double S" also functions as a figure for the text, enacting the narrative code or enunciation through which the text represents itself.[25] In *Sapphira and the Slave Girl,* the "Double S" signifies the novel's doubled narrative structure. Its first half collapses temporal linearity in favor of predominantly narrative *anachronies*—tales told both about the historical past of the novel's story and about the continuous historical present of its narration. The novel's second half, however, rigorously re-establishes temporal linearity. Virtually no disruptions between the story sequence and the narration occur. What happens instead is the gradual absorption of the potential evils within slavery, essentially the novel's plot, into the ameliorative haze of nostalgic remembrance. But what is especially striking about the "Double S" is its appearance in the very middle of the book chronicling Nancy's fear and persecution. The "pleasant feeling one had" in the "Double S" is recalled not only by the countrymen in the quote, but also by the implied narrator who appears as the character-focalizer in the Epilogue. Yet these pleasant feelings of the past, conveyed as stories within the first half of the narrative and as stories narrated to the child-narrator in the Epilogue, exist in tense contiguity to the plot against Nancy that is, essentially, the plotted story of Book Five. Indeed, the past is not so pleasant for every-one, and as a figure for the novel itself, the "Double S" of *Sapphira and the Slave Girl* reveals the internal division between sentiment and slavery that represents an ambivalent and even a contested history in this text.

Despite its twenty-five-year leap forward in narrative time, the Epi-logue of *Sapphira and the Slave Girl* enforces a kind of conventional closure to this novel, much like that of Cather's other late fiction. Formally an epilogue provides an after-history for a fiction, drawing together its narrative strands, and indeed we, with the child-narrator, hear the endings to the stories of characters in the novel proper. We are told, literally, *we* are the narratees, of the histories which have heretofore constructed the story sequence of the novel. And as one long recitation of the past, the Epilogue emphasizes "the pleasant feeling" of memory and narrative re-creation. "The Terrible" has since been encompassed and even nullified by the passage of time, and the emphasis at the end of this novel is on reconciliation. "Nancy's Return," the Epilogue's subtitle, resolves the conflict at the novel's center and provides a conventional happy ending to this particular history. The Epilogue also treats the broader frame of history in its opening pages, detailing the reconcilia-tion between neighbors in Back Creek after the Civil War. Those who sympathized with the idea of abolition, like the postmistress Mrs. Bywa-ters, also hid Confederate soldiers in their houses (274). Fathers re-mained friends though their sons fought on opposite sides of the strug-gle (275). Neighbors of differing political persuasion pulled together to aid a local soldier dying slowly from gangrene (274). Forgiveness and the bridging of differences predominate here, and they underscore the reconciliation between Sapphira and Rachel, as well as between Sapphira and Henry, that immediately precedes them in the narrative.

What might strike the modern reader as somewhat startling in the Epilogue is the complete effacement of the former slaves in the brief history of the war's aftermath. Absolutely no mention of abolition, reconstruction (except for one desultory reference to carpetbaggers), or freed slaves appears. Instead the social reunification that occurs after the Civil War exists entirely between white people. Even Nancy's return to Back Creek is introduced by the narrative as heralding a change in the class differences among white Southerners, with the poor now aspiring to more "extravagant" kinds of leisure, and young farmers signifying their wealth by purchasing "a smart buggy and double carriage" (277). The narrative declares that the chief consequence of the war, rather than the abolition of slavery, was that it "had done away with many of the old distinctions" (277). Like the absence of green vegetation on the "Double S," this disintegration of class differences is also recalled nostalgically by the Epilogue as something that has been lost to the passage of time, but simultaneously preserved in its retelling as a memory and as a story. Just as Nancy's plight is subsumed within the "pleasant" feelings generated by an evocation of the past, so too are the radical differences in race relations subordinated to those of class as a way of maintaining the "pleasant" recall of history that this novel commits itself to re-creating.

Potentially different versions of history are alluded to as well when the child-narrator notes the regional inflection that characterizes northern and southern speech in the word "history" itself: "Whereas Mrs. Blake used to ask me if she should read to me from my 'hist'ry book' . . . , Nancy spoke of the his-to-ry of Canada. I didn't like that pronunciation. Even my father said 'hist'ry.' Wasn't that the right and easy way to say it?" (284). What follows this seemingly insignificant incident is a narration of the histories of the African-American characters from the novel, all of which, though narrated by Till and Mrs. Blake, reiterate the same attitude toward race hierarchy that Henry Colbert endorses in his wife: "Sometimes keeping people in their place is being good to them." Lizzie and Bluebell, Till recounts, though freed, had literally to be driven off the Mill Farm, so desirous were they of staying. Sampson eventually does go to work in a Pennsylvania mill, though he returns to Back Creek after the war just to see the old mill again. He too misses his life in the South, and complains about how industrial mill processing "burns all the taste out-a the flour" (289). But it is the "sad story" of Tap, "the jolly mill boy with shining eyes and shining teeth" (289) that demonstrates most dramatically the prevailing sense that this narrative is overwhelmingly both a southern and a white "hist'ry." For Tap's tale, narrated by Mrs. Blake, illustrates the tragedy that ensues when people are not kept "in their place." Tap's "hist'ry" takes place during "the Reconstruction time," when freedmen were allowed rightful access to public places which, in this novel, are limited to saloons and pool halls. During a drunken fight Tap accidentally kills a man and is hanged for it, despite the Back Creek farmers who testify to his basic harmlessness. The stated moral of this story is that Tap "hadn't been able to stand his freedom," and ends with both Mrs. Blake and Till agreeing that "it was a Yankee jury that hanged him; a Southern jury would have known there was no real bad in Tap" (290). This tale, the last one recounted about an African American in the novel, proves that the past *is* better, for black and white folks alike. *This* is the conceit passed down in the retelling of Tap's "sad story," a conceit that mirrors the novel's overall structure of narrative *anachrony* as an attempt to recapture the antebellum past.

The version of history presented in the novel then is an undeniably white and nostalgic one, despite the claim that the narrator has heard all these "old stories" from Till, whose "keepsakes and treasures" (291) from the past inspire stories about "the Master and Mistress" that become eventually "a complete picture of those two persons," become in fact, the novel itself. Moreover, it is not the child-narrator who ends the narration, but Till. In direct address, Till utters the novel's final sentence, bemoaning Sapphira's displacement from the sophisticated Chestnut Hill to the rural county of Back Creek, "comin' out here where nobody was anybody much" (295). In one respect, there is an obvious irony here because the novel has itself been a panegyric of these characters who become reanimated and who become somebody through a narration that re-creates them from memory. Yet on another level we are asked to believe that the narrative histories that compose the novel *Sapphira and the Slave Girl* have been narrated by a black woman to a white child. In one final doubling, narrator, and perhaps even the implied author, is, simultaneously, the narratee of the novel. And in singling out Till as the authorial origin of the stories narrated in this fiction, *Sapphira and the Slave Girl* attempts to displace the historical and racial conflicts in its story by positing a shared tradition of fiction making. Yet the logic of white superiority evident throughout the novel, the stereotyped representations of its African-American characters, and the endorsement of the hierarchy that underpins the institution of slavery itself make such an attribution suspect at best. Despite the text's desire to balance simultaneously a nostalgic depiction of the South with a story about slavery, and despite its insistence that these stories have been passed down from black to white, *Sapphira and the Slave Girl* resists the textual and racial integration it attempts to claim.

What it demands of the reader, consequently, is an attention to the way in which its discourse of race historicizes whiteness rather than blackness. For *Sapphira and the Slave Girl* is not really about the condition of African Americans in slavery, but about the way (white) versions of history *need* to remember and to represent black people in order to maintain a political, economic, and social hierarchy. It is, in other words, about the historical and textual politics of domination. Memory is the agent of history in this novel and reveals itself to be ideologically selective to the tales it recalls and reiterates, which form the body of its narrative. In dramatizing how history is remembered and reconstructed as fiction(s), *Sapphira and the Slave Girl* does nothing less than dramatize as well the distorting power of the past.

Notes

1. Categorical Cather

1. All quotations are drawn from a phone interview (April 21, 1991), which Ms. Steinshouer was kind enough to allow me to conduct.

2. The Willa Cather Pioneer Memorial (WCPM) was founded in 1955, and in May 1962 it opened the Willa Cather Museum in Red Cloud. In April 1963, the society began to offer tours of the museum and of the surrounding Red Cloud environs, and in the fall of that same year "Catherland" was adopted as the name for the historical and fictional sites the memorial encompassed.

3. The centerpiece for the diorama, "The Sculptor's Funeral," for example, is an old-fashioned casket donated to the WCPM by the Brown Mortuary in Superior, Nebraska.

4. *Willa Cather Pioneer Memorial Newsletter* 7, no. 1 (Spring 1963).

5. *Willa Cather Pioneer Memorial Newsletter* 32, no. 4 (Winter 1988): 39–41.

6. I am indebted to Sharon O'Brien for introducing the idea of "reading communities" into my thinking about Cather and the canon.

7. Barbara Herrnstein Smith, "Contingencies of Value," in *Canons,* ed. Robert von Hallberg (Chicago: University of Chicago Press, 1984), 24. Cf. Herrnstein Smith's expansion of this essay into *Contingencies of Value: Alternative Perspectives for Critical Theory* (Cambridge: Harvard University Press, 1988).

8. Vernon L. Parrington, *Main Currents in American Thought,* vol. 3, *The Beginnings of Critical Realism in America* (New York: Harcourt, Brace and Company, 1927), 383.

9. Sharon O'Brien, "Becoming Non-Canonical: The Case against Willa Cather," *American Quarterly* 40 (March 1988): 110. See also David Stineback's two essays, "No Stone Unturned: Popular Versus Professional Evaluations of Willa Cather," *Prospects* 7 (1982): 167–76, and "The Case against Willa Cather," *Canadian Review of American Studies* 15 (Winter 1984): 385–95, in which he declares that "no major American novelist in the twentieth century has been as misunderstood and mistreated by literary critics as Willa Cather" (385).

10. *New York Times Magazine,* July 10, 1988, p. 24.

11. Alfred Kazin, *On Native Grounds* (1942; New York: Harcourt, Brace Jovanovich, 1970), 251.

12. Sharon O'Brien, *Willa Cather: The Emerging Voice* (New York: Oxford University Press, 1987), 74. The phrase "Epics of Women" is the title of Parrington's chapter on Cather in *The Beginnings of Critical Realism*, 382. Cf. Cecelia Tichi's conclusion in "Women Writers and the New Woman," from *The Columbia Literary History of the United States*, ed. Emery Elliott (New York: Columbia University Press, 1988): "The American land, then, is the center of woman's power in Cather's fiction. Her heroines—the 'Amazonian' Alexandra Bergson of *O, Pioneers!*, Antonia Shimerda of *My Antonia*, Thea Kronberg of *Song of the Lark*—all embody its characteristics. They enact its generative values, its natural cycles, the moods of its changing weather, its very spatial expensiveness [*sic*]" (605).

13. Paul Lauter, *Reconstructing American Literature: Courses, Syllabi, Issues* (Old Waterbury, N.Y.: Feminist Press, 1983).

14. Though Cather appears in some introductory and advanced historical courses in the Lauter compilation [Introduction to American Literature (5); American Literature: Early Modern Period (121); Introduction to Later American Literature (56); American Literature 1865–1914 (99); American Literature 1914–present (124)], her novels are also included in a number of thematic courses, including Regionalism (196), Black and Ethnic Literature (176), The American Dream (210), Her-Land: American Literature of Women and the Land (194), and Twentieth-Century Novels by Women (160). The most recent thematic study that encompasses all Cather's novels without disparaging or dismissing any of them is Susan Rosowski's *The Voyage Perilous: Willa Cather's Romanticism* (Lincoln: University of Nebraska Press, 1986). Conversely, John H. Randall's *The Landscape and the Looking Glass: Willa Cather's Search for Meaning* (Boston: Houghton Mifflin Company, 1960) and even Jamie Ambrosis's recent *Willa Cather: Writing at the Frontier* (Oxford: Berg, 1988) read the later novels as failures within the parameters of their own critical and thematic concerns.

15. The two late novels that do sustain more critical attention and approbation are *The Professor's House* (1925) and *Death Comes for the Archbishop* (1927). Significantly, they are also the only late novels whose protagonists are male.

16. See, for example, William Curtin, ed., *The World and the Parish*, 2 vols. (Lincoln: University of Nebraska Press, 1970); Bernice Slote, ed., *The Kingdom of Art: Willa Cather's First Principles and Critical Statements, 1893–1896* (Lincoln: University of Nebraska Press, 1966); Bernice Slote and Virginia Faulkner, eds., *The Art of Willa Cather* (Lincoln: University of Nebraska Press, 1973); Brent L. Bohlke, ed., *Willa Cather in Person: Interviews, Speeches, and Letters* (Lincoln: University of Nebraska Press, 1986); Willa Cather, *Not Under Forty* (1936; Lincoln: University of Nebraska Press, 1988); and Willa Cather, *Willa Cather on Writing* (1949; Lincoln: University of Nebraska Press, 1988).

17. See, for example, E. K. Brown and Leon Edel, *Willa Cather: A Critical Biography* (1953; New York: Avon Books, 1980), and James Woodress, *Willa Cather: Her Life and Art* (New York: Western, 1975) and *Willa Cather: A Literary Life* (Lincoln: University of Nebraska Press, 1987).

18. Rosowski, *The Voyage Perilous*, x, xiii.

19. Phyllis Rose, *Writing of Women: Essays in a Renaissance* (Middletown, Conn.: Wesleyan University Press, 1986), 150. See also Lillian D. Bloom and Edward A. Bloom, "The Poetics of Willa Cather," in *Five Essays on Willa Cather: The Merrimack Symposium*, ed. John J. Murphy (North Andover, Mass.: Merrimack College, 1974), 97–119.

20. Cather, *Not Under Forty*, 45. All further references to this work will appear in the text.

21. See both Elizabeth Sergeant, *Willa Cather, A Memoir* (Philadelphia: Lippincott, 1953), 34–39, 43, and Sharon O'Brien, *Willa Cather: The Emerging Voice*, 151–52, on Cather's equation of realism with social reportage and muckraking.

22. Janis P. Stout, *Strategies of Reticence: Silence and Meaning in the Works of Jane Austen, Willa Cather, Katherine Anne Porter, and Joan Didion* (Charlottesville: University Press of Virginia, 1990), 67.

23. Hermione Lee, *Willa Cather: Double Lives* (New York: Pantheon, 1989), 17.

24. Robert J. Nelson, *Willa Cather and France: In Search of the Lost Language* (Urbana: University of Illinois Press, 1988), 2. Though Nelson relies extensively on an almost incomprehensible Lacanian analysis for much of his study, his final chapter raises pertinent and unresolved questions in Cather studies with regard to theoretical approaches (127–52).

25. Jo Ann Middleton, *Willa Cather's Modernism: A Study of Style and Technique* (Rutherford, N.J.: Fairleigh Dickinson University Press, 1990), 21. Cf. Lee, *Willa Cather: Double Lifes*, 4.

26. Stevens, quoted in Woodress, *Willa Cather: A Literary Life*, 487.

27. See Ann Ardis's recent study, *New Women, New Novels: Feminism and Early Modernism* (New Brunswick: Rutgers University Press, 1990), and Rachel Blau DuPlessis's *Writing Beyond the Ending: Narrative Strategies of Twentieth-Century Women Writers* (Bloomington: Indiana University Press, 1985). DuPlessis, however, does not include Cather in her assessment of twentieth-century women modernists because she believes Cather's work adheres more to a nineteenth-century sensibility.

28. Hugh Kenner, "The Making of the Modernist Canon," in Von Hallberg, *Canons*, 363–75. All further references to Kenner's essay will appear in the text.

29. See Cather's essays, "My First Novels [There Were Two]," in *Willa Cather on Writing*, 89–97, and "Miss Jewett," in *Not Under Forty*, 76–95.

30. Granville Hicks, "The Case against Willa Cather," was originally published in the *English Journal* and was reprinted in *Willa Cather and Her Critics*,

ed. James Schroeter (1947; Ithaca: Cornell University Press, 1967), 139–47. All further references to this essay will appear in the text.

31. "Escapism," in *Willa Cather on Writing*, 18. All further references to this essay will appear in the text.

32. See Slote and Faulkner, *The Art of Willa Cather*, 150–51, for a panel discussion about whether Cather actually possessed and articulated a theory of fiction.

33. O'Brien, "Becoming Non-Canonical," 117, 118–19.

34. O'Brien notes only that "a new consensus about her literary values has still not emerged, however, in part because evaluations like 'Her art was not a big art' still have shaping power" (ibid., 123).

35. Kazin, *On Native Ground*, 251, 253.

36. Leon Edel, "Homage to Willa Cather," in Slote and Faulkner, *The Art of Willa Cather*, 203.

37. The lone dissenting voice in early Cather criticism is that of Arthur Hobson Quinn, who argues that "it is the usual critical mistake to speak of Willa Cather as though her main significance lay as a representative of the Far West. While she has represented life in that region with unusual insight and sympathy, she has not been limited to that locality, nor indeed is locality an element of supreme importance in her fiction. She is quite unprovincial, and her significance lies much more in the artistry of her method than in her material. . . . her greatest books came after 1922, and . . . none of them owe their power to the description of the farming life of Nebraska" (*American Fiction: An Historical and Critical Survey* ([New York: D. Appleton-Century, 1936], 683, 696).

38. Randall, *The Landscape and the Looking Glass*, 159–60.

39. David Daiches, *Willa Cather: A Critical Introduction* (Ithaca: Cornell University Press, 1951), 132.

40. Lionel Trilling, "Willa Cather," in Schroeter, *Willa Cather and Her Critics*, 153.

41. If this seems hyperbolic, consider my experience during a job interview at MLA with a large and respected state university in 1986. I was asked just what was "an ostensibly bright young woman, as my letters of recommendation claimed, *doing* writing on the lesser novels of Willa Cather?" The implicit suggestion seemed to be that I was not so bright as I thought, especially for choosing an "inferior" group of texts as both a dissertation topic and a marketing strategy. My polite rejoinder that "later was not necessarily synonymous with lesser" met with bemused condescension, if little else. Needless to say, I did not get the job.

42. Carolyn Heilbrun, *Reinventing Womanhood* (New York: W. W. Norton, 1978), 79, 81.

43. Sandra M. Gilbert and Susan Gubar, "Lighting Out for the Territories: Willa Cather's Lost Horizons," *No Man's Land: The Place of the Women Writer in the Twentieth Century*, vol. 2, *Sexchanges* (New Haven: Yale University Press,

1989), 169–212 (quotation is from p. 173). Gilbert and Gubar devote one paragraph to *My Mortal Enemy* (206), and mention *Shadows on the Rock* briefly (210).

44. In *Felicitous Space* (Chapel Hill: University of North Carolina Press, 1986), Judith Fryer discusses at length only *Shadows on the Rock* (319–41) and *Sapphira and the Slave Girl* (262–73).

45. Stout, *Strategies of Reticence*, 68.

46. In her chapter on Cather in *Lesbian Images* (New York: Pocket Books, 1976), Rule argues, paradoxically, against engaging in lesbian readings of Cather's work. Addressing what she sees as the predominantly homophobic origins of the negative assessments of Cather by Lionel Trilling and others, she suggests that "these grossly inaccurate critical generalizations can only be explained by a desire of each of these men to imply that Willa Cather's 'basic psychology,' 'personal failure,' or 'temperament' negatively influenced her vision. What they want out in the light of day is her emotional and erotic preference for women, and, if they cannot have irrefutable biographical facts or cannot use them in print, they will distort their reading of her fiction to make their discrediting point" (78–79).

47. O'Brien, *Willa Cather: The Emerging Voice*, 133–37. See also O'Brien's useful and lucid definition of the term "lesbian," which she argues depends upon a lesbian "sense of self" within a historical and cultural milieu (127–28).

48. The most recent of these is Hermione Lee's *Willa Cather: Double Lives*.

49. Sharon O'Brien, "'The Thing Not Named': Willa Cather as a Lesbian Writer," *Signs* 9 (1984): 576, 577.

50. Perhaps the most literal of such readings is Timothy Dow Adams's "My Gay Antonia: The Politics of Willa Cather's Lesbianism," in *Historical, Literary, and Erotic Aspects of Lesbianism*, ed. Monika Kehoe (New York: Harrington Park Press, 1986), 89–98, in which he argues that "both Jim and Antonia were imagined by Willa Cather as homosexuals" (91).

51. Catherine Stimpson, "Zero Degree Deviancy: The Lesbian Novel in English," in *Writing and Sexual Difference*, ed. Elizabeth Abel (Chicago: University of Chicago Press, 1982), 244, 246.

52. Judith Fetterley, "*My Antonia*, Jim Burden, and the Dilemma of the Lesbian Writer," in *Gender Studies*, ed. Judith Spector (Bowling Green: Bowling Green State University Popular Press, 1986), 43.

53. Bonnie Zimmerman, "What has never been: an overview of lesbian feminist criticism," in *The New Feminist Criticism*, ed. Elaine Showalter (New York: Pantheon Books, 1985), 207.

54. Joanna Russ, "To Write 'Like a Woman': Transformations of Identity in the Work of Willa Cather," in Kehoe, *Historical, Literary and Erotic Aspects of Lesbianism*, 81, 83.

55. O'Brien, "The Thing Not Named," 597, 598.

56. At least a part of this interpretive emphasis can be attributed to the

ambivalence in O'Brien's essay vis-à-vis its own stance toward a lesbian reading. For though O'Brien turns her argument toward ambiguity and openendedness halfway through the essay ["In deciding whether to define Willa Cather as a lesbian writer and then in determining her individual experience of lesbianism, we cannot use silence—her failure to weave the emotional threads central to her life directly into her fiction—as a clear basis for deduction" (ibid., 580)], her wariness at using silence as the basis for interpretation contradicts her suggestive, but nonetheless unambiguous, reading that "the thing not named" signifies lesbianism in the essay's opening pages.

57. Deborah Lambert, "The Defeat of a Hero: Autonomy and Sexuality in *My Antonia*," *American Literature* 53 (1982): 677.

58. Zimmerman, "What has never been," 214.

59. These quotations from *Willa Cather on Writing* can be found in "On *The Professor's House*" (30), "On *Shadows on the Rock*" (14), "On *Death Comes for the Archbishop*" (12), and "On *The Professor's House*" (30).

60. Bohlke, *Willa Cather in Person,* 169. All further references to this work will appear in the text.

61. Susan J. Rosowski, "Willa Cather's Women," *Studies in American Fiction* 9, no. 2 (1981): 274.

62. Gilbert and Gubar, *Sexchanges,* 173. Compare Rosowski's argument that "Cather focuses squarely on the implications for women of cultural myths concerning them" ("Willa Cather's Women," 265).

63. See Susan J. Rosowski's important essay, "Willa Cather's Subverted Endings and Gendered Time," in *Cather Studies,* vol. 1, ed. Susan J. Rosowski (Lincoln: University of Nebraska Press, 1990), 68–88. My own study expands and builds upon much of Rosowski's earlier work.

64. O'Brien, *Willa Cather: The Emerging Voice,* 41.

65. Adrienne Munich, "Notorious signs, feminist criticism and literary tradition," *Making a Difference: Feminist Literary Criticism,* ed. Gayle Green and Coppélia Kahn (London: Methuen, 1985), 250–51.

66. Ross Chambers, *Story and Situation: Narrative Seduction and the Power of Fiction* (Minneapolis: University of Minnesota Press, 1984), 26.

67. See, for instance, the New Historicist approach to Cather illustrated by Walter Benn Michaels's, "The Vanishing American," *American Literary History* 2 (Summer 1990): 220–41.

68. Merrill Maguire Skaggs, *After the World Broke in Two: The Later Novels of Willa Cather* (Charlottesville: University Press of Virginia, 1990), 10.

2. Design, Duplicity, and Reading

1. Phyllis C. Robinson, *Willa: The Life of Willa Cather* (New York: Holt, Rinehart and Winston, 1983), 243–44.

2. Willa Cather, *My Mortal Enemy* (1926; New York: Vintage Books, 1954), 17. All further references to this work will appear in the text.

3. As Merrill Skaggs wryly notes in her recent work, *After the World Broke in Two: The Later Novels of Willa Cather* (Charlottesville: University Press of Virginia, 1990), 94–95: "*Birdseye* reminds us that our narrator passes us information about the Henshawe story tinted by her own vision. And birds see from only one eye at a time—with less broad synthesis than humans are thought to achieve."

4. Susan Rosowski, *The Voyage Perilous: Willa Cather's Romanticism* (Lincoln: University of Nebraska Press, 1986), 147.

5. The critics whose opinions I quote in this paragraph are, in order of the citation: Hermione Lee, *Willa Cather: Double Lives* (New York: Pantheon, 1989), 208; Dorothy VanGhent, *Willa Cather* (Minneapolis: University of Minnesota Press, 1964), 33; Dorothy Tuck McFarland, *Willa Cather* (New York: Frederick Ungar, 1972), 90; Theodore S. Adams, "Willa Cather's *My Mortal Enemy:* The Concise Presentation of Scene, Character and Theme," *Colby Library Quarterly* 5 (September 1973): 138 (also see John H. Randall III, *The Landscape and the Looking Glass: Willa Cather's Search for Meaning* [Boston: Houghton Mifflin, 1960], 234); David Daiches, *Willa Cather: A Critical Introduction* (Ithaca: Cornell University Press, 1951), 101; Randall, *The Landscape and the Looking Glass,* 240; VanGhent, *Willa Cather,* 33; David Stouck, *Willa Cather's Imagination* (Lincoln: University of Nebraska Press, 1975), 125; Randall, *The Landscape and the Looking Glass,* 235; Stouck, *Willa Cather's Imagination,* 117; Merrill Skaggs posits (*After the World Broke,* 87) that Cather based Myra's character on "the actress and author Clara Morris, whom Cather watched as a professional stage presence during her Lincoln days and later came to 'know' as a writer of stories"; René Rapin, *Willa Cather* (New York: Robert M. McBride & Co., 1930), 78; James Woodress, *A Literary Life* (Lincoln: University of Nebraska Press, 1987), 380; Stouck, *Willa Cather's Imagination,* 117; Woodress, *A Literary Life,* 213.

6. Philip Gerber, *Willa Cather* (Boston: Twayne Publishers, 1975), 118; Randall, *The Landscape and the Looking Glass,* 240–41.

7. Stouck, *Willa Cather's Imagination,* 121, 126.

8. Susan Rosowski, "The Novel of Awakening," in *The Voyage In: Fictions of Female Development,* ed. Elizabeth Abel, Marianne Hirsch, and Elizabeth Langland (Hanover, N.H.: University Press of New England, 1983), 59.

9. VanGhent, *Willa Cather,* 33, 35.

10. Rapin, *Willa Cather,* 79–80.

11. Randall, *The Landscape and the Looking Glass,* 241.

12. The most exhaustive treatment of storytelling in the novel is Rosowski's chapter, "*My Mortal Enemy:* The Idolatry of Sentimental Romanticism," in *The Voyage Perilous,* 144–55.

13. Jo Ann Middleton, *Willa Cather's Modernism: A Study of Style and Technique* (Rutherford, N.J.: Fairleigh Dickinson University Press, 1990), 122.

14. Susan J. Rosowski, "Willa Cather's Women," *Studies in American Fiction* 9, no. 2 (1981): 272–73.

15. Roy Schafer, "Narration in the Psychoanalytic Dialogue," in *On Narrative*, ed. W. T. Mitchell (Chicago: University of Chicago Press, 1980), 39.

16. See Barbara Johnson, *The Critical Difference: Essays in the Rhetoric of Reading* (Baltimore: Johns Hopkins University Press, 1980), 105–6. "It would seem, then, that the function of judgment is to convert an ambiguous situation into a decidable one. But it does so by converting a difference *within . . .* into a difference *between. . . .* A difference *between* opposing forces presupposes that the entities in conflict be knowable. A difference *within* one of the entities in question is precisely what problematizes the very *idea* of an entity in the first place."

17. Ross Chambers, *Story and Situation: Narrative Seduction and the Power of Fiction* (Minneapolis: University of Minnesota Press, 1984), 53.

18. See Skaggs's illuminating reading of this important merging in the novel (*After the World Broke*, 99).

19. Skaggs also notes Oswald's femininity in this curious passage (ibid., 96).

20. See S. J. Rosowski, "Narrative Technique in Cather's *My Mortal Enemy*," *Journal of Narrative Technique* 8 (Spring 1978): 141–49, which also locates a contrast between "Nellie's romanticism" and "Myra's emerging realism" (144). Rather than reading this as textual disjunction, Rosowski instead argues that "the development in narrative consciousness lies at the core of the novel, unifying its subject, theme, and structure" (142).

21. Rosowski, *The Voyage Perilous*, 153.

22. Though *My Mortal Enemy* has never, to my knowledge, been read as a lesbian text, its suggestion that same-sex relationships are less conflicted than heterosexual ones makes it a likely candidate for such a reading. A similar claim will appear in *Lucy Gayheart* as well. For discussions on the prominence of romantic friendship as a positive counterpart of marriage, see both Lillian Faderman's *Surpassing the Love of Men* (New York: William Morrow, 1981) and Carol Smith-Rosenberg's "The Female World of Love and Ritual: Relations Between Women in Nineteenth Century America," in *The Signs Reader: Women, Gender and Scholarship*, ed. Elizabeth Abel and Emily K. Abel (Chicago: University of Chicago Press, 1983), 27–55.

23. See Hermione Lee's reading of Myra's power: "She is the playwright and star of her own life, with Nellie as the silent, attentive audience/transcriber of her scenes and speeches, and of the histrionic responses she evokes" (*Willa Cather: Double Lives,* 214).

24. Janis P. Stout, in *Strategies of Reticence: Silence and Meaning in the Works of Jane Austen, Willa Cather, Katherine Anne Porter, and Joan Didion* (Charlottesville: University Press of Virginia, 1990), remarks upon the ambivalence that characterizes Cather's representation of the limitations in women's spheres:

"The mere fact that the imaginations of Nellie and her Aunt Lydia would have been so wholly taken up by vicarious participation in a story of infatuation and elopement demonstrates the paucity of more autonomous sources of interest in these women's lives. The sad fact, of course, is that women like Myra Henshawe perpetuate this impoverishment of possibility even as they chafe under it" (100).

25. See Lee's important and evocative reading of *Norma* in the novel (*Willa Cather: Double Lives*, 215).

26. Richard Giannone, in *Music in Willa Cather's Fiction* (Lincoln: University of Nebraska Press, 1968), 179–83, gives a complex reading of the ways in which the opera informs the novel. See also Harry B. Eichorn, "A Falling Out of Love: *My Mortal Enemy*," in *Colby Library Quarterly* 5 (September 1973):121–38.

27. "To George and Thomas Keats," 21, 27(?) December 1817, *The Norton Anthology of English Literature*, vol. 2, ed. M. H. Abrams et al. (New York: W. W. Norton, 1979), 867.

28. Willa Cather, "The Novel Démeublé," in *Not Under Forty* (1936; Lincoln: University of Nebraska Press, 1988), 50.

29. Chambers argues that "to designate specifically another text or work of art within a text is to invite the reader to correlate that text with the work mentioned (it may be a positive or a negative correlation, or, of course, both) and hence to situate the text in terms of a literary or discursive context that serves as the interpretant or criterion of relevance, and determines the selective process of reading" (*Story and Situation*, 31).

30. Sigmund Freud, "On the Sexual Theories of Children" (1908) in *The Sexual Enlightenment of Children*, trans. Douglas Bryan, ed. Philip Rieff (New York: Collier Books, 1963), 34–35.

31. See Sharon O'Brien, *Willa Cather: The Emerging Voice* (New York: Oxford University Press, 1987), 201, on the symbolic sexual significance of boxes in Cather's fiction. Susan J. Rosowski, in "Willa Cather's Subverted Endings and Gendered Time," *Cather Studies*, vol. 1, ed. Susan J. Rosowski (Lincoln: University of Nebraska Press, 1990), 82–83, also comments on the use of boxes in *My Mortal Enemy*.

32. Janis P. Stout offers what I think is a revealing paraphrase of Lydia's cryptic comment, particularly with regard to Cather's representation of women and power (or lack thereof) in the novel: "A woman may indeed be justified in lying, she seems to say, but more is to be expected of a man. . . . Women have more need to lie" (*Strategies of Reticence*, 101).

33. Stout argues something similar when she asserts that Nellie's later "vision of the Henshawes is clouded by a wish to maintain some shred of the romantic vision she had clung to as an adolescent. Thus even her enlightened view is distanced and, to a degree, undercut" (ibid., 84).

34. Rachel Blau DuPlessis, in *Writing Beyond the Ending: Narrative Strategies of Twentieth-Century Women Writers* (Bloomington: Indiana University Press,

1985), 15–16, traces such a pattern in much of nineteenth-century women's fiction: "Sometimes death comes to a female character who cannot properly negotiate an entrance into teleological love relations, ones with appropriate ends, a character whose marginalization grows concentrically as the novel moves to an end."

35. See Rosowski, who concludes that "in stripping away conventions to reach a meaning so individual that each character—and each reader—must discover it for himself or herself, Cather anticipates later writers who similarly work toward questions rather than answers" (*The Voyage Perilous*, 154).

36. I am using Shlomith Rimmon-Kenan's model from *Narrative Fiction: Contemporary Poetics* (London: Methuen, 1983), which designates the text as "the only one directly available to the reader. It is through the text that he or she acquires knowledge of the story (its subject) and of the narration (the process of its production). On the other hand, however, the narrative text is itself defined by these two other aspects: unless it told a story it would not be a narrative, and without being narrated or written it would not be a text. Indeed, story and narration may be seen as two metonymies of the text, the first evoking it through its narrative content, the second through its production" (4).

37. McFarland, *Willa Cather*, 94.

3. Tales of Telling and Fictions of History

1. I am using Avrom Fleishman's reductive, though useful definition from *The English Historical Novel* (Baltimore: Johns Hopkins University Press, 1971), 4. "When life is seen in the context of history, we have a novel; when the novel's characters live in the same world with historical persons, we have an historical novel." This is not, however, to ignore that all novels are more or less historical, as systems of representation located within and representing a specific culture at a specific time.

2. Willa Cather, *Shadows on the Rock* (1931; New York: Vintage Books, 1971), 3. All further references to this work will appear in the text.

3. "The difficulty in composing was perhaps the main reason why she read so extensively in the *Jesuit Relations,* La Hontan's *Voyages,* Juschereau's history of the Hôtel Dieu at Quebec, the letters of Mother Marie de l'Incarnation, from which she drew the epigraph for the novel, and a lot of secondary works, among them the *Makers of Canada,* which she bought" (E. K. Brown and Leon Edel, *Willa Cather: A Critical Biography* [1953; New York: Avon Books, 1980], 211). Cather also, according to Edith Lewis, reread Parkman's histories of Canada while at the Frontenac library in Quebec (*Willa Cather Living* [1953; Lincoln: Bison Books, 1976], 154). Much work remains to be done on establishing the relation between Cather's own reading of historical material and its influence on the kind of history she retells and reconstructs in *Shadows on the Rock.*

4. Hayden White, *Tropics of Discourse: Essays in Cultural Criticism* (Baltimore: Johns Hopkins University Press, 1978), 122.

5. Willa Cather, "On *Shadows on the Rock*," *Willa Cather on Writing* (1949; Lincoln: University of Nebraska Press, 1988), 14. All further references to this work will appear in the text.

6. Ross Chambers, *Story and Situation: Narrative Seduction and the Power of Fiction* (Minneapolis: University of Minnesota Press, 1984), 29.

7. Cather herself made this distinction when she responded to the difficulty reviewers had classifying *Death Comes for the Archbishop* by preferring "to call it a narrative," because she thought "that term more appropriate." From "On *Death Comes for the Archbishop*," *Willa Cather on Writing*, 12.

8. I am here paraphrasing White's claim in *Tropics of Discourse*, 82.

9. See David Stouck, *Willa Cather's Imagination* (Lincoln: University of Nebraska Press, 1975), 150: "'shadows' suggests the ghosts or an aura from the past, something only experienced through memory or reflection, rather than the full-blooded presence of legend being relived." Also see Judith Fryer's use of memory as a metaphor for fiction in *Felicitous Space* (Chapel Hill: University of North Carolina Press, 1986), 319–22.

10. For example, Edward Bloom and Lillian Bloom argue in *Willa Cather's Gift of Sympathy* (Carbondale: Southern Illinois University Press, 1962), that "the seeming disjunction implied by the term [anacoluthon] she attained by initiating episodes and then disclosing their resolutions in subsequent appropriate phases of the novel" (198).

11. Mieke Bal, *Narratology: Introduction to the Theory of Narrative*, trans. Christine van Boheemen (Toronto: University of Toronto Press, 1985), 105.

12. See, for example, James Woodress's assessment that *Shadows on the Rock* "is definitely the work of an aging author, even though Cather had not yet reached sixty. It is preoccupied with time and eternity" (*Willa Cather: A Literary Life* [Lincoln: University of Nebraska Press, 1987], 433–34), or David Daiches's conclusion that the novel demonstrates "a lowering of the passion and vitality in the character of the writer that is discernable behind her work" (*Willa Cather: A Critical Introduction* ([Ithaca: Cornell University Press, 1951], 128). Fryer's revisionary feminist critique, *Felicitous Space*, answers the charges of "bad" history and the lack of vitality in the text by valorizing female experience as history. Much of the descriptive detail of *Shadows on the Rock* supports her reading of the text as "woman's" history, especially when considered in the light of Cather's comment that "really, a new society begins with the salad dressing more than with the destruction of Indian villages." Fryer's redefinition of history as it is constituted within this novel pinpoints the importance of female tradition as one of the significant, and arguably feminist, themes among Cather's late fiction.

13. Walter Benjamin, "The Storyteller," *Illuminations*, ed. Hannah Arendt, trans. Harry Zohn (New York: Schocken Books, 1969), 91.

14. Sigmund Freud, *Moses and Monotheism*, trans. Katherine Jones (New York: Vintage Books, 1939), 85–86.

15. Chambers argues that "to designate specifically another text or work of art within a text is to invite the reader to correlate that text with the work mentioned (it may be a positive or negative correlation, or, of course, both) and hence to situate the text in terms of a literary or discursive context that serves as the interpretant, or criterion of relevance, and determines the selective process of reading" (*Story and Situation*, 31).

16. I am indebted to Barbara Johnson for her translation of this passage and for her remarks on the nuances of verb tense.

17. Chambers, *Story and Situation*, 33.

18. Edith Lewis reported that during the composition of *Shadows on the Rock*, Cather had installed reproductions of the Lady and the Unicorn tapestries (Musée de Cluny, Paris) "at the foot of the bed, so that when she was reading in bed at night she could look up at them instead of at the blank hotel walls" (*Willa Cather Living*, 158).

19. Another relevant definition of "cast" as a verb is "to make a stereotype, electrotype, or other printing plate from (letterpress matter)." *Webster's Third New International Dictionary Unabridged* (1961).

20. Freud, *Moses and Monotheism*, 52.

21. Paul de Man, *Allegories of Reading* (New Haven: Yale University Press, 1979), 300.

22. *Compact Edition of the Oxford English Dictionary* (1971), s.v. "parabasis."

23. Chambers, *Story and Situation*, 33.

24. Fryer, *Felicitous Space*, 330.

25. See Ann Romines's reading of the way in which "against Cécile's rapt version of Jeanne's legend Cather pits another version: that of Pierre Charron," in "The Hermit's Parish: Jeanne Le Ber and Cather's Legacy from Jewett," *Cather Studies*, vol. 1, ed. Susan J. Rosowski (Lincoln: University of Nebraska Press, 1990), 153–54.

26. Dorothy Tuck McFarland in *Willa Cather* (New York: Frederick Ungar, 1972), 113, also locates a split between Books 1 through 3 and 4 through 6 of the novel, though she defines it as a shift from religious to secular preoccupations.

27. Hayden White sees the choice of one story from many as, in fact, an inevitable occurrence within historical narrative: "In the process of studying a given complex of events, [the historian] begins to perceive the *possible* story form that such events *may* figure. In his narrative account of how this set of events took on the shape which he perceives to inhere within it, he emplots his account as a story of a particular kind. The reader, in the process of following the historian's account of those events, gradually comes to realize that the story he is reading is of one kind rather than another: romance, tragedy, comedy, satire, epic, or what

have you. And when he has perceived the class or type to which the story that he is reading belongs, he experiences the effect of having the events in the story explained to him. He has at this point not only successfully *followed* the story; he has grasped the point of it, *understood* it as well. The original strangeness, mystery, or exoticism of the events is dispelled, and they take on a familiar aspect, not in their details, but in their functions as elements of a familiar kind of configuration. They are rendered comprehensible by being subsumed under the categories of plot structure in which they are enclosed as a story of a particular kind" (*Tropics of Discourse*, 86).

28. Ann Romines has previously noted this "authorial" power of Jeanne Le Ber: "Jeanne chose instead to become that symbolic object. Thus she claimed for herself immortality and meaning, while forfeiting the knowable particulars of a shared, finite, domestic life" ("The Hermit Parish," 152).

29. Susan Peck MacDonald, in "Jane Austen and the Tradition of the Absent Mother," *The Lost Tradition: Mothers and Daughters in Literature,* ed. Cathy N. Davidson and E. M. Broner (New York: Ungar, 1980), 58–59, analyzes this tradition of the absent mother as one of the frequent plot necessities in novels of adolescent female development: "The absence of mothers, then, seems to me to derive not from the importance or unimportance of mothers, but from the almost excessive power of motherhood; the good, supportive mother is potentially so powerful a figure as to prevent her daughter's trials from occurring, to shield her from the process of maturation, and thus to disrupt the focus and equilibrium of the novel. But if she is dead or absent, the good mother can remain an ideal without her presence disrupting or preventing the necessary drama of the novel. . . . The nurturing that we usually associate with motherhood then, seems to have to be withdrawn or denied in order to goad the daughter into self-assertion and maturation."

4. Obscuring Destinies

1. Willa Cather, "The Novel Démeublé," *Not Under Forty* (1936; Lincoln: University of Nebraska Press, 1988), 46.

2. *Ladies Home Journal,* September, October, and November, 1932.

3. Cather, "The Novel Démeublé," 46, 48.

4. See Susan J. Rosowski's discussion in *The Voyage Perilous: Willa Cather's Romanticism* (Lincoln: University of Nebraska Press, 1986) of three women (Mrs. Dow, Mrs. Freeze, and Mrs. Spinny) in an early Cather story, "The Joy of Nelly Deane" (1911). Rosowski argues that these women are the heroine's " 'three guardians,' the women who act as fates directing her in the role she is destined to play" (221).

5. Roland Barthes, "Structural Analysis of Narratives," *Image-Music-Text,* trans. Stephen Heath (New York: Hill and Wang, 1977), 87.

6. Willa Cather, "Old Mrs. Harris," *Obscure Destinies* (1932; New York: Vintage Books, 1974), 75. All further references to this work will appear in the text.

7. See Hermione Lee's *Willa Cather: Double Lives* (New York: Pantheon, 1989), in which Lee discusses "cross-stitching" as it figures in the woman-centered environment of the novella (318).

8. David Daiches, in *Willa Cather: A Critical Introduction* (Ithaca: Cornell University Press, 1951), 162–63, argues that "this kind of handling of chronology—describing the present situation, then back to the past to show in some degree how it developed, then to the present again to show something new, then some more illumination from the past—can be irritating and confusing in inexpert hands; but Willa Cather knows what she is doing. It is a kind of mystery story, the mystery to be solved being the true character of Grandma Harris and her relation to her family. Mrs. Rosen tries to play the detective, but, as in all good mystery stories, it is not the official detective who solves the mystery. No individual, in fact, solves it, unless it be the reader, who, presented with the growing complexity of the situation, eventually sees a pattern rich enough to contain all the disparate elements. The movement back and forth in time helps to enrich the pattern until we can see in it all that we need to see."

9. Rosowski, *The Voyage Perilous*, 196.

10. See Michael Leddy, "Observation and Narration in Willa Cather's *Obscure Destinies*," *Studies in American Fiction* 16 (Autumn 1988): 141–53, who argues that "Cather's trilogy centers on acts of observation and narration, on the discrepancies between the perception of an observing character and the perceptions of a fictional narrator, and on acts of narrative compensation that make up for what observers fail to see" (141).

11. In an interview with Latrobe Carroll, Cather described her method:

I'm trying to cut out all analysis, observation, description, even the picture-making quality, in order to make things and people tell their own story simply by juxtaposition, without any persuasion or explanation on my part.

Just as if I put here on the table a green vase, and beside it a yellow orange. Now, those two things affect each other. Side by side, they produce a reaction which neither of them will produce alone. Why should I try to say anything clever, or by any colorful rhetoric detract attention from those two objects, the relation they have to each other and the effect they have upon each other? I want the reader to see the orange and the vase—beyond that, *I* am out of it. (*The Bookman* 53 [May 1921]: 216)

12. T. K. Whipple, "Willa Cather," *Spokesmen: Modern Writers and American Life* (New York: D. Appleton and Co., 1928), 147–48.

13. Mieke Bal, *Narratology: Introduction to the Theory of Narrative*, trans. Christine van Boheemen (Toronto: University of Toronto Press, 1985), 105.

14. It is also worth noting that Cather's next novel, *Lucy Gayheart,* repeats the motif of those whose place is in the parlor and those who belong in the kitchen, employing, significantly, a cat metaphor. The statement in "Old Mrs. Harris": "She believed that somebody ought to be in the parlour, and somebody in the kitchen," (134), is revised in *Lucy Gayheart* as: "It has always been like that, the parlour cat and the kitchen cat" (*Lucy Gayheart* [1935; New York: Vintage Books, 1976] 170).

15. I am indebted to Susan J. Rosowski for this connection.

16. See Sharon O'Brien, *Willa Cather: The Emerging Voice* (New York: Oxford University Press, 1987), 37–48, for a psychoanalytic analysis of the tensions between Cather and her own mother, Virginia, over the conventions of femininity and gender roles.

17. Janis P. Stout in *Strategies of Reticence* (Charlottesville: University Press of Virginia, 1990), argues that this story "becomes a protest, not merely of the harsh treatment of one old woman but of the condition of women generally. It becomes an appeal for change" (108).

18. Translated by Dillon Wentworth, earl of Roscommon in *The Works of the English Poets. With Prefaces, Biographical and Critical,* vol. 15, ed. Samuel Johnson (London: Rivington and Marshall, 1790), 121.

19. See Susan J. Rosowski's argument in "Willa Cather's Women," *Studies in American Fiction* 9, no. 2 (1981): 273, that in "Old Mrs. Harris," "Cather comes full circle in her concern with what it is to be a woman, presenting female characters who neither follow a traditionally male route toward transcendence nor struggle for individuality against male expectations."

20. J. Hillis Miller, "Ariadne's Threat: Repetition and the Narrative Line," *Critical Inquiry* 3 (Autumn 1976): 69, 75.

5. *Lucy Gayheart*

1. David Stouck, *Willa Cather's Imagination* (Lincoln: University of Nebraska Press, 1975), 214.

2. Bernice Slote, "Willa Cather," *Sixteen Modern American Authors,* ed. Jackson Bryer (Durham: Duke University Press, 1974), 67.

3. Dorothy Tuck McFarland, *Willa Cather* (New York: Frederick Ungar, 1972), 124, 127; Arthur Hobson Quinn, *American Fiction: An Historical and Critical Survey* (New York: D. Appleton-Century, 1936), 694 (Quinn specifically compares *Lucy Gayheart* to *Shadows on the Rock*); John H. Randall III, *The Landscape and the Looking Glass: Willa Cather's Search For Meaning* (Boston: Houghton Mifflin, 1960), 353; David Daiches, *Willa Cather: A Critical Introduction* (Ithaca: Cornell University Press, 1951), 130.

4. Willa Cather, review of Kate Chopin, *The Awakening,* in *The World and the Parish,* vol. 2, ed. William Curtin (Lincoln: University of Nebraska Press, 1970),

697 (originally published in the Pittsburgh *Leader,* July 8, 1899, p. 6). All further references to this work will appear in the text.

5. Sharon O'Brien's "The Limits of Passion: Willa Cather's Review of *The Awakening,*" *Women and Literature* 3 (1975): 10–20, analyzes this issue broadly in the light of Cather's major fiction.

6. See Sharon O'Brien's psychoanalytic reading of Cather's early antifeminism in *Willa Cather: The Emerging Voice* (New York: Oxford University Press, 1987), 77–116.

7. Willa Cather, *Lucy Gayheart* (1935; New York: Vintage, 1976), 5. All further references to this work will appear in the text.

8. Willa Cather, Preface to *The Song of the Lark* (1915; Boston: Houghton Mifflin, 1983). In "Writing against Silences: Female Adolescent Development in the Novels of Willa Cather," *Studies in the Novel* 21, no. 1 (1989), Susan J. Rosowski argues that "*Lucy Gayheart* is [Cather's] nightmare of adolescence, as if she had returned to the idea of the early novel [*The Song of the Lark*] and explored it again, this time to probe its dark possibilities" (69).

9. See Susan J. Rosowski, "The Novel of Awakening," *The Voyage In: Fictions of Female Development,* ed. Elizabeth Abel, Marianne Hirsch, and Elizabeth Langland (Hanover, N.H.: University Press of New England, 1983), 49, in which she argues that the singular difference between the novel of awakening and the male bildungsroman is the former's tendency to keep female protagonists in check.

10. Elizabeth Moorhead, "The Novelist," *Willa Cather and Her Critics,* ed. James Schroeter (1947; Ithaca: Cornell University Press, 1967), 111.

11. Rosowski, "The Novel of Awakening," 49.

12. Ibid.

13. See Susan J. Rosowski's important reading of the "gothic dimensions" of an inherited script for female characters generally and for Lucy in particular in *The Voyage Perilous: Willa Cather's Romanticism* (Lincoln: University of Nebraska Press, 1986), 219–31.

14. "Lucy Gray" is not usually included in the grouping of five other 1799 poems about a "Lucy": "Strange Fits of Passion Have I Known," "She Dwelt Among Untrodden Ways," "Three Years She Grew," "A Slumber Did My Spirit Seal," and "I Traveled Among Unknown Men." In these poems, the female subject doubles as the poet's muse; her death becomes the inspiration for poetic art.

15. Elizabeth Abel, Marianne Hirsch, and Elizabeth Langland, eds., "Introduction," *The Voyage In,* 11.

16. Abel, Hirsch, and Langland argue that for female protagonists, "development may be compressed into brief, epiphanic moments. Since the significant changes are interval, flashes of recognition often replace the continuous unfolding of an action" (ibid., 12).

17. See John J. Murphy, "Lucy's Case: An Interpretation of *Lucy Gayheart,*"

Markham Review 9 (Winter 1980): 26, and Randall, *The Landscape and the Looking Glass,* 355–56.

18. For a different reading of heterosexual romance in the novel, as well as its startling conventionality, see Blanche Gelfant's important essay, "Movement and Melody: The Disembodiment of Lucy Gayheart," in her *Women Writing in America* (Hanover, N.H.: University Press of New England, 1984), 119–43.

19. Richard A. Spears in *Slang and Euphemism* (New York: Signet Books, 1981), notes that "fairy" was a colloquial word in transition during the early 1900s, signifying both a pretty young woman and a male homosexual.

20. Ibid., 334.

21. James Woodress, *Willa Cather: Her Life and Art* (New York: Western, 1975), 251.

22. Willa Cather, "Miss Jewett," *Not Under Forty* (1936; Lincoln: University of Nebraska Press, 1988), 78–79. For an excellent reading of Cather's inheritance of female artistry from Jewett, see Elaine Sargent Apthorp's "Re-Visioning Creativity: Cather, Chopin, Jewett," in *Legacy* 9, no. 2 (1992): 1–22.

23. Willa Cather, "The Novel Démeublé," *Not Under Forty,* 50.

24. Rachel Blau DuPlessis, *Writing Beyond the Ending: Narrative Strategies of Twentieth-Century Women Writers* (Bloomington: Indiana University Press, 1985), 15.

25. An unpublished letter to Carrie Miner Sherwood (Willa Cather Pioneer Memorial, Red Cloud, Nebraska), July 1934. Quoted in David Stouck, "Willa Cather's Last Four Books," *Critical Essays on Willa Cather,* ed. John J. Murphy (Boston: G. K. Hall & Company, 1984), 294.

26. Daiches, *Willa Cather: A Critical Introduction,* 131. See also Stouck, *Willa Cather's Imagination,* 216.

27. Kate Chopin, *The Awakening* (1899; New York: New American Library, 1976), 89, 124.

28. I am indebted to Susan J. Rosowski for this insight.

29. From "A Slumber Did My Spirit Seal," ll. 3–4. Margaret Homans, in *Women Writers and Poetic Identity* (Princeton: Princeton University Press, 1980), identifies a scheme of representation in the Lucy poems that is similar to this Lucy novel: "The Lucy poems image a feminine figure for whom there is no discontinuity between imaginative sympathy with nature and death, and a masculine speaker for whom Lucy's death is non-catastrophic, sanctifying nature as well as darkening it" (21).

30. Susan J. Rosowski, "Willa Cather's Subverted Endings and Gendered Time," *Cather Studies,* vol. 1, ed. Susan J. Rosowski (Lincoln: University of Nebraska Press, 1990), 85.

31. Abel, Hirsch, and Langland, *The Voyage In,* 12. See also Rosowski's argument in "Writing against Silences," that "Cather's novel of conventional female

adolescence seems a fictional form of current theories of deconstruction, for we see Lucy posing before the yawning abyss of indeterminacy and realize that she is herself such an abyss. Lucy is a character so insubstantial that we ask, finally, where she is in her own story" (72).

6. Enslaved by History

1. See Edith Lewis, *Willa Cather Living: A Personal Record* (1953; Lincoln: Bison Books, 1976), 12–13, and James Woodress, *Willa Cather: A Literary Life* (Lincoln: University of Nebraska Press, 1987), 28.

2. Willa Cather, *My Antonia* (Boston: Houghton Mifflin, 1918), 184, 189.

3. Bell Hooks, *Yearning: Race, Gender, and Cultural Politics* (Boston: South End Press, 1990), 54.

4. See Phyllis C. Robinson, *Willa: The Life of Willa Cather* (New York: Holt, Rinehart and Winston, 1983), 6–14, and Sharon O'Brien, *Willa Cather: The Emerging Voice* (New York: Oxford University Press, 1987), 11–30. Other biographers, notably Woodress in *Willa Cather: A Literary Life*, 466–89, and Hermione Lee, in *Willa Cather: Double Lives* (New York: Pantheon, 1989), 357–70, have read the novel not as a psychological profile of Cather's beginning, but rather as a revelation of Cather's final fictional struggle with age, infirmity, and approaching death. David Stouck, in his analysis of Cather's fiction, *Willa Cather's Imagination* (Lincoln: University of Nebraska Press, 1975), 226–28, also begins his analysis of the novel with the Epilogue, and argues that "in her last books Willa Cather was making her peace with life" (228).

5. O'Brien, *Willa Cather: The Emerging Voice*, 29.

6. Judith Fryer, *Felicitous Space: The Imaginative Structures of Edith Wharton and Willa Cather* (Chapel Hill: University of North Carolina Press, 1986), 336.

7. Quoted in Marilyn Arnold, " 'Of Human Bondage': Cather's Subnarrative in *Sapphira and the Slave Girl*," *Mississippi Quarterly* 40 (1987): 323. Arnold argues that the novel, through its incorporation of slavery as both symbol and plot, critiques the "enslavement to a set of manners" (324) that characterizes Cather's South.

8. O'Brien, *Willa Cather: The Emerging Voice*, 29–30.

9. In a letter to Viola Roseboro, February 20, 1941. Quoted in Arnold, " 'Of Human Bondage,' " 325.

10. Elizabeth Fox-Genovese, *Within the Plantation Household: Black and White Women of the Old South* (Chapel Hill: University of North Carolina Press, 1988), 98, 34–35.

11. Willa Cather, *Sapphira and the Slave Girl* (1940; New York: Vintage Books, 1975). All references to this novel will appear in the text. See Merrill Maguire Skaggs, "Willa Cather's Experimental Southern Novel," *Mississippi Quarterly* 35

(Winter 1981–82): 3–14, in which Skaggs argues that Cather invokes southern types, "only to portray them in radically 'uncharacteristic' attitudes and acts" (4). Skaggs focuses primarily on the white characters in the novel.

12. Among Cather's early critics, Maxwell Geismar, in *The Last of the Provincials,* remarked that "there is, altogether too much stress here on the scriptural appearance, the filial loyalty, and the 'childlike trust' of the faithful Negro slaves themselves." Reprinted in and quoted from *Willa Cather and Her Critics,* ed. James Schroeter (1947; Ithaca: Cornell University Press, 1967), 199. Hermione Lee too notes that Cather's portrayal of her "black characters is problematic," yet she insists that "within the limits of her time and type, Cather was trying to make us aware of a monstrous double history" (*Willa Cather: Double Lives,* 365). Minrose C. Gwin, in her *Black and White Women of the Old South: The Peculiar Sisterhood in American Literature* (Knoxville: University of Tennessee Press, 1985), also is troubled by Cather's representation of race. The novel, Gwin argues, "implies that evil can be without serious consequence, that the black woman of the slave society could indeed escape North from a cruel mistress with no serious emotional scars, that slavery usually had no grave and irrevocable psychological effects upon the enslaved" (138). Like Lee, however, Gwin mitigates this assessment with a part-apology, part-explanation of why Cather's novel nonetheless hedges its condemnation of slavery: "Cather's empathy with her strong-willed female character who must face disability and death may account in part for her ambivalent portrait of Sapphira and the mixed nature of Sapphira's relationships with black women" (138). Among Cather critics, the only one who does not seem troubled by the novel's depiction of African Americans is James Woodress, who insists that "Nancy and Till were drawn from real blacks" (*Willa Cather: A Literary Life,* 482), and that the black characters in the novel, "Jezebel, Till, Nancy, Bluebell, Lizzy, Sampson (the mill foreman) are all individuals. There is not a stereotype in the lot, and the accomplishment is a marvel of memory and observation" (488).

13. William Curtin, "Willa Cather: Individualism and Style," *Colby Library Quarterly* 3 (June 1968): 43.

14. Mildred Bennett, *The World of Willa Cather* (New York: Dodd, Mead & Co., 1951), 7.

15. Willa Cather, *Willa Cather on Writing* (1949; Lincoln: University of Nebraska Press, 1988), 16.

16. Woodress, *Willa Cather: A Literary Life,* 481.

17. Lee, *Willa Cather: Double Lives,* 358. Woodress records that Cather "felt that slavery had been neither a torture prison nor a benevolent training school. It had its pleasant domestic surfaces, she wrote Greenslet in response to a letter praising the novel. She did not remember Till, who was Aunt Till to the Cather family, as a person to be pitied, even though she had been a slave most of her life" (ibid., 485).

18. Steven Cohan and Linda M. Shires, *Telling Stories: A Theoretical Analysis of Narrative Fiction* (New York: Routledge, 1988), 84, 85.

19. Quoted in Woodress, *Willa Cather: A Literary Life*, 488.

20. Albert Boime in *The Art of Exclusion: Representing Blacks in the Nineteenth Century* (Washington: Smithsonian Institution Press, 1990), 86–92, analyzes the "minstrel grin" so common in visual representation and argues that the "grinning countenance" was a standard emblem of southern propaganda, which sought to portray African Americans as preternaturally happy and carefree, in direct contradiction to their existence as slaves. Boime also notes that this stereotypical "smile reflected racist anxieties belying real fears of disguised intentions such as plans for collective action" (87). Both of these attitudes seem to be present in the narrative of Jezebel's history.

21. Quoted in Schroeter, *Willa Cather and Her Critics*, 198.

22. I am indebted to Judith Fryer, Cather scholar and bread baker, for pointing out the difference between these two kinds of bread.

23. See Jenny Hale Pulsipher, "Expatriation and Reconciliation: The Pilgrimage Tradition in *Sapphira and the Slave Girl*," *Literature and Belief* 8 (1988): 89–100.

24. Gwin, in *Black and White Women of the Old South*, attributes "the seductions and attempted rape" to "ramifications of Cather's own rejection of heterosexual relationships, her apparent desire to be a man, and the conflicts she seemed to feel about sex" (145–46). Her confusion of lesbianism with "the desire to be a man" is unfortunate, though she too reads the scene as one of seduction rather than rape.

25. See Ross Chambers, *Story and Situation: Narrative Seduction and the Power of Fiction* (Minneapolis: University of Minnesota Press, 1984), 33.

Index

anacoluthon, 60–61, 65, 66, 70, 72, 73–75, 78, 79, 84, 85
antifeminism, 118
antimodernism, 13–14
art, 69–70, 133, 135, 147, 149
Atkins, Zoë, 132
autonomy (female), 124
"awakening" novels, 117–20, 123, 126, 138–39, 141

Bal, Mieke, 98, 99
Barthes, Roland, 91
Benjamin, Walter, 59, 65
Bennett, Mildred, 8, 153–54
bildungsroman, 23, 79, 116, 120, 121, 131, 141, 144
Boime, Albert, 196 n.20

canon, 6–8, 14–15, 16–17, 25, 30
Cather, Willa: *Death Comes for the Arch-bishop*, 7, 60, 178 n.15; early novels, 7; "Four Letters," 22; late novels, 17, 22–25; *A Lost Lady*, 7, 30, 43; *Lucy Gayheart*, 25, 116–49, 170; *My Antonia*, 7, 13, 43, 151; *My Mortal Enemy*, 25, 27–58; *Not Under Forty*, 14; "The Novel Démeublé," 9–10, 35, 89; "Old Mrs. Harris," 25, 89–115, 170; *O Pioneers!* 7, 13; *The Professor's House*, 15, 30, 178 n.15; *Sapphira and the Slave Girl*, 25, 116, 150–76; *Shadows on the Rock*, 25, 59–88, 90, 154, 155, 164; *The Song of the Lark*, 7, 116, 118; "the thing not named," 19, 45, 55
Catherland, 4
Chambers, Ross, 24–25, 33, 46, 61, 68, 73, 185 n.15, 188 n.15
chiasmus, 91, 107
Chopin, Kate, 117–18, 131, 135

Cross, Wilbur, 60
Curtin, William, 153

Daiches, David, 16–17
deMan, Paul, 72
Dies Irae, 110–11, 113
displacement, 105–7, 163, 167–68, 175
doppelgänger, 128, 130
DuPlessis, Rachel Blau, 185–86 n.34

Edel, Leon, 15–16
epilogues, 86, 152, 153, 154, 157, 173–74
escapism, 14

fates, 90
Faust (Goethe), 109–10
feminist criticism, on Cather, 8, 17–18, 23–24
feminization of men, 35, 40–41
Fetterley, Judith, 20
figural embedding, 68–70, 72, 74–77, 83–84
focalizer, 62–64, 72, 89, 90, 92–94, 95, 96, 98–102, 114, 115, 136, 145, 153
Fox-Genovese, Elizabeth, 152
Freud, Sigmund, 46–48, 65–66, 71, 72
Fryer, Judith, 18, 151, 187 n.9, 196 n.22

Geismar, Maxwell, 163, 195 n.12
Gelfant, Blanche, 193 n.18
gender roles, 41, 42–43, 80–81, 124–25, 126–28, 140
Gerber, Philip, 30
Gilbert, Sandra, and Susan Gubar, 18
Gwin, Minrose C., 195 n.12, 196 n.24

Heilbrun, Carolyn, 17–18
Hicks, Granville, 13–14

history, constructions of, 23, 59–60, 66, 71–
    72, 76–78, 79, 87–88, 102–3, 154–55, 157,
    163, 171, 173–76
homosexuality (male), 129, 131
Hooks, Bell, 151

Impressionism, 133–34
interpretation, 28–29, 48, 50, 52–53, 75, 78–
    79, 97, 98, 100, 111, 113, 115, 157
intertextuality, 46, 66–68

Jewett, Sarah Orne, 133
Johnson, Barbara, 150, 184 n.16, 188 n.16

Kazin, Alfred, 7, 15
Keats, John, 45
Kenner, Hugh, 11–13
kunstleroman, 126

Lambert, Deborah, 21–22
Lee, Hermione, 10–11, 18, 30
lesbian, Cather as, 18–19
lesbian feminist criticism, on Cather, 8, 18–22
literal, 89–90, 93, 115, 144

McFarland, Dorothy Tuck, 57
Michaels, Walter Benn, 182 n.67
Middleton, Jo Ann, 11, 32
Miller, J. Hillis, 115
modernism, 9–13
Munich, Adrienne, 24

narrative: anachronies, 155, 171, 173, 175; ana-
    lepsis, 156, 162, 171; authority in, 44, 50, 56,
    83, 85, 94–95, 104, 160; consciousness, 34;
    difference within, 33, 40, 86, 91–92, 114; du-
    plicity, 33; embedding, 73; experimenta-
    tion, 22–23; incongruity, 35; ironic distance
    in, 39, 51, 146, 161; lines, 98, 109, 112–13, 114–
    15, 172–73; metanarrative, 29; overlay, 35;
    prolepsis, 171; self-referentiality, 33, 56, 70,
    164, 172
Nelson, Robert J., 11
Norma (Bellini), 44–46, 54

O'Brien, Sharon, 6, 7, 14–15, 19–20, 21, 151,
    152, 179 n.21, 181–82 n.56, 185 n.31, 191 n.16,
    192 n.5

Pilgrim's Progress (Bunyan), 113
Pound, Louise, 19

power, 43–44, 48, 80, 102–5, 106, 140, 149, 152,
    158, 165–66, 169

race, 150–51, 152–53, 162, 164, 165, 176
Randall, John H., III, 16, 31, 32
rape, 168
Rapin, René, 32
readability, 24–25, 33, 73
reading: coherence, 53; communities, 6, 8;
    contract, 31; contradictions, 32, 56, 97, 106,
    139; limitations in, 34, 91–92, 96–97, 111
religion, 31, 36–37, 54, 55
Rimmon-Kenan, Shlomith, 186 n.36
Robinson, Phyllis, 27–28, 151
romance, 23, 29, 33, 40, 107, 108, 121, 126
Rose, Phyllis, 9
Roseboro, Viola, 152
Rosowski, Susan J., 9, 18, 23, 29, 31, 32–33, 91,
    120, 148, 191 n.19, 192 nn.9, 13
Rule, Jane, 18
Russ, Joanna, 21

same-sex relationships, 42–43
Santa Fe Conference on Willa Cather, 20
sexuality, 82, 108–9, 124–25, 126–28, 163, 165–67
Shakespeare, 54
Skaggs, Merrill Maguire, 26, 183 n.3, 184 nn.18,
    19
slavery, 151, 152, 155, 159, 161, 163, 165, 169, 170–
    71, 173, 174
Sleeping Beauty, 36–37, 41, 54, 57
Slote, Bernice, 116
Smith, Barbara Herrnstein, 6
Steinshouer, Betty Jean, 3–4
Stimpson, Catherine, 20
stories (within narratives), 36–39, 57, 62–65,
    73–79, 91, 143–45, 154, 156–57, 162
Stouck, David, 31, 116, 121, 187 n.9, 194 n.4
Stout, Janis P., 10, 18

Trilling, Lionel, 14

VanGhent, Dorothy, 31–32

Whipple, T. K., 96
White, Hayden, 188–89 n.27
Wilhelm Meister, 109
Willa Cather Pioneer Memorial Society and
    Education Foundation, 4–5
Wordsworth, William, 116, 121–22

Zimmerman, Bonnie, 21, 22